Employee Resourcing

About the authors

Derek Torrington is Professor of Human Resource Management at the University of Manchester Institute of Science and Technology, was a Chief Examiner to the (former) Institute of Personnel Management and is a Companion of the Institute of Personnel and Development.

Laura Hall is Management Training Executive, ICI Pharmaceuticals, an Associate Examiner to and Fellow of the Institute of Personnel and Development.

Isabel Haylor is Personnel Officer with Tameside District Council.

Judith Myers is Lecturer in Human Resource Management at the University of Manchester Institute of Science and Technology and a Member of the Institute of Personnel and Development.

Management Studies 2 Series

The IPD examination system provides a unique route into professional personnel practice. After the Professional Management Foundation Programme, the Stage II syllabus covers the core subject areas of Employee Resourcing, Development and Relations. This Management Studies 2 series forms the essential reading for all students at this level.

Other titles in the series:

Case Studies in Personnel Management
Diana Winstanley and Jean Woodall

Employee Relations
David Farnham

Employee Development
Rosemary Harrison

MANAGEMENT STUDIES

Employee Resourcing

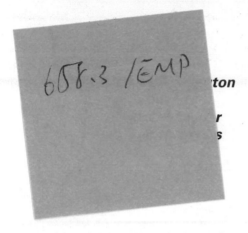

ton

r

s

Institute of Personnel and Development

First published in 1991
Reprinted 1992
Reprinted, with minor revisions, 1995

Phototypeset by The Comp-Room, Aylesbury

and printed in Great Britain
by Short Run Press, Exeter

British Library Cataloguing in Publication Data
A catalogue record for this book is available from the
British Library

ISBN 0 85292 464 X

The views expressed in this book are the authors' own and
may not necessarily reflect those of the IPD.

**INSTITUTE OF PERSONNEL
AND DEVELOPMENT**

IPD House, Camp Road, London SW19 4UX
Registered office as above. Registered Charity No. 1038333
A company limited by guarantee. Registered in England No. 2931892

Contents

Introduction

This book was commissioned by the former IPM to accompany the module of the same name in their professional education scheme and it is organised round the syllabus for both Employee Resourcing I and Employee Resourcing II. It is not a textbook in the conventional sense, but a structure for study.

There are ten *keynote* chapters out of the thirty.

These deal with the main topics in the course and are developed to a normal textbook length. The remaining twenty chapters are shorter and more summary in their treatment. We are anxious to avoid any idea that this is all one needs to read, so all thirty chapters conclude with a number of *study themes* which flesh out the framework that the chapter has provided. Studying the subject really gets under way at the end of the chapter rather than at the beginning.

These study themes take various forms:

First is the *practical learning* approach, where you are asked to work up your understanding of material in the chapter by doing something. Here is an example from chapter 1:

> Interview a friend or colleague in personnel work, either in your own organisation or another, and put the following questions:

(a) How much general influence does personnel have in the organisation?
(b) How much administrative control does personnel have?
(c) What are the three most important initiatives you have taken in the last twelve months? Have they been successful?
(d) What are the three most important initiatives you will take in the next twelve months? Why will you take them?

Use the answers to review your initial understanding of the personnel function.

Many of the study themes take you into *further reading*, where you are asked to read something else, but with specified objectives. Here are examples from chapter 7 and chapter 28:

In *Harvard Business Review* for January/February 1988, Peter Drucker writes on 'The Coming of the New Organization'. Read the article and evaluate his ideas against the reasoning of Handy (1985) or Child (1984).

Read Cherrie and Faulkner (1989) and Thomas (1991). How can safety standards in smaller manufacturing companies be improved? Why are they poorer than in larger companies?

Our third style of study theme is *organisation-based learning*, where you are asked to develop your understanding by thinking through a particular theme by relating it to where you work. In chapter 9 there is this question:

How do you think that your organisation can develop its culture to embrace more thoroughly the concept of social responsibility? What are the pressures in favour and against such a development?

Finally there is the *management problem* approach, where we present you with a typical management problem for which the chapter provides suggestions. This example is from chapter 17:

Do you have someone working for you at the moment who you regard as a poor performer?

Have you talked to them about it?

Have you established a gap between expected and actual performance?

Are the reasons personal, organisational or individual, or a mixture?

Try setting joint goals and a review date together.

As a further practical aid, we have completed some of the shorter chapters with *check-lists* that can help with skills development in the place of work. There are comprehensive lists of references in all chapters.

A
Modern Personnel Management

Chapter 1

The Personnel and Human Resources Function

> Personnel management is that part of management concerned
> with people at work and with their relationships within an
> enterprise. Its aim is to bring together and develop into an
> effective organisation the men and women who make up an
> enterprise and, having regard for the well-being of the indi-
> vidual and for working groups, to enable them to make their
> best contribution to its success.

This was the definition used by the Institute of Personnel Management (now the Institute of Personnel and Development) in 1980 in
a code of professional practice. It is a little too cosy for the 1990s.
Nowadays we are not so inward-looking. All should be well inside
the organisation, but also all must be directed outwards to the
customer, whose satisfaction is the sole meaningful arbiter of success.

Personnel management is the process of making sense of what
people want from their work and what organisations want from
their people, and then getting the best possible match between
those contrasted sets of wants.

What do you want from your work? You want rewards, both
the tangible rewards of money and the intangible rewards of
satisfying work, of status, of people to work with and a sense of
doing something worthwhile. You also want clarity from those
telling you what you have to do, feedback on how you are getting
on and opportunities to develop your career and do new things.
You want to be treated fairly and to feel both security and challenge.

Employing organisations do not exist to meet these aspirations
of the people who work for them, but to satisfy their customers,
to provide value for money, to be efficient and to be cost-effective.
These objectives can, however, only be met through the effective
deployment of human resources. This means basically having 'the
right people in the right place at the right time', but human
resources cannot be deployed in the same way as material or

3

financial resources. What you want from your work has to be at least partially satisfied if your organisation is going to deploy your time and expertise effectively. Personnel management is directed to making a good match between the employee's and the organisation's requirements and then making it better as the needs of both parties to the employment contract alter.

The practice of personnel management varies greatly between different organisations, different corporate cultures and different industrial sectors, and according to the nature of work to be done by individuals. Some organisations have distinctive methods that are governed by foreign ownership or by the political composition of a metropolitan borough council. Some may be labour-intensive, while others are capital-intensive. Organisations in manufacturing tend to operate in many different ways from those that are in retailing. Some categories of employee have terms and conditions of employment that are closely determined by collective bargaining, while other employees negotiate their own individual terms.

Personnel management is not a set of techniques, although all personnel managers need a mastery of methods; nor is it a set of attitudes, although the methods may be misapplied without a clear sense of purpose. Personnel managers have to understand the nature and objectives of their organisation; they have to calculate the human resources requirements and then set up the arrangements to meet the needs: recruitment, training, counselling, negotiating, appraisal, pay and benefits, and many more.

Recently there has been a significant attempt to shake things up within and around personnel management: human resources management has arrived. But has it changed anything?

How the personnel function has developed

Although a particular set of values cannot be ascribed to all members of a group of people at any one time, the development of the personnel function can be illustrated by suggesting the general self-image for personnel specialists that has been dominant at different periods. Each of these self-images still remains as part of the complex of ideas that makes personnel management what it is today.

Looking at the main stages in this development since the nineteenth century, we can see that an almost total preoccupation with employee welfare at the beginning of the period has changed to the present situation where successive waves of management approaches have been adopted in order to get better value for money from employees – although the initial welfare concern remains strong.

The welfare worker

Following the early interventions of the high-profile social reformers like Lord Shaftesbury and Robert Owen, who provided the initial frame of reference for personnel officers to work within, the first people appointed with specific responsibility for improving the lot of employees were welfare officers. They interpreted their role as being to dispense benefits to deserving and unfortunate employees. The motivation was the Christian charity of the paternalist employer, who provided these comforts partly because the employees deserved them but mainly because he was willing to provide them.

The Institute of Welfare Officers (now the Institute of Personnel and Development) was established in 1913, and the welfare tradition remains strong in personnel management. Eighty years ago the emphasis may have been on flowers in the canteen; now it is more likely to be on counselling or establishing workplace nurseries.

The humane bureaucrat

The first phase of personnel work was concerned with the physical environment of work and the amelioration of hardship among 'the workers'. As organisations increased their size, specialisation emerged in the management levels as well as on the shop floor. This led to the growth of personnel work in staffing the organisation, with great concern about role specification, selection, training and placement. The personnel manager was learning to operate within a bureaucracy, serving organisational rather than paternalist employer objectives. For the first time there was a willingness to look at the social sciences for ideas, with scientific management (Taylor 1911), administrative management (Fayol 1949) and the human relations movement (Mayo 1933) all finding enthusiastic devotees among personnel managers.

The current methodology of personnel work was largely developed in this period, and many of its techniques remain at the heart of what personnel managers do.

The consensus negotiator

Personnel managers next added expertise in bargaining to their repertoire of skills. After the Second World War, labour became a scarce resource and trade unions extended their membership. Trade union officials could represent the workforce in a way that personnel managers never could. Union assertiveness meant that employers had to replace unilateral decision and action with bargaining on at least some matters. There was a growth of joint consultation and the establishment of joint production committees and suggestion schemes. When nationalised industries were established, a statutory duty was placed on employers to negotiate with unions representing employees. The role of intermediary became far less pronounced.

The organisation man

The emphasis on humane bureaucracy was then further developed into a preoccupation with the effectiveness of the organisation as a whole: clear organisational objectives were required, and a widespread commitment to those objectives among organisation members. The new approach was also characterised by advocating openness and candour between members of the organisation and a form of operation supporting the integrity of the individual and providing opportunities for personal growth. These ideas seldom had effects beyond the walls of the seminar room in which they were expressed, but the importance of the development was a major change of focus among personnel specialists. After having for so long been identified as people dealing with the rank-and-file employee on behalf of the management, they now began to construe at least a part of their role as being to deal with managers and the integration of management activity itself. It was most obvious in programmes of organisation and management development, and has returned in some of the corporate culture exercises of human resources management.

The manpower analyst

The next distinct historical stereotype is the manpower analyst. The humane bureaucrat was concerned to get a good fit between a particular worker and a particular job: employees were individuals. Trade union representation required personnel specialists to think more collectively: individuals coalesced into manpower. As the rate of technological change began to accelerate and innovation became more necessary, the forecasting of future needs for manpower was added to the personnel specialist's collection of jobs.

The methods were those of manpower planning: to ensure the closest possible fit between the number of people and skills required and those available. The activity has been boosted by the advent of the computer, which makes possible a range of calculations and measurements that were unrealistic earlier.

The human resources manager

The most recent and significant change has been human resources management (HRM), a change of emphasis and attitude towards the employment of people that took the management world by storm during the 1980s. There is now a greater emphasis on strategy than on operations, and a stronger attempt than previously to incorporate personnel thinking into general management and vice versa. HRM is considered in greater detail below.

The above stereotypes have all blended together to make the complex of contemporary personnel management. Although they emerged roughly in sequence, all are still present to a varying degree in different types of personnel post, and the nature of personnel work today can be understood only by an appreciation of its varied components.

HRM – from workforce centredness to resource centredness

Human resources management, or HRM, has come not from within personnel management but from outside. It is a more generalised approach to the management of people, but has significance for the personnel function.

Starting with the standard American sources (Fombrun et al. 1984 and Odiorne 1984) and the main initial British interpretations (Guest 1987 and 1989; Hendry and Pettigrew 1986; Legge 1988), we have a major shift of approach to the employment of people, moving away from the traditional orientation of personnel management, which was concerned with conciliation, propitiation and motivation of employees as a potentially uncooperative *cost*. Instead, those who do the work of the organisation are to be seen as an *asset* in which to invest, so adding to their inherent value and needing less supervision but allowing more scope and autonomy. A less apparent feature of HRM is that some of those who do the organisation's work are regarded as less committed to that organisation through being located at the periphery rather than in the core.

The HRM approach leads to a slight, but significant, difference in emphasis which pervades all activities: the resource required rather than the workforce that is available.

To some extent this is similar to manpower planning, but little use was made of the plans that manpower planning produced and they were usually overtaken by events before their ink was dry. Human asset accounting (Giles and Robinson 1972) was an attempt to make the employment of people more rational but was widely condemned as dehumanising. There is now less justification for that type of scepticism. From the point of view of human well-being, the traditional 'human values' of personnel management were of little value in times of economic recession and organisational contraction. (For that matter, trade union organisation was also of little value.) Throughout the 1980s, jobs were an expense to be reduced and training was a cost to be eliminated; the people who lost their jobs or who were not trained have been victims for whose plight there remains no convincing solution. Furthermore, it is difficult to argue that traditional approaches produced any sort of productive efficiency.

HRM is often connected with the associated fashionable idea of commitment and corporate culture. This tends to be all enthusiasm and superlatives. One of the popular advocates is Tom Peters, and the following list of words and phrases from the contents page of his best-selling book indicate the intensity and almost religious fervour that corporate culture can engender:

> A world turned upside down . . . top quality . . . superior
> service . . . extraordinary responsiveness . . . make sales and
> service forces into heroes . . . encourage pilots of everything
> . . . committed champions . . . purposeful impatience . . .
> empowering people . . . involve everyone . . . celebrate . . .
> lavish . . . inspiring . . . total integrity. (Peters 1989)

This frequently sounds like brain-washing – especially to those who see the world of organisations neatly divided between those with the power and those who do the work. In practice it often seems to emphasise a different split: between core and periphery. Those in the core receive the fringe benefits and management 'care', delivering in return professional competence and a commitment to the organisation and all it stands for. Those on the periphery are paid – sometimes handsomely – to deliver time, labour, professional competence or a mixture of the three, but they are not incorporated into the organisation. Although those on the periphery usually envy the employment security of those in the core, the compensating opportunity of self-reliance and independence may be much more attractive than commitment.

Concepts of personnel management identity

Personnel managers tend to complain about how they are misunderstood and under-utilised, and a part of this tendency has been constantly to turn away from a previous identity in search of a new one. One theme has been to disclaim involvement with employee welfare, even though this remains the most popular component of personnel management in the eyes of everyone else. One of the hardest put-downs for personnel people to cope with is the *odds and ends* allegation, expressed by Peter Drucker (1961, p. 243) as:

> a collection of incidental techniques without much internal
> cohesion . . . a *hodge podge* . . .

As personnel people acquire more and more duties – pensions, share option schemes, profit-sharing, data protection, open learning and so on – this description may seem to be confirmed.

Some people have been attracted by the *employment contract* idea, based on the original concept of Enid Mumford (1972). This sees personnel work as first setting up a series of contracts between employee and employing organisation which describe their mutual expectations, and then ensuring the fulfilment of those expectations.

Similar is the *man in the middle* approach, generally attributed to George Thomason, who saw personnel management as assuming a third-party role between management and employee, especially with the development of legislation. This put personnel managers between the two diverse sources from which they had evolved:

> the one paternalistically oriented towards the welfare of employees and the other rationally derived from corporate needs to control. (Thomason 1976, p. 27)

These last two views partly express the essence of both HRM and personnel thinking, as was also found in the analysis of the personnel function by Karen Legge (1978). She identified two alternative types of personnel people seeking power in organisations. The *conformist innovator* is the personnel specialist who identifies with the objective of organisational success, emphasising cost-benefit and conforming to the criteria adopted by managerial colleagues, who usually have greater power. In contrast, the *deviant innovator* identifies with a set of norms that are distinct from, but not necessarily in conflict with, the norms of organisational success; power is then derived from an independent, professional stance, with managerial colleagues viewed as clients.

While Legge describes a contrast between alternative approaches for personnel people in general, Shaun Tyson (Tyson and Fell 1986) uses a hierarchical classification which relates to the amount of planning involved in different jobs. The *clerk of works* model describes personnel management carried out as administrative support, reactive to the needs of other managers and carrying little authority. The *contracts manager* is also reactive but reacts systematically, rather than spontaneously – by deploying procedures and systems. The *architect* pursues a more creative line, seeking to build the organisation as a whole and working within the dominant coalition of the organisation. This suggests conformist innovation at every level and is attractive to status-seekers because it emphasises 'management' rather than 'personnel'.

Personnel management and the HRM effect

Researchers (for example, Armstrong 1988) continue to point to the ineffectual nature of the personnel contribution to decision-making in organisations and thereby compound personnel managers' convictions about their own inadequacies. Karen Legge (1988) reviewed all the surveys on personnel management in recession and recovery and suggested that personnel management has survived the recession but may be undermined by recovery. Yet current indications are that the personnel profession is thriving. Membership of the Institute of Personnel and Development moved up from 25 000 in 1985 to over 74 000 in 1995. Enrolments for IPD examinations number approximately 8 000 each year, and the number of general personnel and training posts advertised in *People Management* steadily increases.

Those in the personnel function who espouse HRM are usually looking for enhanced status and power. With innovation being the dominant vogue in current management thinking, a change of label implies innovation, even if it is not certain that there is anything different in the package. Others align HRM with the planning and organisational-growth aspects of Tyson's architect in making a further attempt to shed the welfare image, about which the personnel profession continues to be paranoid. Tyson is quite explicit:

> increasingly those in personnel are referred to as 'human resource managers'. Although perhaps an Americanism, this change of title does represent a development of the 'architect' model, with a greater emphasis on internal consultancy and organisation. (Tyson 1987, p. 530)

Considering, however, the history and actual content of personnel work, this is insufficient. Personnel managers have been complaining about their ineffectiveness throughout the period in which they have grown steadily stronger as a professional group and commanded greater influence within the organisation. The membership of the Institute of Personnel and Development exceeds the combined membership of the Institutes of Marketing, Administrative Management, Industrial Managers, and Purchasing and Supply, despite having appreciably higher entry standards. Board-level representation of personnel is now taken for granted to an extent that was unimaginable 20 years ago, when the Donovan Report advocated this bold innovation. It is interesting that the position of trade unions has weakened so significantly during the same period.

Personnel management has grown through assimilating varied evolutionary emphases to produce an ever richer combination of expertise. This is the counter to Drucker's 'hodge podge' charge: the mixture of activities requires a common thread of expertise and understanding as well as an appreciation of many specialisms. Personnel posts would not be found so extensively in boardrooms and similar management assemblies unless they represented a strong expertise that other senior members of the organisation found necessary.

Some current researchers maintain the belief that personnel managers lack organisational power: that they do not have enough influence on selection decisions that continue to discriminate against women and members of ethnic minorities and that they are powerless to prevent a demagogue company proprietor from abrogating collective agreements, for example. Although such a view confirms academic researchers in their comfortable ivory-tower preconceptions, it puzzles most practitioners, because their perspectives are different. Management research usually concentrates on decision-making – especially that carried out at the very pinnacle of the organisational hierarchy. Management is typically seen as a unity to which other people and groups respond. This may be appropriate to make points about grand issues of social inequality, the direction of the economy, profit-centre accountability or strategies in response to European integration, but it is completely remote from the day-to-day issues of getting the job done.

In practice, power is not as strong a feature of the personnel function – or indeed of any management function – as is authority: the authority of expertise. Individual managers, at all levels, spend little time actually making significant decisions: they spend most of their time nudging things to happen, clearing obstructions, calming fears, generating enthusiasm, getting things done. It is interesting that the personal reminiscences of John Harvey-Jones when he retired from the chairmanship of ICI were contained in a book entitled *Making It Happen*; the word 'decision' appears in neither its contents list nor its index.

The main vehicle for making things happen is the personal network of contacts through which the manager seeks favours, information, advice, suggestions and practical help from a great number of people inside and outside the organisation (Kotter 1982). In return, the manager is asked for favours, information, advice, suggestions and practical help. The currency of these exchanges is mainly expertise and only secondly power. The IPM (now the IPD) adopted a policy objective to increase networking among and by personnel professionals.

Some advocates of HRM regard it as a part of a process whereby managers become interchangeable between functional activities, regardless of specialism, so that the overriding expertise is in management rather than in personnel – the responsibility for the time being happening to be human rather than financial or material resources. The risk here is of losing essential expertise. Alistair Mant reminds us of how asset-stripper Jim Slater was asked at his first annual general meeting of Crittall Hope, the window manufacturer, what the company would be making now that he was chairman. His alleged reply was that the company would be making money. The subsequent lack of emphasis on the product led to the decline of the business and the departure of Mr Slater.

The most difficult aspect of management is managing human resources, which are relatively inflexible and where mistakes are hard to rectify. The manager-in-charge-of-personnel-for-the-time-being is likely to lack the essence of what is needed in the same way as did Jim Slater. Twenty years ago there was a widespread Old Joe syndrome: 'We don't know what to do with old Joe, who is a good chap but not much good, so put him in charge of personnel, where his incompetence won't matter.' A wrongheaded interpretation of HRM could produce the Young Nigel syndrome: 'Very bright, but he doesn't know anything.'

HRM is a further aspect of the multi-faceted personnel role, which remains a distinctive management specialism whose practitioners derive their expertise from an understanding of one or more of the ways in which people – individually and collectively – engage with the need to be employed and the needs of organisations to employ them.

The recruitment, development and management of resourceful humans is a more complex, interesting and expert task than the management of human resources. It is needed at all levels in all organisations as a specialist activity, no matter how skilful line managers become. Line managers need from their personnel colleagues a distinctive yet generalised expertise. This is where Legge's categorisation is invaluable. Conformist personnel management innovators do no more than reflect the competences and values of their colleagues. Deviant personnel innovators are able to make a distinctive contribution to the totality of management, which becomes richer and more resourceful as a result.

The personnel function of management

This chapter has so far considered the personnel specialist, but the personnel function of management as a whole is equally important. Each manager has inescapable responsibilities and duties of a personnel type, so personnel management is of interest not only to specialists but to all managers. The degree and nature of the personnel involvement differs, partly for reasons that are specific to the folklore or personalities of the business and partly because of the difference in practice in the particular industry, especially the degree of centralisation or decentralisation.

Sisson and Scullion (1985) carried out research in the largest 100 companies in the United Kingdom and demonstrated how practice varies. Some companies have very large corporate personnel departments, others have a small head-office operation, others have a single corporate-level executive and others have no corporate personnel activity at all. The reason for this diversity is attributed to whether or not the managers at the centre have retained responsibility for a number of critical aspects of operating management as well as discharging responsibility for strategic management.

Where personnel is regarded as a critical function in which a common approach is needed because of the integrated nature of the organisation being a single business, like Marks & Spencer or Ford, then there is the need for a strong corporate personnel function. In the multi-divisional corporation, there is not the same logical need for strong centralisation.

In a book like this, published by a professional body with a vested interest in personnel work as a distinct professionalism, it is inevitable that ideas and explanations will be offered from a standpoint that reflects that interest, but at least one current commentator regards this approach as needing care if a potential trap is to be avoided:

> it will be the policies of the organization that determine the role of personnel managers, as it has been in the past, rather than an idealized model of what personnel managers ought to be. (Sisson 1989, p. 40)

Personnel managers, therefore, must not only have a distinctive contribution to make but must also have a working relationship with other functions which enables that contribution to be made.

Another way in which the organisation of the personnel function varies between organisations is the degree of attenuation, or the 'giraffe effect' (Torrington et al. 1985), which is to be found in a number of organisations where there have been attempts to make the business leaner and fitter. The organisation retains a senior personnel manager with significant rank and responsibility but little specialist support at middle to senior management levels and a personnel administration manager who keeps records and deals with a wide range of routine matters. This type of arrangement requires a strong reliance on consultants and other types of peripheral employee to provide the expertise and the time to deal with those matters which require professional expertise. The greater the degree of attenuation, the fewer specialist roles there will be.

Personnel specialists, like most members of management, feel that they need support 'from the top' to ensure the effective collaboration of their line colleagues. They often believe that without the endorsement of the chief executive they have no influence. As the affairs of the organisation do not necessarily involve them, they usually need to intervene and are apprehensive about being bypassed. Endorsement from the most powerful person available eases the intervention and makes other people likely to welcome it.

It is important, however, not to become overdependent on the goodwill of an individual and risk antagonising other colleagues with whom it is necessary to work on an everyday basis. Pratt and Bennett (1989, p. 10) suggest that the staff specialist will often be younger than the line manager, who

> may feel threatened by the younger man's apparent technical
> expertise, particularly in areas where the line manager is not
> thoroughly acquainted with recent developments . . . The
> specialist is considered to have the ear of senior management
> and is thus somebody to be handled with greater circumspec-
> tion than normally justified by his status.

Personnel people also have the problem that they are often seen
as those who make life difficult – asking for information, requiring
procedures to be followed and inventing time-consuming activities
like performance appraisal, or championing distracting issues like
equal opportunities or job redesign.

The personnel manager will succeed in working effectively with
colleagues only by having useful expertise, and has to earn the
ready cooperation of all members of the organisation, not only
other managers, because of that expertise. Support from the top
is an invaluable aid but a poor crutch.

Some organisations do not have personnel specialists at all,
feeling they do not need, or cannot afford, this type of specialism.
They may use consultants, they may use the advisory resources of
university departments, they may use their bank's computer to
process the payroll, but there is still a personnel dimension to
their management activities. Some personnel professionals (for
example, Lyons 1985) believe that their main purpose is to make
themselves superfluous by getting all their management colleagues
to appreciate the importance of personnel issues. When everyone
is his or her own personnel manager, then the specialist can fade
away. Apart from the obvious fact that this will never happen –
just as the whole world will never be converted to godliness and
righteousness – this is becoming a rare point of view because it
implies that personnel management consists of little more than
having the right ideas. It underrates the extensive knowledge and
practical management methods that have constantly to be put into
operation to get the personnel work of the organisation done.

Study themes

1 Read any two of the following from the references at the end
  of this chapter and formulate your own definition of personnel

management: Armstrong (1988), Guest (1989), Legge (1988), Tyson (1987).

2 How does the American version of HRM differ from the British version?

3 To what extent do you agree or disagree with the following:

> Developing commitment to corporate culture is a confidence trick. It blinds employees to the realities of the business, making them uncritical and compliant. These qualities are unhealthy for the individual and destructive for the organisation.

4 Which of the various concepts of personnel identity do you find most attractive to you personally? What would be a better concept?

5 In your job, how important is your expertise and how important is the degree of support you receive 'from the top' in enabling you to make things happen?

6 Read the references Sisson and Scullion (1985) and Torrington et al. (1985) and sketch a rough organisation chart of the personnel function in your establishment. Consider the degree of attenuation and centralisation of personnel activities in the organisation. What effect do they have on the roles and distribution of responsibility among members of the personnel function? How would roles and distribution of responsibility change with a change in the degree of attenuation or centralisation?

7 Interview a friend or colleague in personnel work, either in your own organisation or in another, and put the following questions:

(a) How much general influence does personnel have in the organisation?

(b) How much administrative control does personnel have?

(c) What are the three most important initiatives you have taken in the last twelve months? Have they been successful?

(d) What are the three most important initiatives you will take in the next twelve months? Why will you take them?

Use the answers to review your initial understanding of the personnel function.

References

Armstrong, P., 1988. The personnel profession in the age of management accountancy, *Personnel Review*, vol. 17, no. 1.

Drucker, P. F., 1968. *The Practice of Management*, Pan Books, London.

Fayol, H., 1949. *General and Industrial Management*, Pitman, London.

Fombrun, C., Tichy, N. M., and Devanna, M. A., 1984. *Strategic Human Resource Management*, John Wiley, Chichester.

Giles, W. J., and Robinson, D., 1972. *Human Asset Accounting*, Institute of Personnel Management, London.

Guest, D. E., 1987. Human resource management and industrial relations, *Journal of Management Studies*, vol. 24, no. 5.

Guest, D. E., 1989. Personnel and HRM: can you tell the difference? *Personnel Management*, January.

Hendry, C., and Pettigrew, A. M., 1986. The practice of strategic human resource management, *Personnel Review*, vol. 15, no. 5.

Kotter, J. P., 1982. *The General Managers*, Free Press, New York.

Legge, K., 1978. *Power, Innovation and Problem-solving in Personnel Management*, McGraw Hill, London.

Legge, K., 1988. Personnel management in recession and recovery, *Personnel Review*, vol. 17, no. 2.

Lyons, T. P., 1985. *Personnel Function in a Changing Environment*, 2nd edn, Pitman, London.

Mayo, E., 1933. *The Human Problems of an Industrial Civilization*, Macmillan, New York.

Mumford, E., 1972. Job satisfaction: a method of analysis, *Personnel Review*, vol. 1, no. 3.

Odiorne, G. S., 1984. *Strategic Management of Human Resources*, Joossey Bass, Chicago.

Peters, T., 1989. *Thriving on Chaos*, Pan Books, London.

Pratt, K. J., and Bennett, S. G., 1989. *Elements of Personnel Management*, 2nd edn, Van Nostrand Rheinhold, London.

Sisson, K., 1989. *Personnel Management in Britain*, Blackwell, Oxford.

Sisson, K., and Scullion, H., 1985. Putting the corporate personnel department in its place, *Personnel Management*, December.

Taylor, F. W., 1911. *Scientific Management*, Harper & Row, New York.

Thomason, G. F., 1976. *A Textbook of Personnel Management*, 2nd edn, Institute of Personnel Management, London.

Torrington, D. P., Mackay, L. E., and Hall, L. A., 1985. The changing nature of personnel management, *Employee Relations*, vol. 7, no. 5.

Tyson, S., 1987. Management of the personnel function, *Journal of Management Studies*, September.

Tyson, S., and Fell, A., 1986. *Evaluating the personnel function*, Hutchinson, London.

Chapter 2

The Personnel Management Role

Notions of the personnel management role vary both within organisations and between them. How are these perceptions shaped and to what extent do they influence the effectiveness of the personnel department as a management function?

To assess the role of the personnel department in the modern organisation, we will consider the following: perceptions of personnel specialists by line and other managers, the power of the personnel department, the professionalism of the personnel occupation and the role of the personnel specialist in the corporate management team.

Perceptions of the personnel management role

The relationship between personnel and line managers

The personnel manager is generally seen as existing to provide a service to line management:

> It is not the personnel manager's job to manage people, but to provide the specialist knowledge or services that can assist other members of the management team to make the most effective use of the human resources – people – of the organisation. (IPM 1974, p. 3)

However, research suggests that many line managers are unclear as to the scope and content of such a service (Legge 1978).

Firstly, all management jobs involve a number of personnel activities. This produces a certain degree of ambiguity as to which aspects of personnel management should be left to the specialists and which aspects should be dealt with by line managers.

Secondly, the personnel specialist is considered by many managers to have a purely advisory role, lacking any real power or authority:

> in the majority of companies, one gets the impression that the personnel manager is a sort of buffer or conduit between the trade union side and those with the real power to authorise settlements. (Jenkins 1973, p. 34)

> Nearly always he is the 'man-in-the-middle'. For management, who pay his salary, he must argue the company case; from the union viewpoint he is expected to negotiate acceptable terms and conditions for staff. If the personnel man adopts a progressive policy, management says 'slow down'. If he goes at the pace of many employers associations, he is accused by the unions of 'lagging behind'. (Dryburgh 1972, p.3)

Because of this image, line management tend to underestimate the importance of the personnel role with respect to organisational decision-making, with the result that personnel is frequently bypassed and not consulted. As we shall see later, this perception of the personnel role creates a vicious circle whereby the lack of credibility in personnel prevents its involvement in decision-making and thus perpetuates the image of the personnel department as a service function of limited importance.

What steps can personnel managers take to promote their image?

A recent article by Davis (1987) suggests that one reason for personnel's poor image among colleagues and line managers is its 'lack of attention to some of the basic concepts of public relations, selling and marketing' (p. 34). Personnel must aim to remove what Davis terms the 'iceberg effect'. Seven-ninths of an iceberg are submerged and out of view – the same may also be said of personnel work. Personnel specialists need to sell, through a process of management education, the full scope of personnel work and responsibility. In addition, personnel managers need to market their ideas more effectively. For example, rather than lingering on the negative effects of not implementing a new system or procedure, personnel needs to highlight, in a positive way to management, any benefits and advantages that such a change might have.

Personnel specialists are essentially providing a customer service to managers. As well as being closely oriented to the needs of management, this service should be actively promoted, reviewed and updated to ensure complete satisfaction. An action plan for the implementation of a customer-orientated personnel service is provided by Humble (1988).

Power, authority and the personnel function

There exists today a traditional stereotype of the personnel department as lacking power and authority. How accurate an assessment is this? What factors determine the importance of a function within an organisation?

Specialist knowledge and expertise

The higher the level of technical knowledge and the more sought-after the professional expertise of a department, the more likely it is that others will depend on it for the achievement of their own goals. Recent developments in the field of personnel, such as new employment legislation, the impending single European market and the European social charter, together with the growing number of personnel managers with professional qualifications, have created a situation in which personnel specialists hold a monopoly on knowledge required by other departments. The personnel department's power is thus enhanced to the extent that it is able to establish 'unsubstitutability' with regard to the provision of particular services or information (Hickson et al. 1971).

Access to information

Much research emphasises the importance of information as a source of power within organisations (see Pettigrew 1973). Such information may be obtained in a variety of ways:

- Managers occupying roles that involve many work contacts across departments or organisational hierarchies are in an ideal position to access valuable information. As we have seen, personnel is often regarded as a communications link between employees and management, with control over the information flow between the two groups. Personnel managers are thus in an ideal situation to gather, manipulate and utilise information to their own and their department's advantage.

- In order to formulate business plans and strategies which can effectively contribute to organisational goals and decision-making, personnel must possess precise information and facts. The increasing application of *computerised personnel information systems* (CPIS) over the last decade has made such hard data available to personnel departments. An example of the contribution to business operations facilitated by CPIS is described by Carolin and Evans (1988) with reference to the new Nissan manufacturing plant in north-east England.

Contribution to organisational goals

Powerful management functions are likely to be those that can show a direct contribution to organisational goals and success:

> . . . personnel managers will be or become more effective in their organisations if they earn the respect of their top and middle management by their ability to help them in the development of human resources to achieve organisational objectives. (Myers 1971, p. 6)

A major problem with this approach is the difficulty in establishing direct causal links between personnel activities and desired organisational goals. While the personnel department may be responsible for designing the systems and procedures which provide the framework for human resources management within an organisation, the department's success is largely dependent upon the ability of line managers to follow such procedures. As Legge (1978, p. 61) points out,

> . . . because personnel is chiefly concerned with providing efficient inputs for use within other functional systems (e.g. those of sales, R and D, production . . .), not for use within its own system, the outputs these resources generate are achieved within, and are seen to be the achievement of these other systems . . . even if employees' ability to achieve required outputs is an indirect result of good personnel management in the areas of recruitment, training and development, and conditions of employment, the specific contribution of personnel is difficult to measure and isolate from effects of market and other organisational factors.

However, as we shall see later, the ability of personnel to contribute directly to the achievement of business goals may be enhanced by the active involvement of personnel specialists in corporate decision-making.

Personnel management and professionalism

In its ongoing struggle to establish credibility within the organisation, personnel has embraced the concept of *professionalism*. This can be defined generally as a means for occupational control (see Friedson 1973), or more specifically in terms of a *trait* model. Legge and Exley (1975) list the following as the most frequently mentioned professional traits:

- skill based on theoretical knowledge;
- the provision of education and training;
- competence evaluated by fellow professionals;
- organisation – that is, a professional culture is sustained by formal professional associations, which have the power to regulate entry to the profession;
- adherence to a professional code of conduct;
- altruistic service.

By adopting the 'professional' label, personnel specialists hope to increase the status and prestige of their occupation and acquire authority, a high degree of autonomy and appropriate economic rewards. A major step towards the professionalisation of the occupation has been the development of a self-regulating, professional body: the Institute of Personnel Management.

The Institute of Personnel and Development

The historical origins of the personnel function can be traced to the industrial welfare movement of the late nineteenth century, when a number of pioneer employers and welfare workers saw the need to improve working conditions within organisations. These welfare workers provided an essential communications link between employers and employees. By 1914 it was estimated that about 24 firms had specialised welfare departments. The previous

year had seen the establishment of the Welfare Workers Association, with a total of 35 members. This association kept the 'welfare
workers' title in a number of different forms until 1931 (Table 2.1),
when it was renamed the Institute of Labour Management; it subsequently became the Institute of Personnel Management in 1946,
and the Institute of Personnel and Development in 1994, which
now has a membership of over 74 000.

Table 2.1
Historical origins of the IPD

1913 Welfare Workers' Association
1917 Central Association of Welfare Workers
1918 Central Association of Welfare Workers (Industrial)
1919 Welfare Workers' Institute
1924 Institute of Industrial Welfare Workers
1931 Institute of Labour Management
1946 Institute of Personnel Management
1994 Institute of Personnel and Development

For the majority of members, entry is through the *professional
education scheme and examinations.* However, competency-based
routes offer an alternative assessment mechanism for experienced
professionals.

The professional education scheme was reviewed in 1988, and a
number of changes were subsequently introduced in 1990. The new
scheme has a modular structure which allows students the choice as
to whether a generalist or a more specialist programme is followed.
This can be seen as a direct response to the growing trend by
personnel practitioners to specialise in a particular area of personnel management, such as compensation, recruitment, training etc.
Through the new modular structure, the education scheme is able
to provide a broad knowledge base for all students, while retaining
the flexibility to cater for individual aspirations.

In addition to training and education, an important role of the
IPD is the continuing knowledge and up-to-date information which
it provides to its members. This is achieved through monthly publications, such as *People Management*; courses; conferences, including the national conference at Harrogate; and the IPD information
and advisory service (Whittaker 1989).

Professionalism in the workplace

The process of professionalism requires an acceptance by others of the role of the personnel specialist as a professional. This presents a number of problems. Firstly, within any organisation there are a number of managers, supervisors and administrators who specialise in areas covered by the umbrella of 'personnel' but who do not see themselves as personnel specialists. It is difficult for such individuals to accept that personnel managers possess a unique body of knowledge and skills, akin to that of, say, doctors or lawyers. The involvement of line managers in personnel management thus undermines the credibility and expertise of the specialist:

> . . . personnel was hindered by the fact that top management felt it knew more about personnel matters than the personnel department. This is unlike management's attitude towards other departments (e.g. engineering, accounting) in which management knows it does not have the expertise of these staff departments. (Ritzer and Trice 1969, p. 68).

Secondly, while it is in the interests of personnel specialists for their occupation to be seen as a profession, such recognition may create a problem as regards relationships with fellow managers. Research by Goldner and Ritti (1970) found that personnel managers in the USA resisted the professional label since they felt that 'to be identified as a part of a "profession" would preclude concurrent identification as general management' (p. 473). Thus, acceptance as a professional may exclude the personnel specialist from the general management team, and effectively prevent personnel from taking an active role in corporate decision-making.

Finally, the body of knowledge relating to personnel is not as technical or exclusive as is the case with other established professions. It is therefore not possible to have total control over entry to the occupation. The result is that there are currently a large number of individuals practising personnel with no recognised personnel qualifications. Such a situation undermines the credibility of the IPD as a legitimate professional organisation.

In an article, Cowan (1988) suggests a number of steps which might be taken in order to improve the professional image of personnel:

- A higher external profile should be promoted through the media. This could also include the appointment of a spokesperson to comment on personnel-related issues.
- Links with universities, business schools and colleges should be strengthened, and the IPD should become more involved in management research.
- Membership arrangements should reflect the changing nature of personnel management.

Personnel management in the 1990s – a corporate role?

Personnel in the 1990s needs to make a direct contribution to the formulation and implementation of corporate strategy and business goals. It is widely believed that one method of achieving this central role in organisational decision-making is the representation of personnel specialists at board level.

A major survey of personnel practitioners in the UK (Price Waterhouse/Cranfield 1990) found that 63 per cent of organisations employing more than 200 people had a personnel representative on the main company board. The larger the organisation, the more likely it was to have a personnel specialist at board level. However, despite board representation, only 62 per cent of these respondents claimed to be involved in the development of corporate strategy from the outset. Another 28 per cent were involved in the consultative stage, while 8 per cent of personnel board directors were involved only in the implementation of corporate decisions. The remaining 2 per cent were presumably not consulted at all.

There is obviously an urgent need for personnel to become more involved in corporate strategy formulation at an earlier stage:

> Personnel directors who remain in their corner nursing their knowledge of the behavioural sciences, industrial relations tactics and personnel techniques, while other directors get on with running the business, cannot make a fully effective contribution to achieving the company's goals for growth, competitive gain and the improvement of bottom-line performance. It is not enough for personnel directors just to understand the business and its strategy; their role must be built into the fabric of the business. (Armstrong 1989, p. 53)

Involvement of personnel specialists at corporate level requires an acceptance by management that personnel can make an effective and worthwhile contribution to company strategy and decision-making. Research by Legge (1978) found that, while managers were content to accept the provision of routine services from personnel, where broader issues were concerned there was a feeling that personnel specialists were 'out of touch with the operating areas of the company' (p. 53).

The above perception of personnel was often a direct result of the failure by senior management to recognise the full scope of the personnel function's role, leading to its exclusion from what were seen as essentially 'non-personnel' business issues. The problem was that such issues invariably had a knock-on effect with respect to the personnel department – for example, production scheduling had implications for recruitment and training. Steps then had to be taken by personnel – usually at short notice – resulting in interim crisis measures which rarely provided a satisfactory or complete solution. This then reflected back on the ability of the personnel function to cope with its responsibilities and led to a lowering of status with regard to further involvement in business decisions. As Legge (1978, p. 55) explains,

> . . . defining the role of a personnel department in narrow traditional terms is likely to be self-perpetuating, as its exclusion from planning and developmental activities is likely to render it even less effective in dealing with those 'personnel' problems recognised as its responsibility, confirming line management in their view that personnel's responsibilities should be of the routine kind.

Increased involvement in corporate decision-making requires a *greater understanding and awareness of business matters* on the part of personnel managers. Indeed, it has been suggested that it may be useful for personnel specialists to spend a period of time in line management, and vice versa. Personnel specialists would acquire valuable business acumen, and line managers would learn about the importance of human resources in the day-to-day running of an organisation (Lucas 1990).

The importance of business knowledge to personnel professionals was emphasised by one personnel director as follows:

> The proportion of senior personnel people who can talk intelligently about business economics and business strategy, who can appear to be businessmen or women first (where their priorities should be) and personnel people second is all too small . . . I think that the profession has a lot to do to raise its standards, to get higher-quality people into it and to ensure that its members are educated generally in business as well as specifically in personnel management. (Armstrong 1989, p. 55)

Failure to take up a more commercial orientation may result in personnel remaining typecast in its traditional, bureaucratic image and effectively excluded from the corporate management team.

Study themes

1   If a total concern for the customer – marketing – is the secret of success, there are new concepts to help the personnel manager from the broader field of managing service . . . A simple model of service management starts with the vital questions: 'Who are our customers? What do they want from us? How are their needs changing? How do we find what these needs are?' Remember that the only business reality is customer perception of value. (Humble 1988, p. 30)

Design a customer-service policy for implemetation within your organisation.
2 Which departments within your organisation are the most powerful? Explain the possible reasons for this with reference to Pfeffer (1981).
3 Compare and contrast the personnel occupation to a well-established profession such as medicine or law. Areas of discussion could include the characteristics of a profession, knowledge base and expertise, ethics, professional association, scope of influence outside the profession.
4 Read Sisson and Scullion (1985) and Purcell (1985). Evaluate the role of the *corporate* personnel department.
5 What do *you* believe will be the major challenges facing personnel managers in the 1990s?

References

Armstrong, M., 1989. Personnel director's view from the bridge, *Personnel Management*, October, pp. 53–5.

Carolin, B., and Evans, A., 1988. Computers as a strategic tool, *Personnel Management*, July, pp. 40–3.

Cowan, N., 1988. Change and the personnel profession, *Personnel Management*, January, pp. 32–6.

Davis, T., 1987. How personnel can lose its Cinderella image, *Personnel Management*, pp. 34–6.

Dryburgh, G., 1972. The man in the middle, *Personnel Management*, May.

Friedson, E., 1973. Professions and the occupational principle, in Friedson, E., (ed.), 1973. *The professions and their prospects*, Sage, London.

Goldner, F., and Ritti, R., (1970). Professionalisation as career immobility, in Grusky, O., and Miller, G., (eds.), 1970. *The Sociology of Organisations*, Free Press, New York.

Guest, D., and Horwood, R., 1980. *The role of effectiveness of personnel managers*, London School of Economics, London.

Hickson, D., et al. 1971. A strategic contingencies theory of intra organisational power, *Administrative Science Quarterly*, vol. 16, pp. 216–29.

Humble, J., 1988. How to improve the personnel service, *Personnel Management*, February, pp. 30–3.

IPM, 1974. *A Career in Personnel Management: what it is and how to train for it*, Institute of Personnel Management, London.

Jenkins, C., 1973. Is personnel still underpowered? *Personnel Management*, June, pp. 34–5.

Legge, K., 1978. *Power, Innovation and Problem Solving in Personnel Management*, McGraw-Hill, Maidenhead.

Legge, K., and Exley, M., 1975. Authority, ambiguity and adaptation: the personnel specialist's dilemma, *Industrial Relations Journal*, vol. 6, no. 3, p. 59.

Lucas, D., 1990. On the road to the top, *Personnel Today*, September, p. 25.

Myers, C., 1971. The changing role of the personnel manager, *Personnel Review*, vol. 1, pp. 6–11.

Niven, M., 1967. *Personnel Management 1913–1963*, Institute of Personnel Management, London.

Pettigrew, A., 1973. *The Politics of Organisational Decision-Making*, Tavistock, London.

Pfeffer, J., 1981. *Power in Organisations*, Pitman, London.

Price Waterhouse/Cranfield, 1990. *Project on International Human Resource Management*, Cranfield School of Management, Cranfield, Bedford.

Purcell, J., 1985. Is anybody listening to the corporate personnel department? *Personnel Management*, September, pp. 28–31.

Ritzer, G., and Trice, H., 1969. *An Occupation in Conflict: a Study of the Personnel Manager*, Cornell University Press, Ithaca.

Sisson, K., and Scullion, H., 1985. Putting the corporate personnel department in its place, *Personnel Management*, December, pp. 36–9.

Torrington, D., 1989. The evolving education programme for personnel professionals, *Personnel Management*, September, pp. 42–5.

Watson, T., 1977. *The Personnel Managers*, Routledge & Kegan Paul, London.

Whittaker, J., 1989. Institute membership: passport or profession? *Personnel Management*, August, pp. 30–4.

Check-list – an evaluation of the personnel management role

The following is a check-list of the main activities undertaken by personnel managers within organisations (see Guest and Horwood 1980):

1 Recruitment and selection
2 Industrial relations
3 Direction and policy determination
4 Health, safety and welfare
5 Payment administration
6 Manpower planning and control
7 Training and development
8 Employee communications
9 Personnel planning and research
10 Organisation design and development
11 Personnel information and records
12 Pay and benefits determination

For each activity, evaluate your own role with respect to the following:

1 Determining requirements
2 Developing policies and procedures
3 Implementing and carrying out policies and procedures
4 Advising
5 Taking part in decision-making

What steps could be taken in order to improve your performance in each area?

B
Human Resource Planning and Organisation

Chapter 3

Changing Ways of Employing People

Organisations adopt employment strategies in response to prevailing labour-market conditions. Such strategies are shaped by economic, technological, political and social factors.

In this chapter we shall examine changes in employment strategy and policy over the last decade, including increased labour flexibility, the development of a segmented labour market and the growing use of subcontractors and external agencies. We shall then go on to review recent political and demographic changes in the United Kingdom and Europe, and consider their likely impact on employment strategy in the 1990s.

Flexible employment strategies of the 1980s

The recession of the late 1970s, together with a number of other factors including increased overseas competition, technological change and reduction in working time, caused a number of companies in the early 1980s to review their employment policies.

A key consideration was *flexibility*. In order to survive after the recession, organisations needed to become much more flexible in their response to external change agents. This is turn required them to be more flexible in their internal organisation, including the deployment of labour.

By changing the way in which work was organised, companies hoped to increase the flexibility of their workforces. Research by John Atkinson of the IMS (1984) suggested that these employer initiatives could be incorporated into a new employment model which moved away from the traditional, hierarchical structure of organisations. Atkinson termed this model '*the flexible firm*' (fig 3.1).

Such a firm consists of three groups of workers:

Core workers comprise the primary labour market. They conduct the key, company-specific activities. If the nature of the operation

Figure 3.1
The flexible firm (from Atkinson 1984)

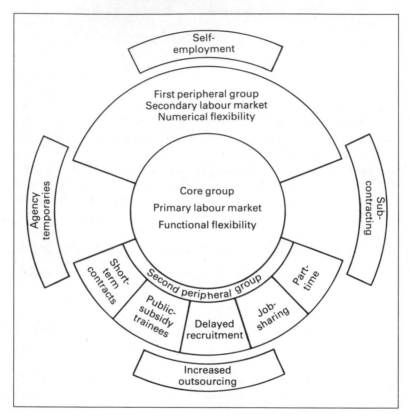

changes, these workers will be expected to learn new skills and accept lateral transfer, often outside their normal skill environment – *functional flexibility*. Core workers are full-time, permanent, career employees – for example, managers and technical staff.

Peripheral workers comprise the secondary labour market. Their jobs are not company-specific and tend to be less skilled, requiring little training – for example clerical and supervisory work. Peripheral workers enjoy a lower level of job security and have less access to career opportunities. This encourages a high level of labour turnover. In some cases an organisation may supplement the flexibility of the first peripheral group with a second peripheral group. These workers are hired on contracts which permit easy adjustment of numbers – *numerical flexibility* – for example, part-timers, job-sharing, short-term contracts etc.

External workers The division of labour into core and non-core tasks highlights the potential role of contractors, agencies and self-employed workers for undertaking routine and specialist jobs – for example, catering, cleaning, road transport, security, public relations, market research etc. Benefits to the employer of subcontracting include improved flexibility and productivity, reduced employment costs, increased resources available for main business activities and enhanced job security for core employees (Evans and Walker 1986). However, there are also a number of disadvantages as regards the widespread use of contract staff (Cross 1986):

- *Cost* Although contract workers may allow short-term savings to be made, long-term costs will probably exceed those of employing an equivalent number of permanent staff.
- *Quality* It is more difficult to monitor work and safety standards of contract staff.
- *Reliability* It is not always possible to assess the reliability of external agents.
- *Employee relations* How will the use of contract workers affect relations with permanent staff and trade unions?

Another issue is the increasing practice of *contracting-out*. Employers shed employees in order to trim headcounts, and then rehire the workers as independent contractors, thereby retaining their valuable skills and background knowledge. This allows greater flexibility for both employer and contract worker – organisations are able to deal more effectively with fluctuating business requirements, and workers are able to offer their services to a number of companies (Clutterbuck 1986).

The consequences of the above employment strategies for workers are considerable. While core employees are afforded permanent, full-time, secure employment, the position for peripheral workers is not as favourable. Peripheral jobs tend to require low-level skills with little training, investment or promotion opportunities. Such workers – particularly part-timers – are also at a disadvantage as regards non-pay benefits and employment rights. However, while the labour surpluses of the 1980s may have facilitated such working arrangements, it is likely that recent political and demographic changes will force employers to develop more varied policies to meet current employee demands and expectations.

Factors influencing employment strategy in the 1990s

Political factors

The Single European Act 1986

> Improvement and harmonisation of living and working conditions throughout the European Community has been part of the Common Market since the EEC Treaty (sometimes called the Treaty of Rome) of 1957, which sets out the principles and framework for achieving a single European market. (Mill 1990, p. 17)

The Single European Act 1986 rejuvenated the original theme of the Treaty of Rome in the form of some 279 measures deemed necessary to achieve a single market in Europe. Such a market will provide Europe with a unique industrial and commercial opportunity, in addition to strengthening political links within the Community. The Act identified 31 December 1992 as a final date by which time all measures should have been adopted.

The move towards the single market led to the idea of a 'social dimension'. It was the European Commission's thesis that employees in the Community would not willingly accept the impact of the economic measures involved in building a single market unless they saw that there was also a social dimension to the process, which guaranteed that employment and social rights would be maintained and, indeed, gradually harmonised upwards across the Community.

Pursuing the objective of giving concrete expression to the 'social dimension', the European Commission lost no time in drawing up a *Community Charter of Fundamental Social Rights of Workers*. A preliminary draft of the social charter was issued by the Commission in May 1989. The final text of the charter was endorsed during the Strasburg summit in December 1989. It sets out a range of basic employment rights under 12 headings:

1 The free movement of workers within the EC
2 'Fair remuneration' for employment
3 The improvement of conditions of employment
4 Social security
5 Freedom of association and collective bargaining
6 Vocational training
7 Equal treatment for men and women
8 Information, consultation and participation arrangements
9 Health and safety at the workplace
10 Young people
11 Retired people
12 Disabled people

Employment strategy and the single European market

The charter is not binding on the member states. Instead, the action program must be approved in the form of individual pieces of legislation by the EC Council of Ministers. However, it is likely that the social charter, together with the Single European Act, will have a considerable influence on employment practices in the UK over the next decade. A review of the likely impact of 1992 is given by Underwood (1989):

- *Recruitment* Although employers have been free to recruit in Europe for several years, a number of problems – language difficulties, choice of advertising media, recognition of qualifications, assessment of work experience – have limited employee movement. However, it is anticipated that the advent of the single market, together with greater European awareness, will prompt an increase in labour movement. UK recruiters will then be forced to compete in a wider market.
- *Health and safety* The European Commission has drawn up a framework setting out employers' responsibilities as regards health and safety. Many of these recommendations are already covered by the Health and Safety at Work Act 1974 – UK

employers may therefore not have to review as many practices as employers in other member states. However, a proactive approach should be taken and any new legislation should be incorporated into current policies.

- *Employee relations* Within Europe, new attitudes to employer–employee relations are developing, and new issues such as the protection of part-time and temporary workers are being discussed. UK employers must therefore face the possibility of some changes in the terms and conditions of their employees.
- *Training* In order to compete in a European market, organisations will need to provide increased vocational training and also language skills for employees.
- *Pay* At present, UK salaries are below European levels. This has obvious implications for remuneration packages, particularly if companies are recruiting outside the UK.

In conclusion, over the next decade employers will be required to adopt an overall employment strategy for Europe, compatible with cultural variations, but flexible enough to meet individual needs.

Eastern Europe

A final consideration is the recent political change in Eastern Europe, including the reunification of Germany. Although a few British companies have been trading for some years in the Eastern bloc, the eight Eastern-bloc countries represent a largely untapped source of business and labour – their population being 43 per cent of that of the 12 member states of the EC. Already there are reports of companies looking to the East in order to fill technical and other vacancies (see *Personnel Today* 1990). The opening-up of this market, together with the increased mobility of Eastern-bloc workers, will undoubtedly effect employment conditions in the rest of Europe.

Demographic factors

There are four major demographic issues facing employers in the 1990s in relation to the external labour market (Atkinson, 1989):

Labour shortages In 1971 there were approximately 900 000 live births in the UK. By 1975, there were less than 700 000 and the birth rate has remained below 800 000 per annum to date (NEDC, 1988). But, although the workforce is growing, it is not expanding quickly enough to cover increasing demand for labour. The 1990s are therefore likely to be characterised by labour shortages, in the same way as the 1980s were characterised by labour surplus.

Age composition The impact of the above population statistics has been highlighted in a recent report, *Young People and the Labour Market* (NEDC):

> Over the next five years the number of 16–24-year-olds in the labour force will fall by 1.2 million, a decline of one fifth – with a decline of 23 per cent in the 16–19-year-old age group. Employers are going to find it much more difficult to recruit sufficient numbers in the future.

Companies that rely on young people in certain jobs, or as trainees for specific career plans, will experience particular problems. However, it is likely that the majority of employers will be forced to review policy as regards the preferred age of new recruits.

Sex composition Due to the decline in population growth, employers will have to rely more on increasing the readiness of all individuals to work. For example, it is estimated that 90 per cent of the expected increase in labour supply to 2000 will be among women. By 2000, women will comprise 44 per cent of the labour force.

Skill shortages Demand for labour in manual and unskilled jobs is likely to continue to contract during the 1990s. However, demand for skilled labour – particularly professional, scientific and technical workers – is predicted to increase. There is, even now, a shortage of graduates – a major source of entrants into skilled occupations.

It is predicted that demographic factors and educational policy will lead to a drop in the number of students attending university and polytechnic, from 124 000 in 1992 to 113 000 in 1998 (Curnow 1989). In addition, there is evidence to suggest that, with regard to new graduates and skilled staff, implementation of the single European market in 1992 will produce a net worsening of supply in the UK, as more potential recruits seek employment overseas (Pearson and Pike 1989). Indeed, the increased willingness of graduates to work abroad is reflected in the success of recent European job fairs (Hall 1990b).

A response to demographic change

Overall, these demographic and labour-supply factors are certain to cause a tightening of labour markets in all parts of the UK. However, what may well exacerbate the situation is the failure of employers to devise and implement suitable responses. Atkinson (1989) has suggested a sequential response by firms to the predicted demographic downturn. His model outlines a progression from short-term to more long-term responses, and from an external labour-market perspective back to an internal one.

Most businesses in the UK are currently 'taking it on the chin'. They are passively responding to the current labour shortages and recruitment difficulties by allowing hiring standards to fall, reducing output, increasing overtime etc. When these methods are no longer feasible, firms will begin to *compete* with each other for the available labour. Tactics here will include the following:

- *Intensifying recruitment efforts* through advertising campaigns and posters, targeting distant labour markets, encouraging relocation/travel.
- *Strengthening liaison with schools, colleges and universities* by introducing work experience and YTS schemes and open-days for local youngsters. Poole (1989) suggests that firms should offer 'rewards' such as sponsorships, donations, prizes etc. to schools and colleges which provide recruits.
- *Increasing pay* Almost all companies will increase pay. This will have a spiralling effect, as an increase introduced by one company will be undermined by the same response from competitors.

Eventually, organisations will find that the growing cost of competing for the available labour will lead them on to find *substitute* workers – that is, to target non-traditional sectors of the labour force:

Women In an attempt to attract women recruits, many organisations are introducing new flexible working arrangements. By targeting recruits who do not fit into the traditional 'nine-to-five' work pattern, companies are able, firstly, to select from a wider labour pool and, secondly, to provide a closer match between working hours and business requirements (such as late-night/weekend opening).

A problem facing many employers wishing to attract women returners is the issue of child-care facilities. Without child care they can both trust and afford, most women are reluctant to return to work after maternity leave. Current provision falls well short of demand – recent estimates cite only 3000 children in workplace nurseries, while 250 000 attend child minders.

For many employers – particularly small firms – the cost of establishing a workplace nursery is prohibitive. Only 9 per cent of employers currently offer child-care facilities. One solution is the pooling of resources with local councils and other employers to set up nurseries:

> Islington Council aims to set up a 40-place staff nursery in partnership with another employer . . . The council will reserve a number of places for staff in hard-to-fill jobs such as teachers. The nursery will be highlighted in advertisements for such jobs. (Hall 1990a, p. 3)

Alternative options include vouchers or cash allowances. If child-care facilities in the UK are to be improved, input is required not only from employers but also from the government. In April 1990, the Chancellor of the Exchequer abolished the tax that employees had to pay on employers' provision of workplace nurseries. However, this concession applies only to nurseries run by employers jointly with other employers, voluntary bodies or local authorities. It is therefore likely to have only a limited effect on the spread of child care and the return of mothers to work.

Older workers Over the next two decades the population of the UK and the rest of Europe will undergo an ageing process. It is predicted that, by the year 2000, the over-65's will make up 15–16 per cent of the UK population (Goetschin 1987). Coupled with a decline in the number of youngsters entering the labour market, these statistics have important consequences for employers.

At present, there are over 10 million pensioners in the UK, together with large numbers of workers who have taken early retirement. For employers faced with a diminishing workforce, the over-50s have become a target recruitment group. The most publicised schemes are those introduced by the large retail chains:

> Two years ago Tesco targeted older people in Crawley with a local advertising campaign. It filled all its vacancies within a week. The success of this campaign encouraged the company to develop a mature entrant programme – life begins at 55 – recruiting up to the age of 69 . . . (Finn 1990, p. 37)

For many mature employees, work provides a necessary social focus, part-time hours being most attractive. Although such recruits may require longer training and a more democratic style of management, the benefits of improved customer service, high staff motivation and reduced turnover outweigh any drawbacks.

A few companies are also considering flexible forms of retirement as a means of retaining the valuable skills and experience of their older employees. For example, older managers can be re-employed as external consultants or assigned to project work. One problem with these schemes is the rigidity of current pension arrangements. However, reforms allowing for 'phased' retirement and part-pension options would encourage the development of flexible retirement. Such policies are of particular relevance in the light of predicted demographic trends.

Students   Many companies are now employing students in part-time and/or vacation work as a means of attracting permanent recruits. This is of particular relevance in view of current graduate shortages.

Employers will finally come full circle, back to their present labour force. Policy initiatives here include the *creation* of enhanced job opportunities and improved worker performance:

• increased training and retraining;

- improved deployment of labour through job restructuring/ multiskilling (see Hendry and Pettigrew 1988);
- development of career programmes and improved promotion opportunities;
- moves towards greater employee participation through team-building and profit-sharing;
- company incentives (loyalty bonuses, non-contributory pension schemes).

Despite extensive publicity regarding the so-called 'demographic time bomb' of the 1990s, research suggests that the majority of employers have taken little or no action to resolve the problem. When action is taken it may be, as Atkinson (1989, p. 24) predicts, 'Too little . . . too late . . . too crude'.

Study themes

1 Consider the advantages and disadvantages of using contract staff.
2 Read the article by Atkinson and Meager (1986). What steps can organisations take to incorporate numerical and functional flexibility into their work systems? Explain what is meant by 'distancing'.
3 Select two recommendations from the European social charter and discuss their impact on current employment policy in the UK.
4 Consider Atkinson's (1989) sequential model outlining employers' responses to current labour shortages. At which stage is your organisation? What recruitment/retention initiatives would you recommend introducing and why?

References

Atkinson, J., 1984. Manpower strategies for flexible organisations, *Personnel Management*, August, pp. 28–31.
Atkinson, J., 1989. Four stages of adjustment to the demographic downturn, *Personnel Management*, August, pp. 20–4.
Atkinson, J., and Meager, N., 1986. Is flexibility just a flash in the pan? *Personnel Management*, September, pp. 26–9.

Clutterbuck, D., (ed.), 1986. *New Patterns of Work*, Gower, Aldershot.

Cross, M., 1986. Flexible manning, in Clutterbuck (1986).

Curnow, B., 1989. Recruit, retrain, retain: personnel management and the three R's, *Personnel Management*, November, pp. 40–7.

Evans, A., and Walker, L., 1986. Sub-contracting, in Curson, C., (ed.), 1986. *Flexible Patterns of Work*, Institute of Personnel Management, London.

Finn, W., 1990. Grey matters, *Personnel Today*, April, pp. 37–8.

Goetschin, P., 1987. Re-shaping work for an older population, *Personnel Management*, June, pp. 39–41.

Hall, L., 1990a. Firm links for kids, *Personnel Today*, April, p. 3.

Hall, L., 1990b. On your marks, *Personnel Today*. March, pp. 18–20.

Hendry, C., and Pettigrew, A., 1988. Multiskilling in the round, *Personnel Management*, April, pp. 36–43.

Mill, C., 1990. How the European Community works, *Personnel Management Plus*, July, p. 17.

NEDO, 1988. *Young people and the labour market*, National Economic Development Office, London.

Pearson, R., and Pike, G., 1989. *The graduate labour market in the 1990s*, Institute of Manpower Studies, Falmer.

Personnel Today, 1990. Engineering search goes to Eastern Bloc, July.

Poole, M., 1989. Time to tackle the labour supply problem, *Personnel Management*, July, p. 79.

Underwood, R., 1989. 1992: new frontiers, new horizons, *Personnel Management*, February, pp. 34–7.

Chapter 4

Changing Ways of Working

As we have seen, employers in the 1990s will be faced with a number of political and demographic changes which will have a profound effect on human resources strategy and planning. Skill and labour shortages will lead to an increasingly competitive environment, forcing many employers to adopt new recruitment and retention policies.

One initiative being taken up by a number of organisations is the introduction of flexible working schemes. Traditionally, the only alternative to full-time working was part-time and/or shift work. However, over the past few years there has been a marked increase in the number of employers offering flexible options to the five-day working week. In the past, such arrangements were rare and tended to be reserved for the exceptional employee unable to conform to the full-time pattern of work. Today, flexitime, job-sharing, term-time working, career breaks, sabbaticals and homeworking are increasingly part of the recruitment package offered by employers, in an attempt to match the needs of current employees and to recruit target groups such as women returners and older workers.

Part-time working

Part-time working has traditionally been viewed as a low-status, secondary form of employment. This is partly a reflection of the largely female workforce involved and the concentration of part-time jobs in the service sector, notorious for its low wages and poor employment conditions. During the last few years, however, there has been a widespread growth in part-time working throughout all sectors of the economy, including banking and professional and scientific services. Department of Employment figures show that the number of part-time workers as a proportion of all employees increased from 19.1 per cent in 1978 to 24.2 per cent in 1989.

Recent changes in the labour market have led to organisations turning to part-time workers as a means of providing a flexible alternative to full-time employees. Advantages include the coverage of absences, peak business hours and holidays; reduced overtime and the provision of trained employees for recruitment to full-time posts. This form of flexible working is also particularly appealing to women, mothers returning to work, the over-50s, disabled workers, students etc., and companies are now directly targeting these workers.

Job-sharing

> Job sharing is a way of working where two or more people share one full-time job between them. Each sharer does half the work and receives half the pay, holidays and other benefits of the job. (New Ways to Work 1989)

Job-sharing potentially gives access to higher-status, better-paid jobs than were traditionally available to part-timers. How a job is shared depends on the needs of the job, the employer, colleagues and the job-sharers themselves. For example, some jobs require a 'hand-over' period of a few hours each week to enable sharers to exchange information, plan future projects etc. Other posts may require only a minimal briefing, often in the form of a phonecall or note. The most common arrangement is for each sharer to work two and a half days a week; variations include mornings-afternoons and alternate weeks or months.

Advantages of job-sharing cited by employers include increased flexibility, peak-period cover, reduced absenteeism, continuity during holidays and sick leave, promotion of equal opportunities and a wider range of skills and experience brought to bear on one job. Many employers also believe that job-sharing improves staff retention and recruitment. Possible disadvantages may include increased administration/recruitment costs, communication problems and additional supervision (New Ways to Work 1989).

From the employees' perspective, job-sharing provides a flexible alternative to full-time working, the sharers retaining the status and promotion prospects of equivalent full-time staff. Many of

these individuals are unab
them the opportunity to pu
or develop another interest.
practice to offer the post to t
jobs have reverted to full-tin
the employer may advertise f
culty in filling these posts, since
part-time work. Indeed, a rec
London boroughs (New Ways to
cent of London boroughs have
increase of 34 per cent since 1987.

Moonlighting

As the number of companies offering part-time hours increases, it is likely that there will be a concurrent growth in the number of workers 'moonlighting' or holding down two part-time jobs. Indeed, shortages of part-timers in the south-east of England have prompted one retailer to target individuals whose present job allows them some free time – for example, shift workers and seasonal workers (see Carrington 1990).

Changes in part-time working

Recent reports (IDS 1990) suggest that the gap between terms and conditions for full-time and part-time staff is narrowing. Currently, employees who work 16 hours a week or more acquire the same employment rights as full-timers, while those working 8–16 hours acquire these rights only after continuous service of five years. Areas now under consideration include pensions, profit-sharing, medical insurance, mortgage subsidies and staff discount schemes. The reasons for this are as follows:

1 Employers do not wish to lose skilled staff who change to part-time work after maternity leave.
2 Increased competition for part-time women workers.
3 Trade unions are promoting the issue of part-time working.
4 The legal climate is becoming less conducive to discriminatory practices against part-time employees, as evidenced by impending legislation in the form of the European Commission's draft

...he and temporary workers (June 1990). ...te that part-timers (working over eight hours ...temporary workers should receive

...nt comparable with that of full-time permanent em-...yees with regard to benefits under any insurance scheme and access to vocational training;
- prior information of full-time permanent vacancies within the organisation;
- proportionate rights, particularly regarding social security, paid leave and allowances based on seniority and dismissal;
- the same health and safety protection as full-timers.

Flexible work patterns

Fixed daily or weekly working hours may not be the most effective means of meeting production and business requirements. More flexible arrangements allow working hours to be considered on a *daily*, *weekly* or *annual* basis, so that work schedules can be altered accordingly.

Flexible working hours

The concept of flexible working hours (FWH) was introduced into the UK in the early 1970s. Today it is estimated that approximately 2 million people in the UK are on flexible hours, the majority being white-collar workers. These new arrangements have proved popular both with employers and employees.

The basic principles of FWH are simple:

> They involve the abolition of fixed working hours and the exercise of choice by the individual employee over his starting and finishing times. Given that he is contracted to work a certain number of hours in a day (or a week, or a month) it is up to him when he attends the place of work, within limits set down by the employer. (IDS 1983a, p. 2)

In general, FWH schemes encompass the following points:

- The hours between which the employee may work – for example, 8.00 a.m. to 6.00 p.m. This is known as the *bandwidth*.

- A time of day when all employees must be present – the *core time* (this excludes business, holidays etc.). Typical schemes have a core time of at least two hours in the morning and two hours in the afternoon.
- The periods of time between the limits of the bandwidth and the core time constitute *flexible bands*. It is during these periods at the beginning and the end of the day that employees may choose when to work. While individuals are not required to be present throughout this time, they must ensure that all contracted hours are completed.
- Each scheme's rules also have a *settlement* or *accounting* period for hours:

  > The settlement period is the time in which employees must complete their contractual hours. For example, if an employee is contracted to work a 35 hour week, in a 4 weekly accounting period he will have to clock up 140 hours on the FWH scheme. (IDS, 1983a, p. 2)

- Employees may accumulate *credit* hours to take off during core time. For example, if they have worked enough extra hours in one period (normally seven or eight), they may be allowed to take a day off in the following period. Most schemes place a limit on the number of these 'flexidays' (usually one or two) that can be taken in any one period.

In order for a FWH scheme to be seen to be fair and accurate, opportunities for abuse must be kept to a minimum. This is normally achieved through the use of efficient time-recording and monitoring systems. The four types of system in use are manual systems, clocking systems, time recorders and computer systems. For many white-collar employees, time-keeping is a matter of trust rather than control. Staff may therefore resent the introduction of systems for recording their working hours. However, the lack of such a system may give rise to suspicions of favouritism or that some individuals are not putting in their full complement of hours.

Many employers regard FWH as an employee benefit and have introduced FWH schemes as a method of attracting and retaining staff. For a full review of the advantages and disadvantages of FWH for both employers and employees, see IDS (1983a).

Compressed working weeks

Compressed working weeks allow for the reallocation of worktime into fewer and longer blocks during the week. Examples include four 10-hour days, the 4½-day week and the 9-day fortnight (see Curson (1986) for a review of schemes currently in operation). Compressed working weeks do not include provision for a reduction in total working hours or increased employee discretion over worktime. Reasons for introducing such schemes have varied from improving employee morale, productivity and recruitment, to reducing overhead costs and levels of absenteeism and overtime. For employees, compressed weeks allow longer periods of leisure time and fewer journeys to work.

The current interest in flexible working arrangements may well lead to an increase in compressed weeks, particularly if these are coupled with greater employee choice as regards options available – for example, introducing a scheme in conjunction with a flexitime system (Harkness and Krupinski 1977).

Annual hours

In the competitive business environment of the 1990s, there will be an increasing need for companies to synchronise employee working hours and the operating profile of the business, in order to reduce costs and improve performance. The 'annual hours' approach has proved to be an effective way of tackling this problem:

> Central to every annual hours agreement is the fact that the period of time within which full-time employees must work their contractual hours is defined over a whole year. All normal working hours contracts can be converted to annual hours; for example, an average 38 hour week becomes 1732 annual hours, assuming five weeks of annual holiday entitlement. (Lynch 1988, p. 36)

The flexible work schedules allowed by the annual hours approach is of particular relevance to the manufacturing sector, which needs to make fullest use of expensive machinery and assets. Not surprisingly, the early exponents of annual hours were the continuous-process industries, such as paper, food, drink, chemicals, oil, glass and cement. These sectors found that such agreements reduced overtime and unit costs, increased flexibility and productivity and reduced absenteeism (Desmonds and Vidal-Hall 1987).

While annual hours may facilitate more intensive use of plant, or longer opening hours in, for example, the retail and service sectors, the full potential of the approach cannot really be exploited unless the company's activity also has a seasonal or cyclical dimension (such as in the leisure and tourist industry). Advantage can then be taken of the fact that the scheme allows more hours to be rostered during the busy periods of the business and less during slack periods. An excellent example of the use of such a rostered scheme is that introduced by the RAC to cover its port services operation (see Lynch 1988).

From the employee's viewpoint, annual hours offer a number of flexible options while guaranteeing a fixed number of working hours per year. In addition, the system maintains a regular monthly salary, regardless of the hours worked during that period.

Organisations may use annual hours as part of a programme of changes towards greater flexibility or as a method of altering the length of the working week, controlling overtime or improving response to variations in business demand.

Term-time working

Term-time working is an arrangement whereby employees are given unpaid leave of absence during school holidays, while retaining the same conditions of service as permanently contracted full-time and part-time staff.

This form of flexible working has long been used by local authorities (see New Ways to Work 1990b) and is now being taken up by private companies, in order to encourage women with older children to return to work.

In 1989 the Alliance and Leicester Building Society introduced term-time working for parents of school-age children:

> Under the scheme, parents of children aged from five to fourteen can work during school terms only. Staff taking this option are given 10 weeks' unpaid leave each year to take

> during the school holidays, on top of which they are expected
> to take at least four weeks of their annual holiday entitlement
> (from three to six weeks depending on seniority and service)
> during the school holidays. This minimum of 14 weeks' holi-
> day amply covers the summer, Easter and Christmas breaks.
> (Spencer 1990, p. 32)

The holiday periods are covered either by rescheduling work or
by taking on casual labour. Although the Alliance and Leicester
scheme was not introduced in response to any immediate recruitment problems, it is part of a long-term initiative to improve
recruitment and retention of staff.

Term-time working provides a flexible option for many working
parents. Indeed, it is noticeable that many of the schemes have
been taken up by both working fathers and mothers. It is also of
particular assistance to single parents, who may not have a partner
available to assist in taking and collecting children to and from
school.

Career breaks

Career breaks allow an employee to take an unpaid break from
work, generally between two to five years, while remaining in
touch with the company (for example, through training/refresher
courses, newsletters, annual reports or working for short periods).
On returning, employees are guaranteed a job at the level of their
original post, plus adequate retraining.

Career breaks were first introduced by the high-street banks to
encourage women to return to work after having a family. The
National Westminster Bank introduced its career-break scheme in
1981. This allows both men and women, at any level, to take up
to five years off to care for children. The use of similar schemes
is now spreading in both the private and the public sector: ICI and
Norwich Union have recently introduced five-year career-break
schemes, and in July 1990 the NHS announced a career-break
scheme for all categories of worker.

However, recent take-up figures for current schemes suggest
that the legal implications of a break in service with regard to
continuity of employment and statutory rights may be deterring
employees from requesting career breaks (see Lucas 1990).

Employers may therefore be forced to review schemes if staff are to be encouraged to take up career breaks.

Sabbaticals

Sabbaticals are extended periods of leave, usually seen as a reward for long service and generally intended to allow the employee an opportunity to pursue outside interests – for example, travel, voluntary work or further education. They can last anything from four weeks to a year and can be paid or unpaid.

Sabbaticals were originally introduced in the USA, where one in six employers now offer them. Although they are still fairly novel in the UK, a number of companies are now considering schemes. May (1985) provides a full review of a sabbatical programme operated by the John Lewis Partnership.

Homeworking

At present there are estimated to be over 2 million people in the UK working at or from home. Homeworking is not an easy or cheap option: it requires the recruitment of suitable workers, effective communication channels and remuneration policies, and the development of progressive training and promotion structures (Rothwell 1987).

Examples of homeworking projects currently operating in the UK include those run by IBM (UK), Digital Equipment Co., Rank Xerox and Texaco. One of the earliest schemes was established by F-International, a computer software company. Approximately 75 per cent of the workforce are self-employed and work from home; 90 per cent are women. Employees are recruited to work on particular projects, for which an hourly rate is paid. On average, individuals work 20–25 hours per week. The scheme requires close supervision and effective communication channels. Advantages of this and other homeworking schemes include increased flexiblity, job satisfaction and productivity (average gains 20 per cent); widening of the labour pool to include homebound workers; improved retention levels and reduced overheads (Kelly 1985).

Successful homeworking requires attitudinal changes on the part of both workers and managers. As Stanworth and Stanworth (1989) explain, homeworkers need not only technical knowledge but also psychological preparation – the ability to 'self-start', to use small-business and time-management skills and to cope with isolation. Many such workers fear that being home-based will result in reduced promotion prospects and marginalisation from the social and political life of the workplace. Personality is also an important factor – for example, an extrovert with high affiliation needs may not easily adapt to home-based work.

As regards managers' attitudes to homeworking, this requires a shift from traditional management methods – often characterised by close supervision of the work process – to a more open style of management whereby workers are given greater autonomy and flexibility. Managers need to develop delegation skills, together with the ability to set joint objectives/targets and to assess individual performance on results.

Study themes

1 The majority of FWH schemes in the UK are for white-collar workers. What problems would you encounter in setting up a scheme for blue-collar workers? How would you solve them?
2 Consider the advantages and disadvantages of homeworking for both employer and employee.
3 Describe the flexible working arrangements currently offered by your organisation (or recommend suitable schemes). Evaluate their effectiveness with regard to improving recruitment and retention of staff.
4 In 1983 the Conservative government introduced the 'Job Splitting Scheme' (see IDS 1983b). Compare the objectives and methods of job-splitting to traditional job-sharing schemes.
5 Read Lynch (1988). Outline the benefits and costs of introducing an annual hours scheme.

Check-list for introducing flexible working arrangements

1 Forms of flexible working

(a) What type of flexible working schemes would be particularly relevant to your organisation?
(b) Are there any jobs that would not be suited to flexible working? Give examples and explain why.

2 Communication and consultation

(a) Have all proposed changes been discussed with employees and trade unions?
(b) How important is flexible working to your employees? Would a survey or questionnaire be helpful?
(c) Devise ways of communicating and promoting new working patterns to employees:

- team briefings,
- poster campaigns,
- newsletters.

3 Management commitment

(a) Explain the reasons behind the introduction of flexible working? Is it related to market and customer needs, internal efficiency/productivity, development in new technology, availability of labour? What are the cost benefits?
(b) Have all line managers been briefed on the implications of flexible working?
(c) What management problems, if any, do you envisage (for example supervision, timekeeping)? How can they be solved?

4 Employee rights

(a) Are flexible working options open to all employees?
(b) Do flexible working options offer the same conditions of service and promotion/training opportunities as traditional full-time employment? If not, explain why.

References

Carrington, L., 1990. Two jobs better? *Personnel Today*, June, p. 37.

Curson, C., (ed.), 1986. *Flexible Patterns of Work*, Institute of Personnel Management, London.

Desmonds, G., and Vidal-Hall, T., 1987. A study of annual hours arrangements in the UK, *Industrial Society*, February.

Harkness, R., and Krupinski, B., 1977. Two surveys – working hours arrangements and shiftwork, *Journal of the Australian Department of Science and Technology*, vol. 3, no. 2, pp. 27–34.

IDS, 1983a. *Flexible Working Hours*, IDS Study 301, Incomes Data Services, London.

IDS, 1983b, *The Job Splitting Scheme*, IDS Study 289, Incomes Data Services, London.

IDS, 1990. *Part-Time Workers*, IDS Study 459, Incomes Data Services, London.

Kelly, M., 1985. The next workplace revolution: telecommuting, *Supervisory Management* (USA), October, pp. 2–7.

Lucas, D., 1990. Breaking up is hard to do, *Personnel Today*, July, pp. 41–2.

Lynch, P., 1988. Matching worked hours to business needs, *Personnel Management*, June, pp. 36–9.

May, S., 1985. Sabbaticals: the John Lewis experience, in Clutterbuck, D., (ed.), 1985. *New Patterns of Work*, Gower, Aldershot.

New Ways to Work, 1989. *Introduction to job sharing*, November, New Ways to Work, London.

New Ways to Work, 1990a. *Newsletter*, vol. 6, no. 1, New Ways to Work, London.

New Ways to Work, 1990b. *Job sharing and flexible working in the London boroughs*, April, New Ways to Work, London.

Rothwell, S., 1987. How to manage from a distance, *Personnel Management*, September, pp. 22–6.

Spencer, L., 1990. Parent power, *Personnel Today*, April, pp. 32–3.

Stanworth, J., and Stanworth, C., 1989. Home truths about teleworking, *Personnel Management*, November, pp. 48–52.

Chapter 5

The Computer: Problem-solving and Control

The computer is used increasingly in personnel departments at both strategic and operational levels, and in 1990 Richards-Carpenter reported that 91 per cent of organisations surveyed used a personnel computer system.

Information about people is stored, monitored and used operationally – for example, as in administrative systems. This information can also be used more strategically, by statistical analysis, to identify current workforce profiles, trends and future models of the workforce. Current and potential problems can be identified, and the implications of a range of solutions can be investigated. The personnel department computer can also be linked with other systems, either internally or externally, and, for example, can send information to banks and receive information from networks holding other human resources data.

The computer has the potential to be the hub of the personnel department, but it is rarely found to be so in practice at present. Hall and Torrington (1989) classify users as stars, radicals, plodders and beginners: of the 35 organisations described in their research, 24 were plodders or beginners where use was very limited. In this chapter we look briefly at system set-up, then in more detail at a range of applications, the Data Protection Act, management and control of the system and its users, and the implications of use for the personnel function.

Set-up and systems

Personnel computer systems can run on mainframe, mini or micro computers, and the choice will depend on a variety of factors. These factors include the hardware already used by the organisation, required links with other systems, flexibility needed, computer capacity demanded in terms of number of employees and

. applications, user population envisaged, finance available and so
on.

Systems can be produced in-house or bought as a package from
a supplier. There are a number of well-tested personnel packages
now available, such as those from Peterborough Software, Percom
and Missing Link. Recent systems all offer interactive computing,
so that users can have direct access into the system via a keyboard
and can request changes and reports which will be processed
immediately, providing information for further amended requests.
Older systems which operate by batch processing would take
periods from 24 hours upwards to days and weeks to provide the
information requested!

The most effective personnel computer systems are those which
include comprehensive personal information on individual
employees together with details of the jobs which they are doing
and the competencies required. It is vital that the database provides for history to be stored, so that as individuals are promoted
there remains a record of their previous post. If *comprehensive*
personal data is included, the system can be used to link a wide
range of factors together in analyses. If the system contains only
limited personal data it would be termed a 'personnel tool'. An
example of such a tool might be an absence system, in which
name, number, grade and absence are recorded. Another would
be a safety system – with name, number, post; safety equipment
allocated with dates; and accident data. Recruitment systems and
training systems are often used in this way and will be discussed
in more detail later in the chapter. These computer tools are most
effectively used when they can be linked into a comprehensive
system, so that information can be uploaded and downloaded and
all computerised personnel data is consistent.

Some personnel computer systems are combined with systems
from other departments, the most common combinations being
with payroll and pensions. In some organisations a *total* organisational system is being developed, rather than separate functional
systems, and personnel data would be included in this as part of
the system. An example of this is the Joint Development Programme at British Gas.

Computer applications

Record-keeping and listing reports

This is the most basic level of personnel computer use: as little more than an electronic filing cabinet and typewriter. Such applications are usually found on a standard database system, such as dBase III, rather than on a specialised personnel system – although some of the older mainframe systems operate only in this limited way. The benefits of use are that lists can be produced of employees in differing order – such as grade order, age order, sickness absence order – and can be combined with other pieces of information about the individual – such as location and years employed. Lists can also be produced of employees in a certain category – for example, lists of women and of men, lists of people with a certain skill, or lists of people over 55 years, say. Lists will generally be totalled at the bottom. These lists can be helpful in a large organisation when looking for potential candidates for a specialised post where certain key skills are required.

Statistical reports, matrices and graphs

These analyses can be much more complex and detailed. Some systems are designed with key reports built in so that at the press of a button a particular report can be processed. This is a great advantage as long as new reports can also be specified as new needs for information are identified – this is not possible with *all* systems. Where reports are identified and produced on an ad-hoc basis, this can be a very time-consuming iterative process, with each report being constantly refined and improved on the basis of the results from the previous report.

At the simplest level, these analyses may summarise the type of data collected in list form (see above). So, for example, bar charts could be produced to represent the number of people in different age bands. Pie charts could be produced to show how the man-power budget is allocated between different departments, or how absence is spread. Stobie (1986) gives an example of how numbers of people against length of service varies according to grade, as illustrated in fig. 5.1.

Employee Resourcing

Figure 5.1

Numbers of staff in each of three groups plotted against length of service

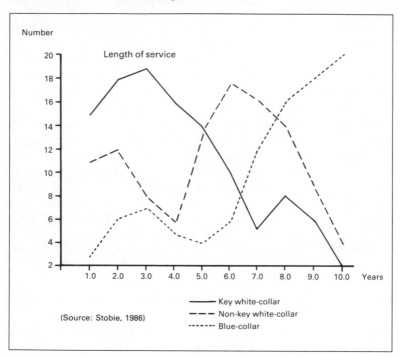

(Source: Stobie, 1986)

——— Key white-collar
– – – Non-key white-collar
······· Blue-collar

A more complex analysis, which one of the authors has seen demonstrated, illustrates absence levels in number of days (banded) against different grades, and number of spells of absence (banded) against different grades. These matrices were analysed by function, department or whole organisation. The bands used to categorise absence behaviour were selected to represent set percentages, so that absence behaviour of, say, the highest 10 per cent of absentees could be described, as could the behaviour of 'average' employees. These bands and their descriptive behaviour were then used as guides by supervisors so that they could identify when absence was greater than average and could follow the prescribed action appropriate to absence level.

Royal Insurance has used statistical analysis to approach career planning (Broomhead 1987). It described what was happening in the organisation by analysing age against salary level. Initially a scattergram was produced, and this was regressed to produce division into deciles. These are shown in fig. 5.2. Having produced these graphs, subsets of the employee population can then be compared against the current total picture. In the case of Royal Insurance, historical data was also available, so these subsets could be compared at different points in time. This approach has been used to compare the position of women, graduates, mature recruits and others.

Modelling

The computer can be used to ask 'what if' questions based on current data in the system. These types of questions are critical in manpower planning, to assess the impact of a variety of scenarios for the future. For example:

- what would be the total paybill if we increased pay by 5 per cent, 6 per cent or 5.5 per cent?
- what would the workforce look like in two, five and ten years' time without taking recruitment into account?
- if we take on 50 graduates this year, how many are we likely to have retained in three, five and ten years?
- if we produce 25 per cent, 30 per cent or 35 per cent more product this year, how many more staff do we need at what grades (based on given ratios of staff to production)?
- given a projection of how the workload varies in peaks and troughs during the day, how many person hours are needed at each time period, and what alternatives are there for providing manpower at each time (testing, for example, different shift start and finish times)?

Mayhew (1987) gives an excellent example of staff demand over the year and staff available over the year and shows graphically where the shortfalls and the surpluses are. Various strategies are then explored regarding how surplus staff time can be used in the slack periods and how additional staff time can be found in the busy periods. Possibilities may involve repositioning holidays and

Figure 5.2
The relationship between age and salary

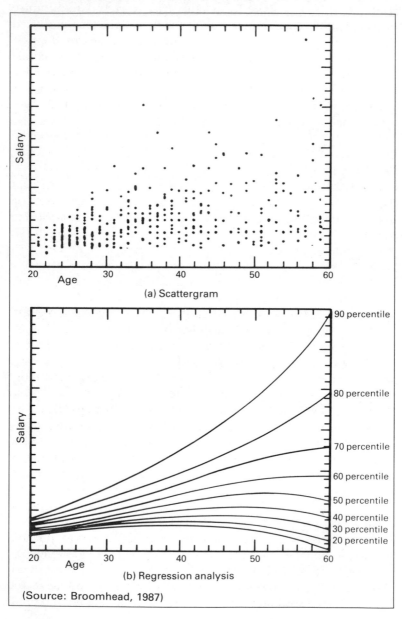

(a) Scattergram

(b) Regression analysis

(Source: Broomhead, 1987)

training events. The effect of each scenario can be graphed until the staff supply line and staff demand line are as close as possible.

Administrative systems

Administrative systems can be devised in any area of personnel where there is an administrative chore. Recruitment and training systems are most common, but systems can be devised for safety and for holiday allocation choices, for example. One of the first systems was the one used for recruitment by Foster Wheeler Energy (Ive 1982). Another well-publicised system is that used by the Bank of England and reported by Hill (1985). These systems involve inputting applications against available posts. Brief individual details would be noted, and actions against the progress of that application would be recorded. Letters that need to be sent are all included in the system. So, when nine applicants need a letter to say that they have been unsuccessful, the letter and the list of names are linked and the system produces that letter individually addressed for each of those names. Records are automatically updated from this process of sending out the letter.

Systems can also accept diary dates so that reminders come up stating that certain things in the recruitment cycle need to happen that day or that week. Clearly there are advantages in accuracy, in time-saving, and in promoting a professional image. In addition, the data in the system can be analysed: at one level to provide indications on workload and trends, and at another to monitor, for example, progress on equal opportunities against targets, if these have been agreed. A currently available off-the-shelf system is SAM (Selection and Matching), produced by Pear Computing.

Increasing use is also being made of training systems, and a good example of this is PS 2000/TS, produced by Peterborough Software. In this system there are two major areas: individual details and course details. In the individual data part of the system, details of the person are needed together with some brief details of his or her current job (for example, job title and number of people managed), and these can be downloaded from the main personnel system. Training needs against individuals can be logged in, together with identified courses, dates and bookings where appropriate. There would also be a training record for all individuals, showing courses that they have attended in the past.

In the course side of the system, courses that are run internally can be specified in full in terms of objectives, duration, tutors, location and so on. Events of each course can be logged into the diary, and rooms and tutors can be booked through the system. The system can also be used to progress nominations, either coming direct or from the individual side of the system. Direct nominations would mean that a name is added to the course list for an event, and this would trigger the individual details to be updated to say that this person has been booked on a course. Course bookings can be done the other way around, through the individual's record, by booking an individual on to a particular event, and this would update the list of attendees automatically. The system has the facility for automatic letter generation, as do the recruitment systems, so that letters for participants can be produced by matching a standard letter with the participants list. Similar diary facilities also exist.

Applications not dependent on a comprehensive employee database

Expert systems

Expert systems are different from database systems in that they contain a knowledge base about a particular topic which comprises judgemental and qualitative information. Green (1987) comments that as database systems store, sort, manipulate and present bits of information, expert systems carry out these functions with knowledge. As database systems enable more efficient clerical, statistical and administrative processes, knowledge-based systems enable more efficient professional processes and decisions. Mitchell (1985) identifies four benefits of expert systems:

- the knowledge base may contain more information about a particular topic than any individual manager has;
- the knowledge can be applied in a logical way to any problem that the manager has in that area;
- the knowledge base can be added to by the manager so that it becomes more knowledgeable;

- the knowledge can be about qualitative areas as well as quantitative ones.

Expert systems have been used in a number of personnel areas – for example, in disciplinary procedures, to identify a structured interview programme for a given job (targeted selection), in job analysis and in organisation design. Systems operate by asking the user appropriate questions and, depending on the answer, can use follow-on questions or move to the next logical area for questioning. In this way the system takes the user through a structured process, which in itself generates learning. Expert systems are not designed to supplant professional judgement but to encourage sound logical thought processes and *supplement* professional judgement.

There are fewer firms involved in this side of personnel computing, and Business Information Techniques Ltd, of Bradford Science Park, has been a leader in the field with its product PARYS. For this and some other systems, some individual data is required – for example, when matching job dimensions and person attributes – and it is possible to download data from the main personnel database to avoid additional inputting.

Text networks

These are internal networks with information such as personnel policy and procedures and a range of on-line forms. Notice-board announcements, management briefings, organisation charts and employee handbooks can also be distributed and used in this way.

Human resource networks

These are similar to teletext and Prestel and contain factual information in the form of text, tables and graphics. They are more common in the USA but are being used increasingly in the UK. Networks are available in the area of pay and benefits data and current employment legislation. The National Training Consultancy has now begun to put its training-course evaluation material on disc, and this will be regularly updated – although not on-line.

Test administration

It is now possible to use computer versions of commonly used selection tests. The tests can be done interactively at the terminal, and the system can then score and carry out analyses and comparisons.

Interactive learning and interactive video

Flexible learning packages often contain interactive computer modules that take the learner through the material and ask check questions at regular intervals. The learner can move backwards and forwards in the package to cover a topic again or to miss out a chunk with which he or she is familiar. These interactive computer modules are often combined with video clips.

These packages – particularly where video is included – take large amounts of time to produce, and only large organisations would produce their own in-house versions. An example of interactive video would be for a time-manager package, and Lifeskills Ltd produces a package named 'Career Builder' which helps the user assess his or her career choices and strengths.

Personal computing

Separately from the personnel database, personnel professionals may use any number of standard wordprocessing, spreadsheet design packages, or electronic mail. With some systems it is possible to download data from the personnel database to use with other PC packages.

Protection of computer data about individuals

The Data Protection Act 1984 was designed to regulate the confidentiality, privacy and security of personal information. There have always been risks with storing individual information, but these have been highlighted with the growing use of computers.

Confidentiality relates to information that is sought, collected or kept by the organisation, the disclosure of which would be detrimental to the organisation itself or the supplier of the information

– for example the guarantee that references requested are in the strictest confidence, in order to protect the reference-writer.

Privacy relates to information sought, collected or kept by the organisation about a past, present or future employee, the use of which which might be detrimental to the individual. Detrimental effects might arise from:

- the information being inaccurate, incomplete or irrelevant;
- the information being accessed by those who should not need to use it;
- the use of that information for a purpose different from the one for which it was obtained.

The Data Protection Act applies to all organisations holding personal data on computer. Personal data has been defined as:

> data which relates to a living individual who can be identified from the information including an expression of opinion about an individual but not any indication of the intentions of the data user in respect of that individual.

All organisations using a computerised personnel database must be registered with the Data Protection Registrar, giving the sources and purposes of the data that is collected. Not only do organisations need to register each purpose of the data, they also need to comply with the eight data protection principles of the Act, which are that personal data will be:

- obtained and processed fairly;
- held only for lawful purposes which are specified in the register entry;
- used or disclosed only in a manner compatible with specified purposes;
- adequate, relevant and not excessive in relation to purpose;
- accurate and, where relevant, kept up to date;
- not kept longer than necessary for the specified purpose;
- protected by appropriate security against unauthorised access, alteration, disclosure or destruction, and against accidental loss or destruction.

The remaining principle states that an individual is entitled to be informed where data is held about him or her and entitled to access the data and, where appropriate, to have the data corrected or erased.

Tarrant (1990) states that a tougher line is now being taken with those who fail to register or to renew their registration, as the Act has been on the statute books long enough for organisations to understand what is required of them. Prosecutions and enforcement notices are increasing.

There are five ways in which the Act can be enforced:

- prosecution in the courts – usually arising from failure to register or using the data for unspecified purposes;
- enforcement notices, issued by the Registrar where one or more of the eight principles has been contravened, and requiring the user to comply;
- deregistration, if the user fails to comply – which may apply to all or part of the data;
- refusal to accept an application to register or to amend a current registration;
- transfer prohibition notices, which prevent the transfer of the data outside the UK.

In spite of some initial concerns when the Act was first put on the statute books, there is evidence to suggest that the vast majority of organisations support its eight principles. Angel (1985) comments that the Act reinforces good personnel practice, and Tarrant (1990) reports a survey regarding the Act referred to by the Registrar in his *Annual Report to Parliament*, the results of which indicate support for the principles but also support for simplifying and limiting current legislation requirements. Changes are presently being considered by the government.

In most cases, concerns from personnel managers were about the right of individuals to see data recorded about themselves. They saw no problem with most of the data, except for appraisal data, data on potential and career planning data, with the result that these are sometimes kept manually. There is some feeling that data on potential may be regarded within the Act as an expression of opinion about the individual and would therefore have to be disclosed if retained on computer. It is interesting to

note that, in most cases, information about top managers is not
held on computer at all.

Design, control and use of personnel computer systems

The way that the system is used depends on its design, how access
is controlled, the ability of staff and the support they receive and
the views of the personnel manager.

Design of the system

To encourage effective use of the system, it needs to be designed
in a 'user-friendly' way. Systems with menus, help screens and
built-in code lists will help the user find his or her way around
more quickly without constant reference to an 'IT-friendly' manual. Sequences for getting into and out of various parts of the
system and routines need to be quick and simple, and it is often
in this respect that some of the older in-house systems fall short.

Another aspect of system design that is important in encouraging use is the ease and speed of updating and report generation.
When systems are operating in real-time and are fully interactive,
changes can be made immediately, and any reports produced will
reflect the current situation. With some systems – for example,
batch systems – changes can only be input periodically. With
others, changes can be made interactively on a downloaded file,
but the master database is perhaps only updated monthly, and this
causes problems for other users who cannot get the up-to-date
information. Where updating can only be done periodically, there
is a need to maintain paper records in addition to those on the
computer, and this brings with it all the disadvantages of duplicate
records and the inability to make the computer the critical and
only source of personnel data. The system is not fully integrated
into the work of the personnel department.

In terms of report production, many systems now have the
capability to produce reports immediately, although we have
heard of cases where limited machine capacity and system design
have meant that the processing and printing out take 24 hours for
a complicated report – the system being unavailable for other
users until the report is completed!

A further common problem with the design of systems is found where more than one computer system is used in the personnel department. In these cases personnel data is fragmented – that is, located in different systems – with the result that reports combining a breadth of different types of information are difficult to produce. Sometimes data is duplicated – with some of the same data being held in different systems, but with no links between the systems. In these cases it is almost impossible to keep data consistent, and input time is doubled.

Access

Access to the system is critical and may be restricted by the philosophy of the personnel department or by the lack of hardware. If prevention is the prevailing philosophy of the personnel department then only limited numbers of personnel staff are allowed to view and use the data, and even fewer are allowed to update records. This prevents many potential users from easily integrating the computer data into their work, and also holds back system development. Force may be an effective philosophy if this is backed by sufficient computer and support facilities and an organisational culture which has fully absorbed the technology. Choice has the advantage of encouraging those who are keen, and builds on personal enthusiasm, but unless there is sufficient training and encouragement the result is that many may avoid the technology, feeling blocked by their lack of experience and a fear of the unknown.

Lack of hardware can also be a block to access and thus affects the way the system is used. If the computer is to be fully integrated into the work of the personnel department, then all staff – *including senior managers and professional levels* – need to have a terminal or PC on their desk via which they can access the system when they need it. This is especially vital for administrative staff who input data – if the system is not available to them when they need it, duplicate manual records will be kept with all the confusion and time-wasting that this entails.

A further aspect of access is the stance that the personnel department takes in respect of users from other departments. Increasingly, line managers from the whole organisation are seen as legitimate users of the personnel database and are vital in that

they – not the personnel department   are the true owners of the
information, the personnel department being the caretakers, coordinators, and developers of the system with a remit to use the
data in a more strategic way. Tannenbaum (1990) discusses the
implications of this expanding and diverse pool of users. He
describes the diversity of users along several dimensions, such as
technical sophistication, knowledge of human resource issues,
focus, method of accessing information and expectations. Recommendations to encompass this diversity include cross-sectional
sampling for computer needs analysis, incorporation of ease-of-
use features, developing an access/data-sharing plan, developing
and conducting multi-level training, establishing a human resources
information centre and keeping up with user expectations.

Training and support

In addition to a well-designed user-friendly system and appropriate access, users also need adequate training and support if
they are to get the best out of the system and contribute to its
development. Hall (1987) identified a distinct lack of formal training in this respect, and Eason et al (1974) talk about the important
role of 'local expert'. A resident 'local expert' is a member of the
personnel department, accessible to all, who is a computer
enthusiast and who is prepared to share his or her learning with
others. Users more easily gravitate to such a person rather than
ringing up IT services or the software house, or delving into a
'user-unfriendly' manual. There is a potential gain for the personnel function where this role is formalised and expanded.

Role and views of the personnel manager

The personnel manager will have a major influence on how the
system is used and developed. Managers who are enthusiastic
about computer use will be looking for new opportunities to relate
the system to their work in order to improve the contribution of
the personnel function. Managers who see personnel and computing as mutually incompatible will reject such connections, or just
not look for them. Managers also affect the development of computer use by their own 'hands-on' use of the system, which puts

managers in a much better position to direct its use in addressing key strategic personnel issues.

Implications of computer use for the personnel function

There are a number of potential implications for the personnel function in organisations where the computer is used to a fuller extent.

Personnel computer use has assisted the development of a human resources approach, as more and better-quality data is available regarding human resources issues and concerns. This results in better monitoring and control of personnel activities and a more quantified view of personnel issues. The personnel function is therefore in a better position to link personnel activities with business objectives, and to be proactive.

Another emerging role is that of information centre, and there is evidence to show that line managers are increasingly looking to the personnel function for key human resources data. In particular, one of the authors has found increasing demands for information from more senior managers intending to use this in a strategic manner.

Some personnel managers have commented that computer use encourages a role of internal consultant in the organisation, as they are seen to have key organisation-wide data, and thus a strategic view. Others have commented that there is a developing role of change agent in IT for those few personnel departments who were not last in the organisation computerisation race.

Computer use has caused some reduction in clerical staff in the personnel function, and this has often been seen as the payback for the cost of the computer system. There is some evidence that remaining clerical jobs have been enriched, and that computer skills are increasingly being valued in the function at *all* levels.

Most importantly, there is some support for the link between *sophisticated* computer use and an improvement in the image and credibility of the personnel function. Looking to the future, the indications are that the personnel function will need to show itself to be professional (businesslike), efficient, skilled and vital to the survival of the organisation. It will need to be in a position to financially evaluate personnel plans and activities, control manpower tightly and be proactive in identifying and solving manpower issues. The potential of the computer to support and enhance these activities is immense, but so far few organisations are exploiting this potential.

Study themes

1 Read Tannenbaum (1990). He suggests six trends in personnel computer use. Analyse each trend in terms of the progress being made in your organisation.
2 Read the article by Huczynski and Fitzpatrick (1989) relating to the cost of absence, and the book by Behrend (1978) relating to absence monitoring. Then design an absence-control procedure appropriate to your organisation and which is feasible if a computer system is used. Specify:
   • which data you would collect, and from whom/where;
   • how you would analyse the data;
   • what procedures you would instigate, and for whom;
   • how you would monitor the effectiveness of the system.
3 Read Hall and Torrington (1989). How would you describe computer use in your organisation, using the four categories they outline? Give examples to support this classification.
4 Thomas (1990) identifies that for personnel managers there is an 'under-investment in learning (vs training)' in relation to use of the computer. How can managers be encouraged and supported in this learning?
5 If you were asked to write on IT in personnel strategy for your organisation:
   • what data would you need to collect?
   • how would you collect it?
   • what major issues and decisions would need to be considered and included?
6 Interview five personnel managers in your own or another organisation. Write a summary paper which compares and contrasts their views on the role of the computer in the personnel function. How do you account for these views?
7 Read Green (1987) and Mitchell (1985) on expert systems in personnel. Identify another personnel area where expert systems are not currently used, and describe

- the type of knowledge that could be put into the system,
- how the system would be used,
- what the advantages of such a system would be.

References

Angel, J., 1985. How to ensure that your software complies with the Data Protection Act, in Page (1985).

Behrend, H., 1978. *How to Monitor Absence from Work: From Headcount to Computer*. Institute of Personnel Management, London.

Broomhead, H., 1987. An approach to career planning, in Page (1987).

Eason, K. D., Damodaran, L., and Stewart, T., 1974. A survey of man-computer interaction in commercial applications, *LUTERG*, No. 144, University of Technology, Loughborough.

Green, H., 1987. Expert systems in personnel, in Page (1987).

Hall, L. A., 1987. *Computer Use in the Personnel Function*, unpublished PhD thesis, UMIST, Manchester.

Hall, L. A., and Torrington, D. P., 1989. How personnel managers come to terms with the computer, *Personnel Review*, vol. 18, no. 6, pp. 26–31.

Hill, M., 1985. The recruitment system of tomorrow, today – design and implementation, in Page (1985).

Huczynski, A., and Fitzpatrick, M., 1989. End of the mystery – calculating the true cost of employee absence, *Journal of Employee Relations*, vol. 11, No. 6, pp. 12–15.

Ive, T., 1982. *Personnel Computer Systems*, McGraw-Hill, Maidenhead.

Mayhew, L., 1987. Manpower profiling, in Page (1987).

Mitchell, H., 1985. Expert systems for personnel work, in Page (1985).

Page, T., (ed.), 1985. *Computers in Personnel – Today's Decisions – Tomorrow's Opportunities*, Institute of Personnel Management, London, and Institute of Manpower Studies, Falmer.

Page, T., (ed.), 1986. *Computers in Personnel – from Potential to Performance*, Institute of Personnel Management, London, and Institute of Manpower Studies, Falmer.

Page, T., (ed.), 1987. *Computers in Personnel – Business and Technology – Achieving Practical Solutions*, Institute of Personnel Management, London, and Institute of Manpower Studies, Falmer.

Richards-Carpenter, C., 1990. The personnel power plant has arrived, *Personnel Management*, July, p. 79.

Stobie, I., 1986. Computer Graphics in Personnel, in Page (1986).

Tannenbaum, S. I., 1990. Human resource information systems: user group implications, *Journal of Systems Management*, January, pp. 27–32.

Tarrant, P., 1990. Personal data: the act begins to bite, *Industrial Management and Data Systems*, no. 1, pp. 11–14.

Thomas, C., 1990. Management development and IT: bridging the gulf, *Industrial Management and Data Systems*, no. 3, pp. 3–8.

Chapter 6

Human Resource Planning and Corporate Planning

Human resource planning (HRP) is directed to ensuring that the organisation meets its goals by developing and implementing the organisation's human resource strategy. There should be no dilemma, therefore, in carrying out HRP as a fundamental part of the corporate planning process. This does not always happen in practice, however.

What does human resource planning include?

The purpose of HRP is to develop schemes for the acquisition, development, management, organisation and use of employees, so that, as with any other valued resource, they are deployed as effectively as possible to the achievement of organisation goals. HRP is concerned with integrating these activities so that they are mutually supportive and make sense within a central philosophy of the way that people should be managed in the organisation.

Human resource planning covers a wide spectrum of activities. At one end there are the traditional manpower planning activities concerned with providing the organisation with the right number of people with the right skills at the right time. These 'hard' activities are dealt with in detail in the following chapter. At the other end of the spectrum are plans and activities which are designed to affect the way that people behave in the organisation and so ultimately affect the organisation's culture. Examples of this 'softer' aspect would be the planning and implementation of a total quality approach, a performance management culture, a 'customer comes first' orientation, the flexible organisation and so on. Bramham (1989) explores these areas in more detail. The development of a learning organisation is another example of a human resource strategy aimed at improving organisational performance.

Whichever end of the spectrum is being considered, there will be implications for the acquisition, development, management, use and organisation of employees. In the acquisition area, for example, implications may be in terms of the definition of the advertised jobs, the numbers of people required, their technical skills, their interpersonal skills, their management skills, their experience, the development opportunities that are used to attract them, the recruitment process used and so on. The emphasis is on ensuring that all activities are consistent with each other and are integrated.

The terminology in the human resource planning area is confusing, and Manzini (1984) comments that it is constantly changing. In this text and others, we use HRP as a term which covers both the hard and soft planning approaches. Other authors, such as Bramham (1989) for example, restrict HRP to the softer aspects.

The management of change has to be a fundamental skill in HRP and its implementation. This applies across all aspects, but is particularly important when dealing with the softer issues. Activities involve analysing environmental influences and trends, identifying where the organisation wants to be (its vision of the future), defining where the organisation is now and agreeing plans to effect the transition. These plans need to take account of the readiness and capability of people in the organisation to change and the nature of the resistance that there will be.

Environmental pressures on HRP

Pressures in the environment have influenced both the way that HRP is carried out and its perceived importance.

Increasing competition in terms of price and quality and of a global rather than a national nature has been identified as a major pressure. The realisation of some organisations that their productivity lagged way behind their competitors – particularly Japanese competitors – has stimulated major re-evaluations of philosophy and practices, resulting sometimes in the phenomena of corporate turnaround. Hill et al. (1988), for example, has identified the need for a shift from short-term to long-term profitability in order to achieve this, Peters (1988) sees that drastic changes in managerial approach are required, and others have identified the vital need to shorten product development cycles. Drucker (1988) argues that if organisations survive they will need to be information-based and operate in a way that is technically and organisationally more complex, with flatter structures and functioning in task teams. Flexibility in all its forms will be vital. Mergers and acquisitions are becoming a way of life. All of these demand the use of different skills and the operation of different organisational cultures. The environment in which the organisation operates creates great implications for the human resources in the organisation, and therefore the way in which they are planned becomes critical.

For Europe there will be pressures, too, from the unification of Europe in 1992, as Sedel (1989, p. 20) explains:

> The European Community is planning far-reaching changes in social legislation that will effect how and where companies locate, and how they manage, develop and pay their employees.

Greer et al. produced an excellent paper (1989) based on their research which indicated a change in emphasis in HRP from a technical approach using sophisticated statistical analyses to an approach centred upon its strategic planning role and more closely linked into the business. So, for example, there is much greater use of succession planning charts and less use of regression analysis. Techniques with shorter planning horizons are used. There was evidence that HRP is interpreted more flexibly and that it is accepted to a greater extent in the organisation, with more involvement of line managers and greater integration with other activities. These changes were in response to greater uncertainty in the organisational environment.

Integration with corporate planning

The description of HRP in this chapter so far implies that HRP and corporate planning should be closely integrated activities. Other writers support this view, such as Bennison (1987) and Bramham (1989). Schein (1986) reported that 40 per cent of respondents to his survey identified the need to integrate HRP with strategic corporate planning as a high priority. Baird et al. (1983) argue that HRP cannot be considered separately, as organisational strategy cannot exist without a human resources component.

In reality the extent to which HRP is included in corporate planning varies considerably. Burack (1985) found that there was much confusion in this area, as he reported that two-thirds of human resource specialists in his survey identified that HRP was included in organisational planning, but only half the business planners, in the same organisations, felt that this was the case. There continues to be considerable scepticism about the incorporation of HRP, resulting from such concerns as:

- the low status of the personnel function;
- the connection of the personnel function with maintenance activities;
- the failure of human resource professionals to understand business issues;
- a lack of identified success criteria with which HRP can be evaluated.

There is, however, evidence to indicate that the consideration of human resource issues within corporate planning is increasing. Greer et al. (1989) identified a greater perceived importance of HRP in organisations and also an increased acceptance and use of HRP techniques. Greater involvement of line managers was also identified, which may be the key to further integration, as Craft (1988) argues that managers need to be convinced of the value of HRP for it to be successfully integrated into corporate planning.

Ulrich (1987) identifies a range of criteria that would encourage acceptance of HRP into business planning. These are:

- ensuring that human resource plans cover a wide range of issues and build in competitive advantage;
- keeping the techniques and plans simple;
- offering choices;
- identifying human resource activities that can be used to accomplish business strategy;

- using business language and rationale;
- raising questions.

The true integration of HRP into the business and the greater involvement of line managers have implications for the personnel role in HRP in the future. A change from a role as controller and co-ordinator to an equal partnership with shared responsibility has been predicted. Greer et al. (1989) also predict that direct personnel involvement in HRP will decrease, but indirect involvement will increase. Tichy (1988) argues that personnel people will be key change-agents in this area. Personnel specialists will need to be proactive and raise the level of line managers' awareness of human resource issues, especially environmental influences and internal trends and the implications of these. Key skills will include the ability to support line managers while at the same time challenging their perspective and encouraging them to consider a wider range of options.

Problems with human resource planning

Integration with corporate strategy and planning

We have demonstrated above how important it is that HRP is integrated with corporate planning. One of the difficulties in achieving this is that the personnel function may not be represented within the organisation at board level. Brewster and Smith (1990) report that about two-thirds of UK organisations in their research had personnel representation on the board, which is less than in other countries in Europe. They also comment that, even with representation on the board, the human resources view is not always integrated into corporate strategic planning. It seems that for many organisations human resources strategy and planning are still seen as things which follow on from corporate strategy and planning, rather than things which contribute to it.

Uncertainty and the complex nature of the human resource

Not only does HRP have to respond to, and try to predict, the environment which is increasingly uncertain, it also is about the planning of people who are unpredictable in themselves. This is much more difficult than planning the financial aspects of the organisation. In other respects, too, planning for people is more difficult than planning for money, as Hussey (1982) noted:

- people are different from each other and are therefore not interchangeable;
- people are needed in a specific place at a specific time, but they are difficult to move around;
- a surplus of people is a drain on profits;
- as people are human beings, they have a right not to be treated casually.

Planning can therefore only be effective if it is viewed as planning a range of possibilities for contingencies that may arise. It is also a requirement that planning is done on a continuous basis. Planners also need to take account of the implications that changes will have on people.

Terminology and change

The third major group of difficulties with HRP, as we mentioned earlier in this chapter, is the lack of consistent terminology, the use of complex techniques and the changing emphases within HRP itself.

Greer et al. (1989) identified some of these issues in their research, and a number of others too. The main difficulty with HRP that they identified was that business operating plans were not sufficiently precise. Their summary of HRP problems is shown in Table 6.1.

Study themes

1 Read Sedel (1989) on the implications of the unification of Europe. What problems and opportunities will result from this for your organisation? What contribution does HRP make to solving the problems and capitalising on the opportunities?

2 Read Brewster and Smith (1990) on corporate strategy. Their Table 2 shows the differences between UK, France, Germany, Sweden and Spain with reference to written and unwritten personnel strategy. How would you account for these differences?

Table 6.1

Human resource planning problems

Major Problem Areas	Percentage of Firms Reporting Problems
Lack of Precision in Business Operating Plans	53.7
Inadequate Line Management Interest	43.3
Inadequate Link with Strategic Planning	38.8
Accuracy of Forecasts	35.8
Inadequate Data Base	29.9
Acceptance of Human Resource Planning	25.4
Expense	9.0
Other	9.0

n = 67. Only responses from companies that conduct HRP are included.

(Source: Greer et al, 1989)

3 Describe the highest level in your organisation at which the personnel function is represented. What role does the personnel function play at this level, and what are the implications for HRP in your organisation?

4 In moving to a customer-oriented organisation, what implications are there for human resourcing and what issues and options need to be considered in a human resource plan?

5 What is the balance between the softer and the harder aspects of HRP in your organisation? Justify your answer with examples, and explain why you feel that this situation has arisen.

References

Baird, L., Meshoulam, I., and De Give, G., 1983. Meshing human resource planning with strategic business planning: a model approach, *Personnel*, vol. 60, pt 5, pp. 14–25.

Bennison, M., 1987. Manpower planning and corporate policy: making the connections, *Manpower Policy and Practice*, autumn. vol. 3, no. 1, pp. 18–21.

Bramham, J., 1989. *Human Resource Planning*, Institute of Personnel Management, London.

Brewster, C., and Smith, C., 1990. Corporate strategy: a no-go area for personnel? *Personnel Management*, July, pp. 36–40.

Burack, E. H., 1985. Linking corporate business and human resource planning: strategic issues and concerns, *Human Resource Planning*, vol. 8, pt 2, pp. 133–45.

Craft, J. A., 1988. Human resource planning and strategy, *Human Resources Management: Evolving Roles and Responsibility*, Bureau of National Affairs, Washington DC, pp. 47–87.

Drucker, P. F., 1988. The coming of the new organisation, *Harvard Business Review*, vol. 66, no. 1, pp. 45–53.

Greer, C. R., Jackson, D. L., and Fiorito, J., 1989. Adapting human resource planning in a changing business environment, *Human Resource Management*, vol. 28, no. 1, pp. 105–23.

Hill, C. W., Hitt, M. A. and Hoskisson, R. E., 1988. Declining US competitiveness: looking for new models of organisations, *Academy of Management Executive*, vol 2, no 12, pp. 51–60.

Hussey, D., 1982. *Corporate Planning: Theory and Practice*, 2nd edn, Pergamon Press, Oxford.

Manzini, A. O., 1984. Human resource planning: observations on the state of the art and the state of practice. *Human Resource Planning*, vol. 7, pt 2, pp. 105–10.

Peters, T., 1988. Leadership excellence in the 1990s: learning to love change, *Journal of Management Development*, vol. 7, no. 5, pp. 5–9.

Schein, L., 1986. Current issues in human resource management, *Conference Board Research Bulletin*, no. 190.

Sedel, R., 1989. Europe 1992: HR implications of the European unification, *Personnel*, October, pp. 19–24.

Tichy, N. M., 1988. Editor's note, *Human Resource Management*, vol 27, pp. 365–367.

Ulrich, D., 1987. Strategic human resource planning: why and how? *Human Resource Planning*, vol. 10, pt 1, pp. 37–56.

Chapter 7

Manpower Planning

In this chapter we explore the elements of traditional manpower planning. The emphasis is on ensuring that the organisation has the right number of people with the right skills in the right place at the right time – a major challenge! This is the 'hard', numbers, end of human resource planning, but there are clearly links and overlaps with the 'softer' aspects. Bramham (1989) comments that, although he sees a fundamental difference in approach, processes and purpose between these two areas of planning, there are also important areas of interconnection. The two areas cannot be entirely separated, as each plays a part in the other.

The purpose of manpower planning is to avoid situations where, for example,

- excessive overtime is being worked because insufficient staff have been recruited;
- there is overstaffing creating demotivation and a drain on profits;
- the organisation cannot pursue new ventures or initiatives because the required skills have not been recruited or developed; or
- most of the staff are, for example, located in Glasgow but most of the work is for products that are produced in the Manchester plant.

Manpower planning framework

Before looking in detail at each of the elements of manpower planning, it is useful to develop a framework in order to understand how they fit together. Figure 7.1 shows a simple model of the manpower planning process. The first thing to note is that the organisation and its manpower exist within an environment, and that environment will have implications for every element of manpower planning. As the environment changes, so different pressures arise that need to be taken into account when each element is considered.

Figure 7.1
A simple model of manpower planning

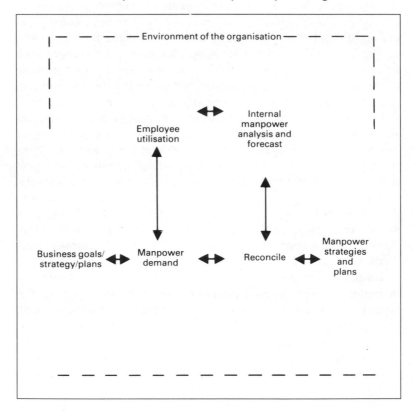

Central elements of the process are the *goals*, *strategy* and *plans* of the organisation. We have already considered in chapter 6 the extent to which people planning is integrated into corporate planning. This business information is vital, whatever the level of integration, whatever the stage in the process at which the human resources function is involved, and whatever the detail of corporate plans. It is this information on what the organisation intends to achieve over the next, say, one to five years that is used to project the quantity and quality of human resources that are required over that period – *employee demand.*

Another consideration in determining employee demand is the *utilisation of employees.* The nature of the work and the way it is structured will affect the number and type of employees required. So, for example, tasks may be delegated, changed or added in; the time spent on tasks may change, and tasks may be carried out at a different level of the organisation than in the past. The way that employees are used will change due to new legislation (such as health and safety legislation), conscious attempts to provide more motivating jobs, new materials and equipment, new processes and other approaches to increase the productivity per person.

The next element in the model is the *analysis of current employees and the forecast* of what is likely to happen to those employees within various future time-frames. Analyses may involve a breakdown of the ages and skills of employees and past trends of leaving the organisation or of promotion. The analysis of what has happened in the past can be projected forwards to predict what the human resources of the organisation will look like if there are no interventions such as recruitment and development or other organisational or external changes which may affect them.

These predictions of the shape of the future workforce can then be compared with the indicated demand for human resources, to identify anticipated over- or under-staffing and skills match. In an attempt to reconcile demand with supply, *external sources of manpower* may need to be investigated on an international, national, regional or local level, depending on the nature of the skills required. Factors in the environment, such as the unification of Europe in 1992, would need to be taken into consideration.

Although we have presented these elements in a logical sequence, clearly there is no one start or end point but rather a process of working through the elements and continually feeding back the prediction made and testing it against the other elements. Potential plans can be tested to identify whether, if carried out, they would enable the demand and supply predictions to be reconciled. The plans may include plans about acquiring new staff, developing and training staff, paying staff, utilisation of staff, reduction of staff, assessment of staff and so on. A vital factor is that these plans should be mutually supportive and make sense as a total package.

Much of the analysis that needs to be done for effective manpower planning can be done most efficiently by computer, and this has been described in chapter 5.

Manpower planning elements

Defining organisational goals and strategy

The information available in this area can be at vastly different levels. At a broad and high level there may be information such as a strategy to shorten product development times, acquire another business, merge with another business, achieve excellence in customer service or be regarded as the industry best in the development of people. At a more detailed level there may be anticipated sales of each product, or specified levels of customer service, anticipated numbers of research trials and anticipated numbers of customers and clients. This more detailed information is more likely to refer to a shorter time-frame and is more likely to change rapidly in response to factors in the environment or internally. Factors affecting the detail may be the activities of a competitor, a change in legislation, a change in the success of one of the organisation's other products/services or in anticipated products/services, changes in the price of oil or activity on the stock market.

Alongside this business information will be other information such as manpower budget information, and this too will have implications for the manpower planning process. There may be restrictions on the money available for manpower, although there will be choices about how that money is distributed and used. If finance is a sensitive issue then there may be strict control from the centre. Other scenarios include departments owning their own manpower budgets but being required not to go over budget, or perhaps being required to make a percentage cut in order to protect profitability. In easier and freer times, departmental budgets may be allocated but there may be little control of overspending. Any restrictions on money will challenge the individuals involved in manpower planning to produce creative plans, and utilisation can become a central issue. Creativity can be stifled if manpower budgets are based on headcounts rather than money value.

Deriving manpower demand

There are two approaches to forecasting manpower demands – objective and subjective.

Objective methods

Statistical methods depend on the assumption that past trends hold good for the future. If there is a lack of information on the goals and strategy of the organisation, or if the goals indicate the continuation of current growth levels, a simple extrapolation of employee number trends can be carried out. This technique is based on past and current trends for people demand. The most common variation looks at people demand over time – sometimes called time trends or time series – influences that may affect people demand are not considered. An example of this technique is shown in fig. 7.2. The biggest problems with this method are

Figure 7.2
Time trends

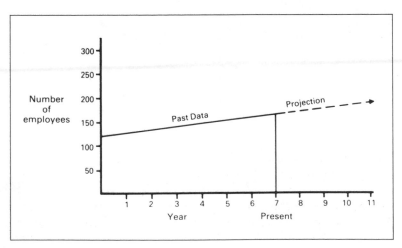

that no account is taken of the effect of environmental or internal changes, and that historical figures of people employed do not necessarily reflect people demand.

A more sophisticated approach involves deriving demand from specified organisational goals and changing circumstances. Models can be produced to take account of customers to be served, air passenger miles anticipated, sales targets or production forecasts. Models can be designed to take account of more than one governing factor and can be based on constant ratios or on variable ratings which take account, for example, of economies of scale. They can also be designed to take account of changes in employee utilisation resulting from different working methods. Comparisons between different scenarios can be produced and displayed graphically, as shown in fig. 7.3.

Work study is another objective approach; it depends on the analysis and grouping of tasks and the minimum time required to

Figure 7.3
Projections which take account of changing circumstances

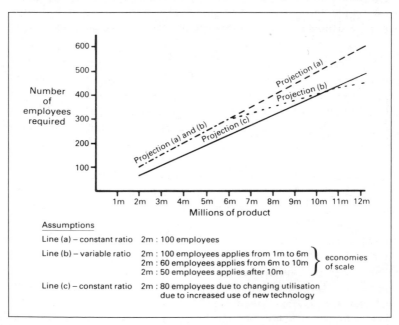

Assumptions

Line (a) – constant ratio   2m : 100 employees

Line (b) – variable ratio   2m : 100 employees applies from 1m to 6m   ⎫ economies
                             2m : 60 employees applies from 6m to 10m   ⎬ of scale
                             2m : 50 employees applies after 10m   ⎭

Line (c) – constant ratio   2m : 80 employees due to changing utilisation
                             due to increased use of new technology

perform them. Further information on work study can be found in chapter 13 on job design and in Currie (1963).

Verhoeven (1982) argues that, although this approach appears to be objective, it is in fact subjective because there is much individual judgement in the way that timing standards are produced and tasks are grouped. Similar activities have been labelled job analysis, activity analysis and task analysis, as described by Walker (1980), and these can be carried out at any level of the organisation.

Subjective methods

Managerial judgement is perhaps the most common subjective method; it is an inductive method based on past experience and knowledge of current organisational goals. This method can be approached from the 'bottom up', with supervisors and middle and junior managers sending their judgements up the organisation to stimulate discussion. It can also be approached 'top down'. Greer et al. (1989) found, in their survey, that supervisor estimate was the method most often used for estimating employee demand, with almost 70 per cent of organisations declaring this approach. Stainer (1971) comments that managerial judgement is often used alongside other approaches.

The Delphi technique is a specialised form of managerial judgement whereby managers independently and anonymously answer questions about projected manpower demand. They are fed back a compilation of all answers and are asked to give their views again. Gradually the views become closer. Although often discussed, Greer et al. demonstrate that this method is little used.

Judgements are required not only about the number of employees that are needed: quality is also a key issue. What skills are demanded of employees in the future? For example, an organisation which is reducing the product development cycle may want to approach this by heavy emphasis on cross-departmental task and project teams. The implications for this in terms of the skill demand would be for interpersonal and project management skills, such as influencing, coordinating, generating commitment and motivation, communicating, training others and so on. Skills selected for and developed in the past may well have been related to technical and scientific excellence, which would be insufficient for the future. The demand in terms of human resources is for a different portfolio of skills.

Employee utilisation

The ways that employees are used is a critical influence on the number and quality of employees that are required.

Reorganisation　Organisations are constantly reorganising themselves in order to become more effective and efficient. Departmental boundaries may be moved, and departments may be merged, separated or relocated. Hierarchies may be reduced or expanded. Functions may be centralised or decentralised. Functional structures may be changed to regional structures, and so on. All of these have implications for productivity in terms of quality and quantity.

Job redesign　More detailed changes in work organisation often respond to the need to provide motivating jobs – for example, through job enrichment, job enlargement and autonomous working groups as described in chapter 13. Tasks may be moved into and out of jobs, and the new jobs may require very different skills than the old – and a different number of employees.

Slimline initiatives and total quality initiatives　Tasks that are unnecessary may be deleted, and the work is then often reorganised in a more streamlined way. Accountabilities are clarified and duplication of activities is avoided.

Organisation and management development　Managers may be developed individually or in groups, and organisation restructuring may follow as part of this process. Introduction of new appraisal systems could also be included here, and also the introduction of performance management.

Bonus, productivity and incentive schemes　These may all affect levels of productivity per person. They may also affect quality of output!

Flexible arrangements　Altering times and periods of work, employing part-time or seasonal staff and employing staff on bases other than a full-time permanent contract will all have effects on quality and quantity of production.

Introduction of new technology, new materials and new equipment These will require a different set of skills and knowledge and will usually enable the same output to be achieved from fewer employees.

Analysing and forecasting internal employee supply

Analysis of current employees and a forecast of what will have happened to these employees at some point in the future is mostly carried out by quantitative techniques, although qualitative approaches are important too.

Analysis of characteristics of current employees

Current employees can be analysed in terms of age, sex, length of employment, experience and skill level and so on. The analysis usually involves grouping or banding numbers of employees into usable categories, and the data is often presented as a bar chart and referred to as a 'profile'.

Analysis can be carried out using two factors at the same time – for example, looking at an age profile for the total organisation and then breaking this down by grade, department, sex, experience or whatever is seen as a critical influencing factor. This sort of analysis can identify gaps in the organisation, or future or potential problems. For example, the age profile in an organisation which is to downsize by 30 per cent might indicate an ageing workforce with many close to retirement. An initial reaction might be that the downsizing process could be managed mainly through retirements and early retirements. However, further analysis might identify that the age profile varies considerably with grade, and that the previous strategy would create problems for the organisation. See fig. 7.4.

Figure 7.4
Age & grade analysis

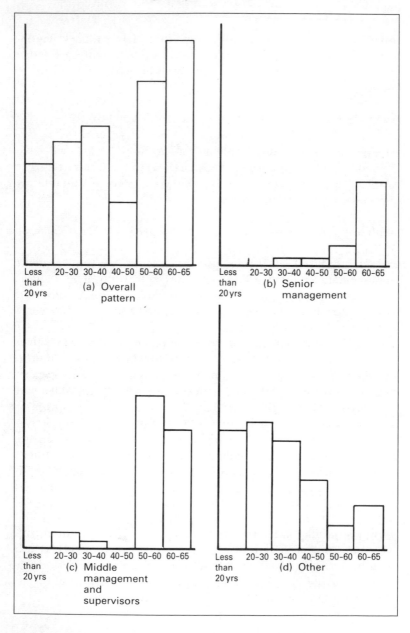

Analyses of employees leaving the organisation

Analyses of the rate at which staff leave the organisation can be projected forwards to indicate the number of staff employed at a future date due to natural wastage with no recruitment. A variety of measures have been developed to produce this information.

The annual labour turnover index – sometimes called the percentage wastage rate – is the simplest technique and expresses the number of staff leaving each year as a percentage of the total number employed. An example is given below. The disadvantage with this method is that it takes no account of length of service, which can have an influence on turnover. There is no way of knowing whether ten people left the same post or whether ten people left ten different posts, but the actions to deal with the problem would be different for each of these situations.

$$\frac{\text{Leavers in year}}{\substack{\text{Average number of staff in} \\ \text{post during the year}}} \times 100 = \substack{\text{Percentage} \\ \text{wastage} \\ \text{rate}}$$

The stability index gives a slightly different perspective; it looks at the number of staff who could have remained with the organisation throughout the whole of the year compared with the number who actually did. No account is taken of joiners during the year, and this analysis does therefore take account of the problem identified above.

$$\frac{\substack{\text{Number of staff with one} \\ \text{year's service at date}}}{\substack{\text{Number of staff employed} \\ \text{exactly one year before}}} \times 100 = \substack{\text{Percentage} \\ \text{stability}}$$

Bowey's stability index uses the same perspective but attempts to take into account length of service as well (Bowey 1974). It uses length of service of all current staff added up over a period (say two years) and expresses this as a percentage of the total service the staff could have had if they had worked the full period.

Formula

$$\frac{\text{Length of service in months over a 2 yr period of all current staff, added together}}{\text{Length of service in months over a 2 yr period of a full complement of staff added together}} \times 100 = \text{Percentage stability}$$

Example

If full complement of staff = 50
and of present staff of 49 there are 40 with 24 months each
2 with 18 months each
4 with 10 months each
2 with 3 months each
1 with 1 month

$$\text{index} = \frac{1043}{1200} \times 100 = 87\% \text{ stability}$$

The census method analyses leavers over a short period of time (say a year) and categorises them in terms of their length of service at their termination. A bar chart is usually produced to display the data.

The retention profile produces an analysis of staff who remain with the organisation classified by year of joining and expressed as a percentage of all joiners in that year. See fig. 7.5 for an example.

Cohort analysis can be applied to a homogeneous group of people – often new graduates who join the company at the same time. A graph can be produced to show the numbers who remain in the organisation year by year. The *half-life* expresses the time taken for the group to have lost half of those present at the beginning.

Qualitative analysis of staff leaving the organisation can be obtained through exit interviews.

Figure 7.5
Retention profile

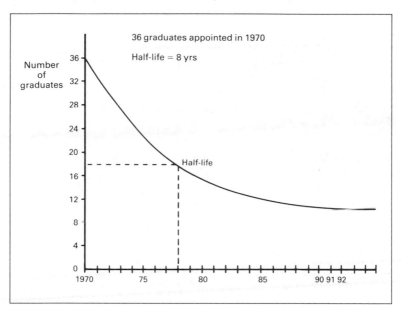

Analysis of internal movements

Statistical methods are often used in this context and are usually more complex than those techniques used to analyse wastage. One of the simpler techniques is the *stationary population* model, whereby joiners from a defined year or years in the past are described in terms of the numbers still employed and their present level of employment.

A more sophisticated variation of this is collecting and analysing this data over a period of, say, four years for a defined group – often graduates. The data will represent all movements of the group, whether promotions or sideways transfers or out of the organisation. A model of the organisation can then be produced showing the groups of jobs in the organisation or function with arrows showing the direction in which people have moved and the numbers who have moved in this way. Thick arrows can be used to represent heavy movement and thin ones to represent minor movement. In this way the flows around the organisation can be presented pictorially. Further analysis can be carried out to break down this picture by sex, age band or department/function. Comparisons can then be made which may indicate blocks or problems – for example, that there is less movement for women than for men. The reasons for differences can then be investigated. General promotion patterns can be considered and analysed, as these will impact on other human resource activities. Patterns need to be evaluated in terms of whether movements are too restricted or too free.

Qualitative techniques involve the use of succession planning and replacement charts. These charts identify roles in the organisation together with the skills and experience required. The present post-holder is identified together with an expectation of when he or she might move on, due to either retirement or a promotion or sideways move for development. Successors are identified in the categories of 'ready now', 'possible now' and 'possible later'. This can form the basis of a plan to develop successors so that they are well prepared when the opportunity comes – which may, of course, be before the date expected if employees in key positions decide to leave the organisation. The technique also identifies the gaps where there are few if any successors and where individuals will have to be recruited to meet the demand. Greer et al. (1989) found that this method was used by 66 per cent of respondents in order to identify manpower supply, and was used by almost as many to identify employee demand.

The environment and forecasting external manpower supply

Monitoring environmental trends and potential changes is crucial to manpower planning. These will impact on the freedom and flexibility that the organisation has to make choices and on situations which may need to be addressed particularly in recruitment. Thorough analysis of external supply will help employers answer questions such as:

- if we need to buy in people with skills in quality assurance in IT, what will it cost us?
- how easy will it be for us to find biometricians?

- if we changed our working hours, could we enlarge our labour market for assembly workers?
- as we lack skills in IEF (information engineering facility) for the production of IT systems and there are few people available nationally with these skills, what can we do internally to develop them?

Overview

At a broad-brush level, organisations need to be aware of the social, political/legislative, industrial and technological scene as well as movements and activities of competitors. In particular, one aspect of the social environment is critical, and that is labour-market issues.

At a 'helicopter' level, there are four major changes that will have an impact on organisations in the 1990s:

- *Labour shortages* The birth rate is slowing down, although not at a consistent or smooth rate. The implication of this is that, although the working population is still growing at present, the workforce size will reduce in the future.
- *Age composition* The workforce is ageing and it is more and more difficult to recruit younger people.
- *Sex composition* Partly due to the decline in population growth and changing social attitudes, women are becoming a larger proportion of the workforce than before. It is predicted that by 2000 they will comprise 44 per cent of all the workforce.
- *Skills shortage* Demand for unskilled labour will gradually decrease and demand for specialist/technical/professional skills and high-level management potential will increase. Pearson and Pike (1990) suggest that the UK may have even greater problems in this area, as 1992 may mean a net loss of people with such skills.

Types of labour market

Labour markets have been defined as a general geographical and/ or occupational area of labour supply and demand. They can be classified geographically at local, regional, national and increasingly international levels. Occupationally they can be classified by specialist or grouped occupations, such as biostatisticians, mass spectroscopists, graduates or clerical workers. There are some choices over how the labour market is defined – for example, being less restrictive about the previous experience needed for a post and being more prepared to train internally. Some factors are fixed, such as legislative requirements and those connected to the willingness of individuals to apply for vacancies. For example, for junior/clerical/secretarial/production-worker roles a local labour market would be in existence with individuals not being prepared to travel more than, say, a maximum of eight to ten miles to reach work. Moving house in order to accept a new job would be very unusual for this group. Senior management roles, on the other hand, would relate to a national and sometimes international labour market.

Each market has its own characteristics – different methods of dealing and different issues will be critical in each. In a local labour market, issues such as opening/closures of nearby work-places, transport and housing patterns, local unemployment levels and local education/training opportunities would all be examples of relevant information.

In understanding the appropriate labour market, information needs to be collected about pay, conditions/benefits and numbers of vacancies broken down by industry. Two key sources of information are *Employment Gazette* and *New Earnings Survey*, both published by the Department of Employment.

Reconciling the analyses and making plans

As we described earlier, the elements of manpower planning are not independent and cannot be progressed in a logical sequence and then completed. The whole process is one of continuous feedback and of testing different scenarios to analyse their implications and the feasibility of potential plans. It is important to devise a strategic approach to issues raised by the planning process – for example, an organisation may need to decrease employee numbers but at the same time be experiencing skills shortages in some areas. The plans need to be linked so that they are mutually supportive and indicate a sense of direction rather than ad-hoc responses to a series of individual issues. This sense of direction is important in the motivation of human resources staff in giving them a benchmark to test their solutions to ad-hoc problems which arise.

When the possibilities have been carefully assessed, plans can be produced in a variety of areas:

Supply plans

These may cover the timing of and approach to recruitment or downsizing, and also promotions, transfers and retention. For example, with an increasing shortage of graduates, the organisation may decide to redefine the labour market by including excellent A-level students and offering them the chance to pursue a degree while working for the organisation. Another organisation may tackle a similar issue by enticing graduates by long-term professional development and well-structured career progression schemes.

Organisation/structure plans

These plans may include the existence, remit and internal structure of departments or businesses. They may also involve the redefinition of jobs. For example, one company decided to stop carrying out internal audit on a regional basis but instead to carry this out centrally in order to improve consistency and cut manpower costs.

Employee utilisation plans

In the above example, 600 regional jobs were cut to 200 central jobs and new skills were needed as the use of IT in the activity increased. There are implications here for redeployment, redundancy and retraining.

Training and development plans

Training implications can arise from most changes – in the case above, for example – and the timing of training can be critical. In the supply-plan example, the implication is for clear development programmes to be worked out in advance so that graduates are clear on what they are being offered. There are also budgetary implications in resourcing these programmes.

Communications plans

Any planned changes need to be communicated to employees, and the way in which this is done is critical. For successful implementation, plans need to allow time for employees to express their concerns and their needs.

Appraisal plans

What is assessed in the organisation needs to be related to what is valued and what is seen as important in the achievement of corporate goals. If the development of people is seen as key then managers need to be assessed on the extent to which they do this as well as the extent to which they meet task demands.

Pay plans

It is often said that what gets rewarded gets done. In the above appraisal example, managers would also need to be rewarded as well as assessed for their people development activities. Another determinant of pay plans is the market rate for skills in terms of pay and benefits.

Study themes

1 What *sources of information* are available to organisations which will help them to identify environmental trends in the four areas identified in this chapter: social, technological/industrial, legal/political, activities of competitors?
2 Read chapter 7 of Walker (1980) on work analysis. Use exhibit 7.3 on page 153 of this, entitled 'Aspects of work that can be analysed', to analyse your own job.
3 Design a process to help managers think more flexibly about ways in which they can expand the labour market for a group of jobs where present supply is inadequate to meet demand.
4 The census method of analysing employee turnover was men-

tioned but not illustrated in this chapter. Carry out a census analysis for a department or function in your work organisation (or for the whole organisation, if you wish). Determine your terms of reference so that there are sufficient leavers in the analysis to indicate an overall pattern. Use a bar chart to display your data.

5 Read Hall (1989). Table IV in this describes the succession processes in two different organisations. Describe the succession process in your organisation along the same lines but giving examples to support your statements. What are the implications of the succession process in your organisation?

6 Read Napier (1989). What potential implications are there for the manpower planning process where a merger or acquisition has just taken place?

7 Draw a plan of the promotion and transfer and exit moves within your personnel department over the past three years. What conclusions can you draw from this data, and what recommendations would you make for the future?

References

Bowey, A., 1974. *A Guide to Manpower Planning*, Macmillan, London.

Bramham, J., 1989. *Human Resource Planning*, Institute of Personnel Management, London.

Currie, R. M., 1963. *Work Study*, Pitman, London.

Greer, R., Jackson, D. L., and Fiorito, J., 1989. Adapting human resource planning in a changing business environment, *Human Resource Management*, vol. 28, no. 1, pp. 105–23.

Hall, D. T., 1989. How top management and the organisation itself can block effective executive succession, *Human Resource Management*, vol. 28, no. 1, pp. 5–24.

Napier, N. K., 1989. Mergers and acquisitions, human resource issues and outcomes: a review and suggested typology, *Journal of Management Studies*, vol. 26, no. 3, May, pp. 271–89.

Pearson, R., and Pike, G., 1990. *The Graduate Labour Market in the 1990s*, Institute of Manpower Studies, Falmer.

Stainer, G., 1971. *Manpower Planning*, Heinemann, London.

Verhoeven, C. T., 1982. *Techniques in Corporate Manpower Planning*, Kluwer Nijhoff, Boston/The Hague/London.

Walker, J. W., 1980. *Human Resource Planning*, McGraw-Hill, New York.

Chapter 8

Organisational Structure

Organisation is both the act of organising and the state of being organised. For managers it is therefore the process of getting things done by deploying resources, determining what work other people should do and making sure that everything fits together effectively so that the whole is greater than the sum of the parts. For all employees it is the state of being part of a social group created and maintained for the purpose of achieving specific objectives that can be achieved only by the working together of people holding different yet complementary roles. Organisation involves specialisation, coordination and hierarchy.

Specialisation

Specialisation is the grouping together of a collection of activities that are carried out by a person or people in such a way that that collection of activities is different from those of other individuals or groups. In some instances that collection of activities is developed into a professional or an occupational skill.

A supermarket deploys the majority of its personnel in one of three activities: warehousing, shelf-stocking and check-out. Effective operation requires the correct allocation of people to each set of activities to ensure a smooth and swift flow of satisfied customers through the store. Some employees will be trained to carry out two or three of those specialised duties, so that the manager has maximum scope for flexibility in determining who does what. When employees can discharge only one set of duties, then specialisation becomes more difficult.

Some of the persistent operational inefficiencies of manufacturing have been blamed on the protective or restrictive practices of skilled workers in certain trade unions. These have been used to protect the security of employment of those following particular trades – for example, plumbers and electricians are the only people permitted to do jobs classified as belonging to people with their particular trade training.

In a similar way managers professionalise their jobs – for example, those reading this book are probably following a course of action that will invest them with specialised skills and areas of knowledge that others do not possess, feeling that this will give them security of employment and comprehensible career prospects.

Recently there has been a general move towards greater inter-changeability amongst those with craft skills and those in manage-ment positions. The overall management problem is to maintain maximum flexibility at the same time as ensuring the necessary provision of specialised expertise.

Coordination

Coordination is making the specialisations fit their activities together so that there is a work flow or other form of balancing such that organisational objectives are achieved. There is little purpose in the warehousing operation in the supermarket being extremely efficient in providing a neat, spick-and-span warehouse if the goods required on the shelves are not there ('Sorry, we're dealing with wines and spirits at the moment; no more margarine until this afternoon').

There is always a temptation for those who make up a team or department to be inward-looking and take a self-sufficient view of their work. One way of overcoming this is to have the mission and objectives of the organisational unit as a whole clear and con-stantly reinforced, so that those in the warehouse construe success as a successful store rather than a neat warehouse. The difficulties with this are its intangibility as a process and the resistance that is often encountered. Simply producing a mission statement or a policy or an enthusiastic poster is not sufficient to orient people towards organisational unit objectives: it requires commitment, which in turn requires a willingness to be committed.

> High commitment is concerned with both behavioural com-mitment to pursue agreed goals and attitudinal commitment reflected in a strong identification with the enterprise (Guest 1989, p. 42)

and

> attitudinal commitment is essentially concerned with the
> strength of the individual–organization linkage. Mowday,
> Porter and Steers (1982) identify three key decisions: identifi-
> cation with the organization's values and goals, a desire to
> work hard for the organization, and a desire to stay with the
> organization (Guest 1989, p. 43)

However logical the objective, the clear facts of the situation are
that many people at work are bored or alienated, perhaps feeling
that they have been badly served by their employer or being
cynical about the employer's competence and integrity.

Most of the methods of organisation design deal with coordination, such as the organisation structure, working procedures,
decision-making machinery and the appointment of coordinators.

Hierarchy

A hierarchy is any system of people or offices graded in rank
order. In working life the term is usually applied to the upper part
of the organisational pyramid and those office-holders possessing
the greatest power and influence. A significant feature of this
power is the responsibility for the actions and decisions of subordinates that is held by the superordinate. The value of hierarchy
is the way in which it clarifies roles as well as distributing authority,
but it also presents major problems of organisation. Where the
hierarchy is steep, with a large number of different levels, there
is a tendency to overmanagement, with much interference by
superordinates (or bosses) in the work of subordinates. In turn
this generates unnecessary administrative work and controls,
which create a need for extra personnel as well as slowing down
decision-making and administrative procedures.

There has long persisted the idea that there is an optimum 'span
of control', so that no manager should have more than five or six
direct subordinates. This idea has been carefully studied by
researchers and it is certainly not generally valid. Flatter hierarchies
with fewer levels are thought to improve communication and
generate greater individual autonomy and responsibility. There
can, however, be a case for a steeper hierarchy (and narrower

span of control) when problems being encountered are unfamiliar or when subordinates are not fully trained.

> As organizations grow from small units up to about 1000 employees, their number of hierarchical levels generally rises from the four levels of chief executive, departmental heads, supervisors and workers typical of the organization employ- ing one or two hundred persons, to about six levels at about the thousand mark. The rate of increase in levels which typically accompanies larger size is, however, a decreasing one. Even at 10 000 employees the norm is only around seven or eight levels. (Child 1984, p. 59)

Few aspects of management practice have been so severely criticised in recent years as hierarchy:

> The traditional corporate hierarchy is rapidly crumbling, and title or formal position count for less anyway, in a world of negotiations involving internal collaborations or strategic alliances or the formation of new ventures. (Kanter 1989, p. 361)

Throughout the 1980s, organisations were made 'leaner and fitter' by cutting out layers of middle management and shortening the lines of communication, until the term 'middle manager' almost became a term of abuse; admitting to being one was similar to admitting to having a communicable disease. Allied with this was a move to make individuals more accountable and empowered:

> [Managers] must learn to operate without the might of the hierarchy behind them. The crutch of authority must be thrown away and replaced by their own personal ability to make relationships, use influence, and work with others to achieve results. (Kanter 1989, p. 361)

The reduction of the levels of hierarchy is thus associated with the development of a different type of expertise by managers. This change of emphasis has been widespread and almost certainly beneficial both to managers and to the organisations they serve, but enthusiasm for cutting hierarchy has to be tempered by com- mon sense. Philip Beresford and Chris Blackhurst analysed the reasons behind the failure of some of the heroes of the enterprise culture of the 1980s, and one of their key conclusions was that these people of considerable talent:

> failed to put in place the organisational structures to enable their businesses to survive without them. While they absented themselves on the next acquisition, their businesses floundered. (Beresford and Blackhurst 1990)

In contrast there are businesses that are less spectacular but enjoy continuing success due to the creation of 'well-oiled management structures'. Such structures avoid the extremes of hierarchical rigidity but still enshrine hierarchical principles.

Hierarchy is not only a method of giving differential status and authority to people in an organisation: it is also a method of limiting a person's authority and power in relation to others. Most importantly, hierarchy is a method of ensuring that those of relatively higher status are made responsible for their actions. The differential status of hierarchy limits the power of individuals and makes them responsible for what they do. There is always a tension between giving people scope and preventing abuse. It is important that company directors should have scope to move quickly and take initiatives in developing their business: it is equally important that they should be strictly accountable for their stewardship, so that funds are not misdirected nor criminal activity authorised. It is important that members of the armed forces should be able to deal with terrorist attacks: it is equally important that their use of firearms should be according to strict rules and authorisation by someone of appropriate rank.

Organisational structure

The most common type of organisational structure is the *bureaucratic*, which is formal and mechanistic, exhibiting the characteristics of bureaucracy. In popular usage this term is frequently used pejoratively to describe administrative inefficiency and delay, with a bureaucrat being seen as an unimaginative figure who is shielding personal incompetence behind a mass of rules and paperwork. Human beings are depersonalised, because the maintenance of the administrative system itself becomes more important than the interests and personalities of the people who operate the system or who seek service from it.

Behind the popular distaste, however, lies an important method of organisation which has been viewed as indispensable for the rational attainment of the goals of any organisation. The German sociologist Max Weber (1947) identified the following characteristics:

- defined areas of duties for each role in an organisation;
- a hierarchy of responsibility;
- clear rules regarding appointments and promotions;
- appointments and promotions based on technical qualifications;
- a fixed salary paid according to rank;
- a separation of office from office-holder so that there is no change in organisation when a person leaves or is promoted.

Weber saw this as an ideal type of organisation because it freed employees from nepotism and overdependence on the whim of superiors at the same time as producing a disciplined and ethical mode of conduct, but later analysts have pointed out that the need to confirm closely to rules leads people to sustain the system rather than serve the people who use it.

Although Weber described bureaucracy as an ideal type of organisation, that did not mean that it was necessarily a practicable type of organisation. It requires a degree of stability that few organisations enjoy, and it ignores the extent to which many people see their place of work as an arena in which they will achieve significant features of their personal growth and discover their identity.

Bureaucracy had been vilified in political discussion as indicating:

> not merely a class of officials but certain types of centralised social order, of a modern organised kind, as distinct not only from older aristocratic societies but from popular democracy.
> (Williams 1983, p. 49)

But, despite its many flaws, bureaucracy remains a basic form of organisation that is appropriate for many types of undertaking.

Where the organisation has a need to move fast and make major decisions that depend more on flair and judgement than on the measured weighing of alternatives, then the structure will be *centralised* – relying on key, powerful figures with all decisions made in the light of central expectations. This is more appropriate for an entrepreneurial type of undertaking that is still trying to become established. The lack of a track record and conventions, as well as the lack of tried and tested rules, makes all members of the organisation relatively dependent on guidance from the centre. The founding entrepreneur may often be reluctant to lose that central role of being closely in touch with everything and making all key decisions. This is the challenge of needing to lose control of a small organisation in order that a growing organisation can acquire the management that it needs: decentralisation.

When there is reliance on diverse professional specialisations and well-established functional expertise, then the bureaucratic structure will be *decentralised*, with greater use of procedures and committees and less dependence on precedents. There may be one of two emphases: function or product. In *functional organisation*, people are grouped according to the expertise they share in a function such as marketing or personnel. In *product organisation*, people are organised around product lines first, functional specialisation second. Power and responsibility are distributed away from the centre, so as to make use of expertise and allow scope for delegation.

The principles of bureaucracy remain the most common principles for managing organisations, especially those that are large and stable, although reservations about the effectiveness of bureaucracy and the associated principle of hierarchy grow steadily.

The *matrix* form of organisation attempts to overcome some of the inflexibility inherent in bureaucracy by combining a functional structure with a product structure. There are two sets of overlapping hierarchies, one at right angles to the other. The vertical hierarchy is the orthodox ranking and reporting relationships of functional specialisation, while the horizontal hierarchy links together people from different functions to share full responsibility for a particular project requiring skills from each.

Matrix organisation is a form that most managers find attractive, because it emphasises expertise and enables people at all levels of management to carry realistic responsibility and see the impact of their own ideas and decisions. It has, however, begun to lose favour because of high support costs and unwieldly administration.

Some people believe that matrix organisation will have a new lease of life as business becomes more international in emphasis, as standard bureaucracy will not work at all in this situation:

> operations which cross national boundaries will almost inevitably run with matrix structures, whether or not they are called that. Dotted lines; more than one boss; activity-based working groups whose members have a primary reporting relationship in many different parts of the organisation; more time spent consulting and agreeing and building consensus than in issuing or receiving command-type instructions. (Vineall 1988)

None of the above forms of organisation is perfect for all situations, and this leads to much discussion about new forms of organisation that will suit the needs of the future as well as coping with the problems that have been experienced so far. The line of argument is frequently to suggest an approach which is different from what has been tried in the past, just as matrix organisation was a reaction against bureaucracy. But there are also aspects of current and evolving business activity that have to be incorporated in any new type of structure.

Organisations are becoming increasingly oriented towards the customer, whether that customer be someone buying a loaf of bread or an airline ticket, a corporation contracting for the supply of capital equipment or a patient awaiting surgery in a hospital, the readers of a national newspaper or the spectators at a football match. This increased emphasis on the importance of the customer and of meeting the customer's needs has been a salient feature of the rise of the marketing emphasis in organisations for some time, but it has gradually had the effect that preoccupation with internal affairs and organisational politics has become less because those working in the organisation have become more outward-looking than inward-looking and relative status in the hierarchy has become less important. This is a trend rather than a complete change, so that relative hierarchical rank, for example, still matters, but it matters less than it did.

Running a business requires an increasing variety of skills and competencies, and management cannot master all the specialised expertise that has to be deployed. This has two main results.

Firstly, it is necessary to rely on all the members of the organisation to know what they are doing, to be competent and to get on with their jobs with the minimum of supervision. Secondly, a single business is seldom big enough to employ all the experts it requires, so many skills have to be bought in from consultants or contractors. This makes the job of organisation a job of organising diverse inputs, many of which are temporary and expensive.

Gradually, computerised management information systems are becoming able to provide the quality of control data that can take much of the seat-of-the-pants element out of management control and make it less vulnerable to the whim or prejudice of individual managers. It becomes possible to agree objectives for individuals and sections that are clearer and more realistic, with less subsequent argument about whether or not the objectives have been achieved. The organising process has to coordinate a widening variety of elements, and the improvement of control systems makes this more possible and shifts the management emphasis in organisation away from supervision and hierarchy towards performance.

Drucker (1988) suggests the need for a considerable reduction in the number of layers in the management hierarchy, with the idea that the organisation of the future will be like a symphony orchestra, with a team of highly skilled experts who know exactly what to do but depend on a conductor to provide coordination and to enliven the performance. Performers specialising in a particular instrument form self-managed working groups without any reliance on a hierarchical management structure above. That attractive idea is slightly weakened, as Drucker concedes, by the fact that a business does not have the main coordinating mechanism of the symphony orchestra: the score to read from (although the computerised management information system is getting close). Kanter (1989, p. 116) feels the idea does not go far enough:

> For corporate players to make beautiful music together they must achieve a balance between concentrating on their own areas of skill and responsibility and working together with others. They need to do their own jobs well while keeping an eye on what might be useful for someone else . . . They need to simultaneously focus and collaborate. They must function in many roles: as soloist, ensemble players, and members of the orchestra.

The analyses of some economists (notably Marglin 1974 and Williamson 1975) have provided a different approach to understanding organisations and the working relationships within them, as they look for rational explanations of behaviour. The entrepreneurial, bureaucratic and matrix forms all take hierarchy as a given and the guiding principle is to identify who is responsible to whom, just as the law sees employees as servants of a master – the employer – and the legal basis on which most of us work is a contract of employment. It is just as reasonable to start analysing without the hierarchical idea being taken for granted. Instead the processes of people dealing with each other in organisations are conceptualised as a series of transactions. This produces a choice, as the working relationship can either be set in a market, where one buys services from another, or it can be set in a hierarchy, where one obtains work from another.

Marglin (1974) argues that management hierarchies were set up at the time of the Industrial Revolution in order that entrepreneurs could exploit labour more effectively. Relying simply on market mechanisms and putting out work to craftsmen working in their own cottages did not provide sufficient supply, as an increase in the price paid by the manufacturer met with a reduction in the volume produced, because the suppliers preferred to increase their leisure rather than their income. The reason for the development of factories and control of process through a management hierarchy was thus, according to Marglin, a response to inadequate market mechanisms rather than because developments in technology required larger-scale operations. This in turn suggests that conventional hierarchy could nowadays be substituted to a great extent by subcontracting and cooperative working.

There are some signs of a new form of organisation evolving. It has some features of the matrix form, and fundamental to its operation is the core/periphery split that is described in chapter 3. The core contains all those activities which will be carried out by employees within a tight-knit, cohesive organisational structure with a strong corporate culture and considerable attention to the career and competence needs of employees. On the periphery will be those less crucial or less specialised activities that are put out for tender by contractors.

There are difficult decisions about which activities should be in which area. The core should contain those skills which are specialised to the business and therefore not readily available elsewhere. It will also contain those people who have sensitive or confidential information, like the chief brewers who are privy to the secret formula that produces a particular beer. Logically, all the other activities are put in the periphery, including those requiring a high degree of expertise but in an area that is not specific to the organisation. This type of split can lead to an efficient, streamlined organisation, but there can still be the problem of an unexpected shortage of people to provide peripheral skills.

In approaching privatisation, several British water authorities reduced their complement of civil engineers, because they were expensive and the work could be done on an occasional basis by consultants. Gradually, however, there developed a shortage of civil engineers in the consultancy firms, so that the simple rules of the marketplace ceased to operate. Few consultancy firms were large enough to employ trainees in the same way that the water authorities had done. It may be true that the consultants had been exploiting large employers like water boards for many years by allowing them to train personnel and then poaching them, but the problem remains. Should water authorities now employ more civil engineers in their core?

Organisation design

Designing the organisation is creating the structure or changing it. The first requirements are *differentiation* and *integration*. Differentiation is making the arrangement for an individual job or task, while integration is coordinating the output of all the individual jobs so that the whole task is completed satisfactorily.

Methods of differentiation and integration vary according to the predictability of what has to be done. Waiters in a restaurant have their activities integrated by a tightly specified system for taking orders from customers, passing those orders to the kitchen in strict sequence, taking completed orders to the table and then clearing the table. Their activities are differentiated by two definitions of territory: the kitchen is the territory of the chef, not the waiter, and each waiter has a set of tables to service in the territory of the customer, which the chef rarely enters. Their activities are further differentiated in their dealings with the customer, where they have considerable latitude to use personal, idiosyncratic social skills to persuade the customer to spend money, not complain, be quick and come again. The only uncertainty is the behaviour and reaction of the customer.

That basic organisation design has scarcely altered for 150 years: the jobs may be complex, but the organisational system is simple. In contrast, jobs in social work or marketing, for example, have greater unpredictability and a constant flow of new problems. This type of situation produces frequent redefinition of job boundaries, great individual autonomy and a tendency to flexible networks of working relationships rather than rigid hierarchies. The organisation of marketing departments differs considerably one from another and is frequently being altered.

There are four fundamentals in organisation design:

- *Task identity and job definition* – deciding what jobs need to be done, making clear what the jobs consist of and how they adjoin other jobs, and avoiding gaps or duplication.
- *Structure* – grouping together different jobs into groups or departments or teams, using the bases of function, territory, product or time period. A further structuring device is hierarchy, as described above.
- *Decision-making complexes* – where organisation affairs are pushed along by decisions that cannot be made by individuals but only by groups of people representing different interests and areas of expertise.
- *Procedures* – the administrative devices for putting plans and policies into operation. These are described in chapter 11.

Organisational change

Organisations have a built-in rigidity and resistance to change. This is partly because their members have the same basic conservatism as all human beings and fear the loss of what they know and understand at the same time as being concerned over a sense of loss:

> Change threatens the investment one has already made in the status quo. The more people have invested in the current

system, the more resistant they tend to be toward change. Why? They fear the loss of status, money, authority, friendships, personal convenience, or other benefits they value. (Robbins 1983, p. 457)

The resistance is also partly due to the feeling that so many hearts and minds have to be won over in the need for consistency and fairness. How far can you change the organisation of your section without all the other sections changing as well and in the same way? Introducing change can therefore be one of the most daunting tasks facing any manager – particularly for personnel managers, who are likely to be altering things that come closest to the sense of security and personal competence that individual people feel. Despite the difficulty, the need is inescapable. As Edmund Burke said, a state without the means of change is without the means of its conservation.

There is, however, a risk that change is introduced simply for the sake of change, like putting up a new set of curtains. This can unsettle people unnecessarily and put undue emphasis on novelty and fashion: there is no more fatal strategy than digging up plants to see if they are growing. Any move towards organisational change has to be carefully thought out and thoroughly justified. You do not introduce a matrix structure of organisation, or stress counselling, or performance-related pay simply because everyone else is doing it: you introduce the change because it is appropriate for your organisation going about its own distinctive business.

A range of approaches to reduce resistance to change have been proposed by Kotter and Schlesinger (1979):

Education and communication   If we fear the unknown, our fear may be reduced when the unknown is explained to us. What is the justification for the proposal? How will it work? How will it affect me/us? What will be the benefits? Providing accurate and believable answers to those questions will reduce resistance if lack of information is the cause of the problem. It will not help if providing more information increases the degree of resistance.

Participation   There is an old axiom that people will support that which they have helped to create. If those who are to be involved in the change are involved in the process of deciding what the change should be, they are likely to be committed to it and to its implementation. It may not be quite the change you wanted, and the consultation may take a long time, but the change should work. If the participation process is seen as a sham and you simply do what you were going to do anyway, then resistance may be greater.

Facilitation Skills training and personal counselling can help people cope with the implications of change.

Negotiation A much more machiavellian approach is to 'buy off' resistance by offering inducements to the individuals and small groups who are focusing it. This is a highly political approach and will probably be construed as bribery if you offer the production manager a larger company car and new office furniture in exchange for dropping objections to a new shift-working arrange-ment. You have shifted the debate away from the merit of the change toward measuring the cost of human frailty. You also run the risk of being blackmailed by other powerful people on other matters later.

Manipulation This is altering or embellishing information to make it more attractive. The positive aspects of the proposed change are emphasised and explained in detail, while the aspects that will be unattractive to the audience being addressed will be glossed over, ignored or misrepresented. Another method of manipulation is the empty threat. 'If we don't do this, we shall be out of business in a month' may jolt people into acceptance of a new strategy, but would be exposed if the initiative were not accepted and the problem did not materialise.

Coercion 'Do this, or else' is the bluntest of all approaches. It has the merit of being straightforward and honest, but has all the obvious drawbacks that any coercive strategy contains: you need considerable power and you have to be able to survive after the change having alienated those who have been coerced.

To most people the first three approaches are more appealing than the last three, but there is not always the time or the room for manoeuvre that they require.

Organisation is about getting things done: organisational change is not simply about getting things done differently, it is about the redistribution of power. Power redistribution is always resisted by those who are going to get less. In the good times there is more potential power for everyone, as there is expansion, growth, lots of promotion prospects and plenty of money for new initiatives, so resistance to change is muted. In the bad times there is potential power loss for everyone, as the opportunities are squeezed. This is when organisational change is really difficult.

Study themes

1 Read Drucker (1988) on 'The coming of the new organization' and evaluate his ideas against the reasoning of Handy (1985) or Child (1984).
2 How does the analysis of Mintzberg (1983) provide useful ideas for your understanding of how organisations work?
3 Consider the advantages and disadvantages of hierarchy after reading either Blau (1966) or Robbins (1983).
4 In studying the different types of organisation described by researchers and management theorists, most managers tend to say, 'Where I work it is a mixture of all those different types.' What is the practical value to you, in your job, of the theoretical distinctions?
5 Handy (1985, pp. 195–6) describes 'the person culture' as a form of organisation. What signs of this do you find in your working situation?
6 Buchanan and Huczynski (1985, pp. 414–19) summarise the scheme of Harold Leavitt for dealing with change containing the four interacting variables of people, technology, structure and task. Read the passage and compare the approach with that of Kotter and Schlesinger (1979). Think of an innovation you want to introduce and consider how you would use these ideas in introducing the necessary changes.

Check-list for reviewing the organisation of your department or section

1 The purpose of the department or section

(a) Does it meet a basic business need – like sales or production – or is it intended to make things run more smoothly – like personnel? Is it necessary?

(b) Is it set up on the basis of *outputs* – like business objectives to be achieved – or on the basis of *inputs* – like people and problems? Are the outputs already being produced elsewhere?

(c) Does the department exist to deal with matters which other managers find uninteresting or unattractive? If 'yes', are the reasons good enough?

2 The activities to meet the purpose

(a) Does the section bring together those who share a particular *skill* or those with a particular *responsibility*?

(b) What activities have to be carried out to meet the purpose?

(c) How many people with what experience and qualifications are needed for those activities?

(d) How many ancillary employees are needed? How can that number be reduced? How can that number be reduced further?

(e) Are all the identified activities needed? Is there any duplication with other sections and departments? Is there a better way?

3 Grouping the activities

(a) How much specialisation is needed? How will this specialisation affect job satisfaction, commitment and efficiency?

(b) Are boundaries between jobs clearly defined and in the right place?

(c) Will job-holders have the amount of discretion needed to be effective?

4 The authority of job-holders

(a) Do job titles and other 'labels' indicate satisfactorily what authority the job-holder has?

(b) Do all job-holders have the necessary equipment – like keys, computer codes and information – for their duties?

(c) Do all job-holders have the required authorisations – like authorisation to sign documents – that are needed?

(d) Is the authority of any job-holder unreasonably restricted?

5 Connecting the activities of job-holders

(a) Do job-holders know what they need to know about the activities of their colleagues?

(b) Are there enough meetings of staff, too few or too many?

(c) Are there enough copies of memoranda circulated for information, too few or too many?

(d) Are job-holders physically located in relation to each other in a way that will assist communication between those who need frequently to exchange information?

References

Armstrong, M., 1988. *A Handbook of Personnel Management Practice*, 3rd edn, Kogan Page, London, chapters 6, 7, 10.

Beresford, P., and Blackhurst, C., 1990. Fallen idols, *The Sunday Times*, 4 March.

Blau, P., 1966. *The Dynamics of Bureaucracy*, 2nd edn, University of Chicago Press, Chicago.

Buchanan, D. A. and Huczynski, A. A., 1985. *Organizational Behaviour: An Introductory Text*. Prentice Hall, London.

Child, J., 1984. *Organization: a Guide to Problems and Practice*, 2nd edn, Harper & Row, London.

Drucker, P., 1988. The coming of the new organisation, *Harvard Business Review*, January/February, pp. 45–53.

Guest, D., 1989. Human resource management: its implications for industrial relations and trade unions, in Storey, J., (ed.), 1989. *New Perspectives on Human Resource Management*, Routledge, London.

Handy, C. B., 1985. *Understanding Organizations*, 3rd edn, Penguin, Harmondsworth.

Kanter, R. M., 1989. *When Giants Learn to Dance*, Simon and Schuster, London.

Kotter, J. P., and Schlesinger, L. A., 1979. 'Choosing strategies for change, *Harvard Business Review*, March/April, pp. 106–14.

Marglin, S., 1974. What do bosses do? in Gorz, A., (ed.), 1974. *Division of Labour*, Harvester Press, Brighton.

Mintzberg, H., 1983. *Structure in Fives: Designing Effective Organizations*, Prentice-Hall, Englewood Cliffs, New Jersey.

Mowday, R. T., Porter, L. W., and Steers, R. M., 1982. *Employee-organization Linkages: the Psychology of Commitment, Absenteeism and Turnover*, Academic Press, New York.

Robbins, S. P., 1983. *Organization Theory: the Structure and Design of Organizations*, Prentice-Hall, Englewood Cliffs, New Jersey.

Vineall, T., 1988. Creating a multinational management team, *Personnel Management*, vol. 20, no. 10, October.

Weber, M., 1947. *The Theory of Social and Economic Organisation*, Free Press, New York.

Williams, R., 1983. *Keywords*, Fontana, London.

Williamson, O. E., 1975. *Markets and Hierarchies; Analysis and antitrust implications*, Free Press, New York.

Chapter 9

Organisational Culture

Organisational culture is a pattern of shared values, beliefs and habits adopted by the people who make up an organisation. This interacts with the formal structure and procedures in producing behavioural norms to determine, for example, how people treat each other, the nature of working relationships that should be developed and attitudes towards change. The nature of an organisation's culture is seldom properly understood, as it is a composite of economic and social influences outside the organisation, as well as the formal structure, management strategy and other features of the organisation itself.

Corporate culture

Corporate culture is an expression of management objectives in trying to shape the culture of the organisation – and therefore the behaviour of its people – so that customers will be more likely to buy, prospective employees more likely to seek jobs and existing employees more likely to be committed to the organisation's cause:

> research dominates that a good organisation which is well known is admired more and liked better than an equally good company which is not so well known. It will attract more and better people to work for it, can more readily make acquisitions and more effectively launch new products: it will perform better. (Olins 1989, p. 53)

Corporate culture can be expressed and reinforced in various forms, such as formal statements of policy and the company logo, stationery and uniforms. Alternatively it can come from the stories that circulate or the way in which influential individuals model behaviour for others. Even where staff accept the authority of

managers and their right to manage, there is always some reluc
tance by members of staff to commit themselves wholeheartedly
to the enterprise (Anthony 1986, p. 41). Attention to corporate
culture can enhance commitment, but the management approach
must be comprehensive and *committed*. A biological metaphor is
apt: plants respond healthily to a total environment that is appropriate to their growth. In organisational life we have had too many
artificial fertilisers that assume that healthy growth will follow
from a large enough dose of a single stimulant.

National influences on culture

The United Kingdom is not Japan or Germany or the United
States, so many of the initiatives developed in those countries will
not readily transplant to a British cultural context, no matter how
attractive they may seem.

> high among the internal checks upon British economic growth
> has been a pattern of industrial behaviour suspicious of
> change, reluctant to innovate, energetic only in maintaining
> the status quo. (Wiener 1985, p. 154)

In the UK change in industrial matters is slow, but it still takes
place. The *enterprise culture* of the 1980s produced a sudden
increase in the number of small and specialised new businesses;
an associated shift in expectations among many young, upwardly-
mobile people who increased their interest in careers; mentoring;
customised pay arrangements and networking. By the end of the
decade the enterprise emphasis had begun to wane, but people
remained more willing to take risks in order to get what they
wanted out of life.

By the 1990s *concern for the environment* had developed
rapidly, becoming an issue to which corporate culture had to
respond. There is concern not only about the ozone layer and the
greenhouse effect but also about being part of an operation causing excessive noise, dirt, smells or other inconvenience to fellow
citizens. This is now broadening into a more general concern with
social responsibility, as people increasingly look to their workplace
for their personal opportunities to do what is worthwhile. There

is a nice irony in the growing pressure from within commercial organisations to be socially responsible at the same time as public-sector organisations have to become commercially efficient.

International influences on culture

International cultural issues are difficult to understand. The Japanese have produced the most dynamic economy in the world in such a short time that Europeans and Americans have tried to copy their methods, but the methods work well only when applied to the Japanese, who maintain the values of an agricultural, feudal nation in which the group is always more important than the individual, so that losing face is a humiliation much greater than in other cultures.

Arabs have a tradition of hospitality to guests that can make them deeply offended when invitations are declined, and they go to great lengths to avoid conflict.

> The Arab executive is likely to try to avoid conflict . . . on an issue favoured by subordinates but opposed by the executive, he is likely to let the matter drop without taking action . . . He values loyalty over efficiency. Many executives tend to look on their employees as family and will allow them to by-pass the hierarchy in order to meet them. (Barratt 1989, p. 29)

The Americans believe in individual autonomy – provided it operates within a clear set of rules – so that American children are taught very early the value of 'doing their own thing' and acquire the extraordinary self-confidence that Europeans are churlish enough to term arrogance. In France, however, there is

> a duty of moderation in acts susceptible to hinder the situation of others. This attitude of moderation is not explicitly codified, neither is it codifiable, but it indicates a certain tendency in French culture. (Poirson 1989, p. 7)

The history of the European Community in attempting to establish a supranational institution is one of constant but reluctant recognition of the stubbornness of national differences and the accentuation of regional differences among, for instance, the Basques and the Flemish.

The first appreciation of international cultural differences in management circles came with the study by Geert Hofstede (1980) of 116000 questionnaires completed by people working in 40 different countries. He concluded that national cultures could be explained by four key factors:

- *Individualism* is the extent to which people expect to look after themselves and their family only – compared with collectivism, where people expect to discharge a wider social responsibility because others in the group will support them. Collectivists owe total loyalty to their group.
- *Power distance* measures the extent to which the less powerful members of society accept the unequal distribution of power.
- *Uncertainty avoidance* is the degree to which people accept the uncertainty of the future and take risks, while others have been socialised to be anxious about this and seek the security of law, religion or technology.
- *Masculinity* is the division of roles between the sexes. In cultures where men are assertive with dominant roles, these values permeate all the organisations that make up the society. Where women have a larger role, values move towards concern for the quality of life and of relationships.

   Hofstede showed clear cultural differences between nations – an example being that Austria, Italy, Japan and Venezuela scored high for masculinity, while Denmark, Norway, Sweden and Yugoslavia scored low.

Gender and corporate culture

Corporate cultures are usually dominated by traditional male values of rationality, logic, competition and independence, rather than the traditional female values of emotional expression, intuition, caring and interdependence (Marshall 1985). This is because positions of influence are held largely by men, but it is by no means clear that male values are necessary for business success. Women wishing to succeed in these organisations have to adopt male values to do so. Only where an organisation is set up from scratch by women will it develop a different culture:

> Women . . . are now doing remarkably well in the firms they have set up themselves. Here, they don't have to play the male game according to male rules. They are free to make up their own rules, make relationships rather than play games, run their businesses more on a basis of trust than of fear, cooperation rather than rivalry . . . (Moir and Jessell 1989, p. 167)

Goffee and Scase (1985) found extensive evidence of women being very successful when able to operate outside a male-dominated culture.

Developing organisational culture

Schein (1985) explains that an organisation needs to develop a culture which enables it to adapt to its changing environment, at the same time as building and maintaining itself through processes of internal integration. He believes that there are primary and secondary mechanisms in development. The primary mechanisms are:

* what leaders pay most attention to;
* how leaders react to crises and critical incidents;
* role modelling, teaching and coaching by leaders;
* criteria for allocating rewards and determining status;
* criteria for selection, promotion and termination.

This line of argument contains problems. Firstly, overemphasis on 'leadership' can develop a culture of dependence on those more senior in the hierarchy. There are limits to what can be achieved by hierarchical means, as we saw in chapter 8.

Secondly, it is easy to confuse cultural leadership with position leadership: those who are most effective in setting the tone of an organisation may not be those in the most senior posts. Elevated position in a hierarchy may help, but does not guarantee effective cultural change. Organisational culture involves all members, and change is effective only when there is wide agreement about, and ownership of, the change to be introduced.

A third difficulty is the assumption that the culture of an organisation is identical in all its areas. In fact all organisations contain subgroupings, each with a distinctive culture depending on its members' views, the nature of its expertise or tasks, its history and so on. When this variety is respected, the culture of the organisation as a whole will be quite different from that in an organisation where such variety is suppressed.

Schein's secondary mechanisms for the development and reinforcement of culture are:

- the organisational structure;
- systems and procedures;
- space, buildings and facades;
- stories and legends about important events and people;
- formal statements of philosophy and policy.

These introduce a wider range of possible actions, but it is interesting that he places last what many managers regard as the most important method of changing *corporate* culture. The formal statements must, however, avoid conflicting with the cultural change that is being attempted. Similarly with organisational structure. A bureaucratic structure, for example, will undermine any moves to introduce a corporate culture emphasising risk-taking and personal initiative.

Culture and strategy

If a business is to achieve its business objectives, there is a need to develop an appropriate cultural emphasis among its people, and changes in corporate culture are most likely to succeed when there is a strategic aim to justify the changes. Miles and Snow (1978) drew the comparison between 'defender' organisations, in which the strategies were low-risk and involved reusing well-tried solutions, and 'prospector' organisations, taking greater risks and looking for new opportunities. The culture of the first was conservative and secure; the culture of the second was innovative and novel.

Just as organisational structures have to suit the business environment, so culture has to suit strategy. But we have seen that culture change is slow and difficult. It is important to be absolutely sure that changes in strategy and related attempts to change culture are really necessary, and not just a managerial whim 'to shake things up'.

Without the central sense of unity that culture can provide, organisations are no more than a collection of people who would rather be somewhere else because they lack conviction about what they are doing. The effective organisation has a few central ideals about which there is a high degree of consensus, and those ideals are supported and put into operation.

Study themes

1 Read the book by Olins (1989) and chapter 7 of Handy (1985). How would you define the difference between organisational and corporate culture?

2 How do you think that your organisation can develop its culture to embrace more thoroughly the concept of social responsibility? What are the pressures in favour and against such a development?

3 Relate the Hofstede (1980) explanation of cultural differences to your own experience and understanding. How helpful do you find his four factors in enabling you better to understand your situation?

4 Think of your working experience and of your observations of public life around you. Who provides cultural leadership without having position leadership? Why and how do they do it?

5 Read either Tiger (1970) or chapters 11 and 12 of Moir and Jessell (1989). Where are there signs of female values in your organisation? How could they spread further in the organisation? What would be the effect of such a spread on the success of the organisation?

6 Kanter (1989, pp. 361–5) believes that the demands of the future will require seven particular qualities from managers. How many of these seven qualities have you got? How appropriate are they for where you are in your organisation now, and

how necessary do you think each of them will be in your future career?

7 It has been suggested that organisations with the best health and safety record are those with a safety culture. How would you set about developing a safety culture (*not* safety rules and procedures).

References

Anthony, P. D. 1986. *The Foundation of Management*, Tavistock Publications, London.

Barratt, A., 1989. Doing business in a different culture, *Journal of European Industrial Training*, vol. 13, no. 4, pp. 28–31.

Goffee, R., and Scase, R., 1985. *Women in Charge*, Allen & Unwin, London.

Handy, C. B., 1985. *Understanding Organizations*, Penguin, Harmondsworth.

Hofstede, G., 1980. *Culture's Consequences*, Sage, Beverly Hills.

Johnson, G., and Scholes, K., 1989. *Exploring Corporate Strategy*, Prentice-Hall, Hemel Hempstead.

Kanter, R. M., 1989. *When Giants Learn to Dance: Mastering the Challenge of Strategy, Management and Careers in the 1990s*, Simon and Schuster, London.

Marshall, J., 1985. Paths of personal and professional development for women managers, *Management*.

Miles, R., and Snow, C., 1978. *Organisational Structure, Strategy and Process*, McGraw-Hill, Maidenhead.

Moir, A., and Jessel, D., 1989. *Brain Sex*, Michael Joseph, London.

Olins, W., 1989, *Corporate Identity*, Thames and Hudson, London.

Poirson, P., 1989. *Personnel Policies and the Management of Men*, trans. Thierry Devisse, École Supérieure de Commerce de Lyon, France.

Schein, E. H., 1985. *Organizational Culture and Leadership*, Jossey-Bass, San Francisco.

Tiger, L., 1970. The biological origins of sexual discrimination, *The Impact of Science on Society*, vol. 20, no. 1.

Wiener, M. J., 1985. *English Culture and the Decline of the Industrial Spirit, 1850–1980*, Penguin, Harmondsworth.

Chapter 10

Communications and Teamwork

Communication is the process of transferring signals, whether between one machine and another or between human beings. Within the human context, the process of communication does not relate simply to the actual transfer of the message:

> True communication is not simply passing information. It is much more concerned with the transference of understanding. (Crossan 1987, p. 28)

All decisions in the human communication process on encoding and channels of communication are related to the required outcome. In other words, as a result of the exchange of signals, there has to be

> some change in the recipient at one (or more) of three levels – those of understanding, acquiescence, and action. The assessment of whether communication is successful or not usually relies on criteria related to these three factors in the intention. (Thomason 1988, p. 401)

The person who initiates the signal has to decide the most effective way in which to encode the message and then transmits it, via the most appropriate channel available. The exchange is completed when the person to whom the message is dispatched receives it and if that person can then decode it.

All these stages of the communication process will be affected by the previous experience of the parties concerned in relation to communication. When encoding the message, the sender must ensure that it is phrased in such a way as to gain maximum effect. This will include decisions on the use of jargon; how to make the message both relevant and simple, without being too repetitious; and how to emphasise the most important aspects of the message. The sender will then choose the most suitable channel of communication – this may be oral, written or non-verbal, or may combine verbal and non-verbal elements. The decoding of any message which is communicated orally will include a response to the non-verbal gestures (for example, a smile or a frown, tone of voice or hand movements) which accompany the message. The interpretation of the signal will also depend on the recipient's perceptions of the sender and on previous experience of the outcome of similar communications.

The message to be transmitted may not reach its destination if there is any form of barrier to communication. This barrier could be an interference with the communication process, such as distracting noise or inattention on the part of the recipient, but barriers to communication can also result from lack of skill of the sender of the message, an incorrect assessment of the level of understanding of the recipient, the use of unfamiliar jargon in the message and the overloading of the system with too many messages at one time.

Another most important aspect of communication is the feedback mechanism, which all such processes must include. Within the human communication system, the success of the communication will be judged by the recipient's reaction to the exchange. This will also show the sender how to adapt the message or whether the channel should be changed to reinforce it. When such an exchange is required in the future, the sender will have learnt valuable lessons on the best way of achieving this.

The relationship between communication and information can be very misleading. While improvements in information technology have resulted in increased availability of and access to information, the level of interpersonal communication has not increased to the same extent. Drucker (1974) notes the existence of a major communications gap in organisations and states that there is a basic misunderstanding of the nature of communication. When there is an exchange of information between individuals, he argues that it is the recipient of the information who communicates and that the sender of the message only 'utters'. If there is no receiver, then no communication has taken place:

> Unless there is someone who hears, there is no communication, only noise. The communicator cannot 'communicate'; he can only make it possible, or impossible, for a recipient . . . to perceive. (Drucker 1974, p. 504 in Sigband)

The information which is communicated is a major element in a power relationship and establishes the owner of that information as the dominant person in the communication process. Not only is that person responsible for deciding what information is released, but the timing of the release can be used to tip the balance of power in the owner's favour, especially in sensitive situations such as during pay negotiations.

Organisational communications

Communication between those who work for an organisation is essential to the organisation's survival, and Klatt et al. (1985, p. 302) point to four basic purposes of communication in organisations – coordination, problem-solving and innovating, leading, and appraising and regulating. Mintzberg (1973, p. 171) considers that a manager's work is essentially involved in communication, and he estimated that around 80 per cent of a manager's time is spent in verbal contact, though Torrington and Hall (1987, p. 73) comment that much of this time is spent inefficiently and ineffectively.

Methods of communicating can exist on a formal and/or an informal basis. Informal systems will exist with or without management support, and the grapevine is often seen to be one of the speediest methods of communicating – if rather unreliable on details! Sometimes, the grapevine is deliberately used by management to 'test the waters' for a proposal, before suggesting an idea formally. In research carried out by Davis (1953), a correlation was found between the levels of use of both the formal and informal channels of communication. An increase in effective formal systems coincided with an active grapevine. This is contrary to the view of some managements that the establishment of communication systems will rid the organisation of its grapevine.

Recently, there has been a growth of formal communication systems devised deliberately to transmit organisational information. These can be established to relay information either to interested individuals or to groups employed in the organisation, such as managers, workers or shop stewards, and may also be used to inform external interested parties such as customers, suppliers, trade unions or the wider public. For example, a company newspaper, while being produced essentially to inform employees of recent developments in the company, may achieve a wider audience through extended mailing lists or by being placed in reception areas of the organisation.

The communication systems in an organisation can process information downwards, upwards or laterally. Downward systems – from top management through the hierarchical structure to the shop floor – depend for their successful operation on an uncomplicated organisational structure. Upward systems – passing information from the shop floor up to the highest levels – can suffer from delays, and messages may be edited by managers on their upward passage, but they are gaining in popularity. Lateral systems – between departments or different specialist groups – deal with the most neglected direction of information flow, and these are rarely found. The most popular existing systems are based on the downward flow of information and incorporate only a single direction of flow. Most organisations use a number of different channels of downward communication, though few have developed one or more reliable upward systems, thus the two-way flow of information is restricted.

Communication can be written, such as notices on open noticeboards, internal memos, company newspapers, letters to employees' homes and employee reports; or oral, by face-to-face contact with senior management, immediate superiors or trade union officials; or by the use of audio-visual materials, loudspeakers and videos. While written communications have the advantage of being consistent in the information given to all employees, oral communication has developed general popularity. Employees state a preference for acquiring information through contacts with department heads or through team meetings (MORI, 1989, p. 42), and also for passing views and information back to management in that way (KPMG Peat Marwick 1990, p. 20).

The establishment of networks for communicating in organisations has been one of the recent growth areas in human resources management, and it is seen that over 50 per cent of the companies surveyed in all the main industrial sectors have a formal communications policy governing these networks (KPMG Peat Marwick 1990, p. 19). There has been a recognisable shift in the way that managements in the UK choose to communicate organisational information – from the reliance on indirect communication through trade union representatives to union members, who are employees of the organisation, towards the creation of direct channels of information from management to all their own employees. The increase in management interest in communicating with their employees is recognised in various surveys of the last ten years (Batstone 1984, Millward and Stevens 1986, Edwards 1987, Townley 1989). It is also noticeable that larger financial resources are being committed to such schemes, with an increasing number of individuals being appointed to sole responsibility for communication at senior management level (IPM 1981).

These communication initiatives are attributed to a combination of factors (Townley 1989, p. 337). These include the following.

1 The moral right to information

Employees are considered to be one of the parties interested in the well-being of the organisation, who should receive information in the same way as shareholders. This view was prevalent in the 1970s, in the aftermath of the Bullock Report, and resulted in a number of pieces of legislation, the only surviving one being that on 'disclosure of information to trade union representatives' (Employment Protection Act 1975).

2 An interest by management in communication as an educative process

It is argued that information supplied by management will enable workers to supplement shortfalls in their knowledge, resulting in more realistic bargaining and influencing the behaviour of employees at work. This unitarist concept is dependent on the acceptance by employees that employers are a credible source of information, and on the assumption that the effects of such information will always be as management wishes – both doubtful propositions!

3 An interest in communication as a method of increasing organisational commitment

The view that increased commitment will stem from a number of elements, including a feeling of belonging (Martin and Nicholls

1987), is much discussed in the literature. Whether being given information without an attendant increase in decision-making power will add to feelings of commitment is an open question.

4 An increased focus on communication due to the pressure of existing or anticipated legislation

Existing legislation on communication includes the provisions of Section 1 of the Employment Act 1982, which requires all companies with over 250 employees to state in their annual reports the action taken in the previous financial year to develop systems for providing employees with information on matters of concern to them, and Section 17 of the Employment Protection Act 1975. The latter statute deals with the information which must be disclosed to trade union representatives for the purposes of collective bargaining ('disclosure of information').

Anticipated legislation is contained in the proposals of the European Community to extend the information and consultation rights of employee representatives in multinational companies (draft European Company Statute) and those with over 1000 employees (draft Fifth Directive) and generally (Charter of Minimum Social Rights).

The existing British legislation has affected only those organisations which were willing to move in this direction, and reaction in Britain to the suggested EC legislation has been firmly against any mandatory rules in this area (Brown and Rycroft 1990, p. 26), while encouraging voluntary extensions of communication and consultation.

5 An attempt by management to undermine or bypass the trade unions

It has also been argued that the move towards the wider dissemination of information is an attempt by management to undermine or bypass the trade unions as providers of information. While there is no doubt that the increase in the use of direct communication systems has coincided with a time of declining power for the trade unions, this decline is claimed (Marchington and Parker 1990) to be a consequence but not an objective of the introduction of such systems.

6 Helping the organisation through changes

Does the introduction of direct communications systems herald a new management style representing the human resources management school, or is it a convenient tool for managements in times of great change? Though there are notable instances of the existence of a new and strategic approach to personnel policies, including communication, the main evidence (Storey and Sisson 1990, Myers 1991) suggests a more piecemeal approach, which involves the use of communication as a tool for helping organisations through times of great change or difficulty. Introduction of communication systems at such times can, however, add to management's problems, by making employees question the managerial motives for their introduction and therefore querying the validity of the information given.

In introducing any communication system, but especially a direct one, an organisation must consider the following:

1 *To whom the information is addressed* It is usual to try to make any direct system available to all employees within the organisation, although, because of shift work, unsocial hours or inaccessibility, this is not always convenient.
2 *By whom the information should be given* Because of reports that employees prefer to receive information from their own superiors (MORI 1989, KPMG Peat Marwick 1990), direct systems such as team briefing (Grummit 1983) use the immediate superior of the team as the briefer to provide the contact point for regular information-giving. This will operate successfully only if that person is able to communicate effectively while understanding the information to be conveyed. Training for superiors in the skills of communicating and in interpreting financial information is essential.
3 *The type and format of information to be conveyed by the system* Organisations often assume that the information that they wish to provide is the kind and in the form that employees wish to receive. Research has shown that employees receive information on such areas as major changes in work organisation or working methods and on terms and conditions of employment, but only limited information on finances and investment plans

(Millward and Stevens, 1986). On the other hand, employees would be interested in information on company plans for the future, how well the individual is doing in his or her job and how well the company is competing in its markets (MORI 1989, p. 40). In the team briefing system, 70 per cent of the information given in the brief is related to that specific work group and 30 per cent is more general company information. The way in which the information is presented is also most important, and audio-visual presentations and videos may assist in this area.

4 *Credibility of information* A number of factors will help with the level of credibility – if information is given at regular intervals and not solely at strategic times; if the information can be questioned and answers are available; if the provider of the information has credibility in his or her own right.

5 *Feedback* A direct communication system should provide opportunity for the receivers of the information to query and make comments on suitable topics. It is important to ensure that any questions which cannot immediately be answered receive prompt attention. The reaction of employees to the subjects discussed at their group meetings and the questions raised can provide valuable feedback data for management.

6 *Timing* The communication system should be based on regular group gatherings, at a frequency related to the amount of relevant information available.

7 *Top management commitment* Any communication system is expensive to the organisation in terms of the time and resources required to keep it operating. It also requires the continuing enthusiasm of top management to provide the information, training and facilities necessary.

8 *Monitoring* Any system needs to be examined from time to time to see if it is operating effectively. The use of an upward communication system, such as an attitude survey, can produce useful insights into this, while management can check on its progress by examining it in operation.

9 *Relationship to other communication systems* No organisation should put all its efforts into one system only; within its communications policy, an organisation should consider by which methods it will pass which items of information and to whom.

10 *Relationship to personnel policy* A communication policy

which forms one part of a considered philosophy will be more successful than one which is an ad-hoc response to particular problems.

The success of any communication system is difficult to judge, and very few organisations conduct regular surveys of their system's operation. This is partly because it is hard to isolate the impact of the communications system from that of other personnel policies and also because few organisations specify targets for achievement by the communicators by means of the system. It will be interesting to see whether the increased interest in communications outlasts the times of economic difficulty – and, if so, whether there will be changes in management style and the levels of decision-making as a result.

Team briefing

The most popular system of direct communications in operation in Britain is team briefing, which has been developed and popularised by The Industrial Society (Grummitt 1983). It consists of a series of regular meetings of some 30 minutes' duration at which the leader of the group passes on company-related information to small groups of employees. This information is passed down through a cascade system until it reaches all parts of the organisation. The leader of the team, or briefer, also adds on other local relevant information and fields questions from the team. Part of the success of the team briefing system lies in the successful operation of the team and the effectiveness of the team leader.

Teamwork

Within any organisation, there are many teams or groups – both formal and informal. The establishment of formal teams within the workplace has recently become increasingly popular. This is based on the view that a team can operate more effectively than the same team members functioning as individuals. There are, however, particular occasions when an individual can perform better alone:

> Problems to which there is likely to be only one correct
> solution are more effectively tackled by individuals. (Hogg
> 1990)

Many problems faced by organisations are so complex that they require more than one individual to work on them. There are also certain organisational structures where teamwork is necessary to achieve the organisation's objectives, such as in combining the talents of both functional and specialist workers. It is also noteworthy that many organisations have experimented with establishing team activities – either as part of the production process (for example, grouping the machinery on the shop floor to form a nucleus for the team) or by setting up teams which operate outside normal production (such as quality circles or project teams).

The creation of a team does not guarantee its successful operation: it takes a considerable period for a team to develop its own identity and procedures for functioning. Handy (1990) has identified four stages of team development: forming, storming, norming and performing. An effective team must contain people whose talents and abilities are complementary but not identical to each other. They must, between them, fulfil most of the basic roles of team members, as described by Belbin (1981). There must be known objectives for the existence of the group, and procedures for reaching decisions. There must also be ways of dealing with conflict within the group, and an appreciation of the strong points of each member, leading to the application of the individual talents of its members to the benefit of the team. The decisions of the team will be based on the knowledge of all its members, and ideas of the team will have been thoroughly discussed and evaluated before being put into use. Those decisions, depending on how they have been reached, will also have the commitment of all the team. Members of an effective team will receive satisfaction from that membership.

There can also be problems emanating from team decision-making. Within the team – as, for example, in a jury – there could be pressures to conform and accept a majority decision, in order to preserve the group identity, even though those who are unsure disagree with that decision. The effectiveness of the team can also be reduced if it is dominated by one individual who does not allow full discussion of all views. There can be a tendency in teams to support one's corner so enthusiastically that one forgets the aim of reaching the best solution – and this whole process is extremely time-consuming.

In industry, the main examples of teamworking are members of the board, (representing different functional and specialist skills), project teams for limited periods and formal production teams as seen in Japan and Sweden. Teamworking can affect recruitment policies, the nature of supervision, the need for common terms and conditions for all in the team, and the importance of multiskilling or at least an appreciation of others' specialisations. The availability of relevant information will also be important to the success of the team.

Study themes

1 You are asked by senior management in your organisation to put forward a proposal for the introduction of a direct communications system. Give your main arguments.
2 What methods can be used to monitor the effectiveness of the communications systems in a large organisation?
3 'High-level teams go through the same processes of development as other teams, but the consequences of their actions are obviously magnified by their seniority.' (Hogg 1990). Consider how this statement applies to a board of directors.

References

Batstone, E., 1984. *Working Order*, Blackwell, Oxford.
Belbin, M., 1981. *Management teams*, Heinemann, London.
Brown, R. and Rycroft, T., 1990. *Involved in Europe*, Discussion Paper No. 12, British Institute of Management, London.
Crossan, D., 1987. A company employee communications strategy, *Management Decision*, vol. 25, no. 3, pp. 28–34.
Davis, K., 1953. Management communication and the grapevine, *Harvard Business Review*, September–October.
Drucker, P., 1974. *Management: Tasks, Responsibilities, Practices*, Heinemann, London.
Edwards, P., 1987. *Managing the Factory*, Blackwell, Oxford.
Grummitt, J., 1983. *Team Briefing*, Industrial Society Press, London.

Handy, C., 1990. *Understanding Organisations*, Penguin, Harmondsworth.

Hogg, C., 1990. Team building. *Personnel Management* Factsheet 34, October.

IDS, 1988. *Teamworking*, IDS Study 419. Incomes Data Services, London.

IPM, 1981. *Practical Participation and Involvement, 1 Communications in Practice*, Institute of Personnel Management, London.

Klatt, L., Murdick, R., and Schuster, F., 1985. *Human Resource Management*, Merrill.

KPMG Peat Marwick, 1990. *Employee Involvement: shaping the future for business*, Confederation of British Industry, London

Marchington, M., and Parker, P., 1990. *Changing Patterns of Employee Relations*, Harvester Wheatsheaf, Brighton.

Martin, P., and Nicholls, J., 1987. *Creating a Committed Workforce*, Institute of Personnel Management, London.

Millward, N. and Stevens, M., 1986. *British Workplace Industrial Relations, 1980–1984*, Gower, Aldershot.

Mintzberg, H., 1973. *The Nature of Managerial Work*, Harper, London.

MORI, 1989. *Blueprint for Success*, Industrial Society Press, London.

Myers, J., 1991. *A Study of Direct Systems of Communication between Employers and Employees*, Unpublished M.Sc. thesis, UMIST, Manchester.

Storey, J., and Sisson, K., 1990. Limits to transformation: Human resource management in the British context, *Industrial Relations Journal*, vol. 21, no. 1, pp. 60–65.

Thomason, G., 1988. *A Textbook of Human Resource Management*, Institute of Personnel Management, London.

Torrington, D., and Hall, L., 1987. *Personnel Management, a New Approach*, Prentice-Hall, Hemel Hempstead.

Townley, B. 1989. *Employee Communication Programmes*, in Sisson, K., (ed.), 1989. *Personnel Management in Britain*, Blackwell, Oxford.

Chapter 11

Work Systems and Administrative Procedures

Business administration systems are of key importance to all organisations. Such systems allow managers to organise the business and exercise control over it. Carter (1982) suggests that business administration can be studied in terms of *systems theory*. The business or work-centre is viewed as a black box in which inputs received from the environment are converted to outputs and transmitted back to the environment (see fig. 11.1):

To describe all the inputs and outputs of a modern organisation would be an extremely complex task. A simpler alternative is shown in fig. 11.2. Here we see the main inputs of labour, equipment and materials, together with the main outputs of profit and product. Control over this system is exercised by the board of directors and senior management. Their role is to measure the output, compare it with the planned output and implement any adjustment required to keep the business on course.

If we were to consider *all* the subsystems operating within a business organisation, we would find that, while some of the inputs and outputs are of a physical nature – for example, labour, raw materials and products – the majority of subsystems within a modern organisation are concerned with data and information processing.

Administrative procedures

Procedures, in common with other forms of planning, seek to avoid the chaos of random activity by directing, coordinating, and articulating the operations of an enterprise. They help direct all enterprise activities toward common goals, they help impose consistency across the organisation and through time, and they seek economy by enabling management to avoid the costs of recurrent investigations and to delegate authority to subordinates to make decisions within a frame of policies and procedures devised by management. (Koontz and O'Donnell 1972).

Figure 11.1
Simple Model of Systems Theory

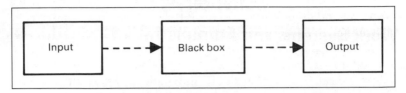

Procedures are a vital part of every business activity: they are used in the acquisition of resources, the provision of information for decision-making and the distribution of goods and services.

Figure 11.2
The systems view of a modern business (from Carter 1982)

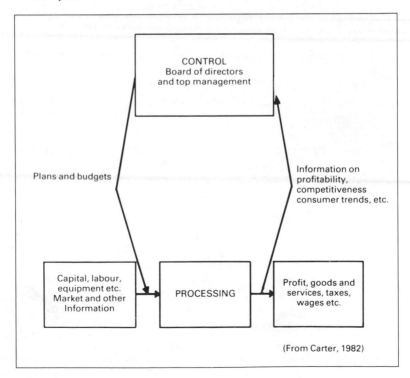

(From Carter, 1982)

The majority of procedures involve the collection and processing of data and the communication and presentation of information. Through a series of sequential steps, they allow a variety of tasks to be accomplished, from placing a new starter on the payroll, to allocating a manager a car-parking space.

In the light of the above, it is surprising that administrative procedures are rarely discussed. One reason may be that they are often considered as being dull and unnecessarily bureaucratic, particularly by those individuals that use them. Procedures are, however, of fundamental importance to the success of all organisations.

Advantages of procedures

1 *Reducing the need for future decisions*   Once a procedure has been established, it may be used time and time again. For example, the procedure for advertising a job may be used each time a vacancy arises. The establishment of standard operating procedures allow tasks to be accomplished as efficiently and quickly as possible.
2 *Consistency*   Procedures allow consistency to be achieved by organisational departments, employees and customers. Such consistency can contribute to a fairer working situation within the organisation and thus safeguard against employee disputes or grievances.
3 *Autonomy for organisational members*   Clear and effective procedures allow subordinates to process work without constant referral to senior management. Such procedures should also permit flexibility, so that exceptional or difficult situations can be easily dealt with.
4 *Management control of operations*   By using procedures to delegate work to subordinates, managers are able to continue with the task of running the organisation. They are, however, still able to monitor the progress of administrative work, since many procedures require approval in the form of authorised signatures (particularly those dealing with pay-related matters).

Disadvantages of procedures

1 *Relevance*   Procedures need to be used with care and should

be applied only to those situations where a procedural solution is appropriate. There are several sources of useless procedures: procedures may become obsolete without being discontinued; procedures may lose relevance by relying on out-of-date information; clerks and administrators may attempt to build up their standing within an organisation by creating a number of complex and irrelevant procedures (see Koontz and O'Donnell 1972).

2 *Duplication* Overuse of procedures can lead to the duplication and overlapping of tasks, creating problems within and between departments.

3 *Complexity* Procedures should avoid being too complex. They should be kept simple and straightforward so that they can be easily understood by all those using them.

4 *Response to change* There is a danger that, through organisational custom and practice, procedures may become somewhat rigid and inflexible. In order to remain competitive, organisations must be able to respond quickly to changes in the external environment. It is therefore important that procedures should be flexible enough to be able to handle such changes effectively. In addition, any changes to existing procedures or the introduction of new systems should be accompanied by full staff consultation and training (Mann 1967).

Types of procedure

Task performance procedures These are standard operating procedures which allow the completion of a particular task – for example, the manufacture of a product or the processing of an invoice. Some task performance procedures are general – for example, typing a script on a wordprocessor – while others are more specific – such as typing a script using the correct letterheads, layout and style of address (Cyert and March 1963).

Planning and expenditure authorisation procedures Procedures are used in the implementation of corporate plans. This includes the meetings at which plans are agreed, the format of meetings and the subsequent setting of budgets to cover any new proposals.

Information and coordination procedures　All organisations rely on the gathering, manipulation, dissemination and storage of information. Examples of procedures used for information and coordination purposes include:

- *Team briefings* – usually conducted at a departmental level. Must be regular in order to be effective.
- *Minutes and memos* – often circulated to a wide distribution list with notes for action.
- *Storage of information*　In most organisations the procedures for record- and report-keeping serve two main purposes: reference and prediction of future trends and events.

Mutual control procedures　These are procedures which allow two parties a certain amount of control over each other. They are most common between employers and trade unions, but are also found between employers and employees. Examples include grievance and disciplinary procedures.

A *grievance* procedure is the method by which an employee raises a complaint or expresses a dissatisfaction about working terms or conditions. Through a series of steps, grievance procedures allow an individual to pursue an issue at various levels within the management hierarchy. A grievance should, in the first instance, be raised with the individual's immediate supervisor. If an acceptable solution is not reached at this level, the grievance may be taken to the next level of management, and so on until it is resolved. A detailed investigation of grievance procedures undertaken by Thomson and Murray (1976) suggests that the components of a procedural structure may be broken down into five main areas: basic structure, the roles of participants in procedure, the scope of procedure, procedural differentiation and the impact of the procedure. Other factors which may affect the operation of a grievance procedure include trade union representation and communications and information networks.

Disciplinary procedures are used by employers to deal with unsatisfactory employee performance. (The disciplinary process is considered in more detail in chapter 17.)

Mutual control procedures provide a valuable method of dealing with problems in which both management and employees have an interest. It is important that such procedures are periodically reviewed, in order to ensure their continuing effectiveness and acceptance.

Methods of producing procedures

There are four main methods of producing procedures (Torrington and Hall 1987):

- *Check-list*   A number of check questions/items are set up which require the individual to work through them in sequence in order to achieve the procedural outcome. See fig. 11.3.
- *Modelling*   A typical procedure is drawn up and used as a model which can be modified and changed to suit a variety of situations. Examples include discipline and grievance procedures.
- *Flowcharting*   This is the most complex procedure, usually retained for those situations involving a number of people and departments. See fig. 11.4.
- *Task logic*   This is a method of work study and associated techniques which uses the logic of the task to dictate the actions to be followed in task performance. (For a detailed review, see Larkin 1969.)

Study themes

1 Describe a task performance procedure currently in use within your organisation. What are its advantages and disadvantages? Could you suggest any improvements?
2 Read Thomson and Murray (1976). What do you consider to be the key features of an effective grievance procedure?
3 Consistency in many procedures is achieved by the use of carefully designed forms. These forms allow the preprinting of fixed data so that only variable data has to be entered; they provide instructions to the user regarding data required and present the data in a standard format. With the above in mind, design a form for the requisition of stationery supplies. Reference may be made to fig. 11.4.
4 Construct a check-list for this chapter.

Figure 11.3
Induction check-list for new employees

Health and safety

1 Explanation of emergency evacuation procedure
2 List of first-aiders on site
3 COSHH regulations and their implications
4 Accident reporting procedure
5 Occupational health services

Code of conduct

Signed undertaking by employee regarding confidentiality and disclosure of information

Employee benefits

1 Company pension scheme
2 BUPA
3 Personal insurance plan
4 Occupational sick pay scheme

Staff rules

1 Disciplinary and grievance procedures
2 Internal promotion policy
3 Data protection
4 Overtime rules
5 Equal opportunity policy
6 Security arrangements
7 Canteen facilities
8 Parking

Figure 11.4
Procedure for requisitioning stationery supplies

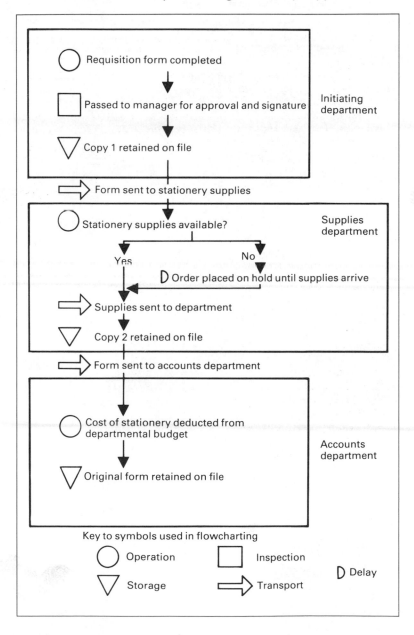

References

Carter, R., 1982. *Business Administration*, Heinemann, London.

Cyert, R., and March, J., 1963. *A Behavioural Theory of the Firm*, Prentice-Hall, Englewood Cliffs, New Jersey.

Koontz, H., and O'Donnell, C., 1972. *Management*, McGraw-Hill, New York.

Larkin, J., 1969. *Work Study, Theory and Practice*, McGraw-Hill, London.

Mann, D., 1967. *Effective Administration*, Macmillan, London.

Thomson, A., and Murray, V., 1976. *Grievance Procedures*, Saxon House, London.

Torrington, D., and Hall, L., 1987. *Personnel Management: a New Approach*, Prentice-Hall, Hemel Hempstead.

Chapter 12

Job Design

When an individual does not perform well in a job, it is often interpreted as a lack of knowledge/skill/ability on the part of that individual. However, an American management consultancy carried out some research on job performance and found that 80 per cent of factors affecting performance were to do with the definition or design of the job, and only 20 per cent resulted from lack of skills or ability. The way that jobs are designed is therefore of critical importance to the organisation.

In chapter 8 we discussed organisation design and identified the design of individual jobs as a component part of this. This chapter looks in more detail at what job design involves and at different perspectives and approaches to job design. In particular, we concentrate on the design of jobs to increase the motivation of the job-holder.

What is job design?

Job design is the process of allocating tasks/activities, methods and relationships to identified roles in the organisation, in order to improve individual and therefore organisational performance. It has been referred to as work design, work structuring (not to be confused with organisational structuring), job redesign and work redesign. Different writers, researchers and practitioners have different perspectives on job design, and historical trends can also be identified.

Historical trends

Many, but not all, of the current approaches to job design are based on the perspective that jobs need to be designed to meet technological and organisational requirements and *also the social and personal requirements of the job-holder.* This emphasis is based on the work of people such as Davis (1966).

Historically a much narrower definition of job design has been used. Robertson and Smith (1985) quote a US study in 1955 where the criteria for job design were

- maximum specialisation, limiting the variety of tasks;
- maximum repetitiveness;
- minimum training.

Taylor (1911) designed jobs that required minimum intelligent thought by the doer and were based on the requirements of the technology.

These designs were based on the idea that people had a purely instrumental approach to work and wanted nothing more from it than money. Changing and increasing expectations from employees, and an understanding that individuals may require satisfaction from the job itself, have encouraged organisations to look more carefully at what motivates people at work and to take this into account when designing jobs.

Four approaches to job design

Campion and Thayer (1989) report the findings of their research which uncovered four approaches to job design, each emphasising different outcomes for the individual and the organisation. They have also produced a questionnaire, fig. 12.1, which enables managers to compare the different approaches. Using and expanding on their classification, the four approaches can be described in the following way;

The motivational approach

This approach is based on research into what motivates people at work. There are a variety of theories which may be used to identify the factors in a job which will motivate people to perform that job well. Maslow (1943), for example, suggests that, as long as physical and survival needs are met, individuals will look for opportunities for social interaction in their work, for recognition

Figure 12.1

Four approaches to job design: a questionnaire

MOTIVATIONAL APPROACH

1) *Autonomy:* Does the job allow freedom, independence or discretion in work scheduling, sequence, methods, procedures, quality control or other decisions?
2) *Feedback:* Do the work activities provide direct, clear information about the effectiveness (in terms of quality and quantity) of job performance?
3) *Achievement:* Does the job provide for feelings of achievement and task accomplishment?

MECHANISTIC APPROACH

1) *Job specification:* Is the job highly specialized in terms of purposes and/or activity?
2) *Skill simplification:* Does the job require relatively little skill and training time?
3) *Repetition:* Does the job require performing the same activity or activities repeatedly?

HUMAN FACTORS APPROACH

1) *Lighting:* Is the lighting in the workplace adequate and free from glare?
2) *Equipment usability:* Is the equipment needed on this job easy to learn and use?
3) *Attention requirements:* Is the amount of attention needed to perform this job minimal?

BIOGRAPHICAL APPROACH

1) *Strength:* Does the job require little muscular strength?
2) *Seating:* Are the seating arrangements of the job adequate (with ample opportunities to sit, comfortable chairs and good postural support)?
3) *Climate:* Is the climate at the workplace comfortable in terms of temperature and humidity, and is it free of excessive dust and fumes?

(Campion and Thayer, 1989)

that they have done a job and for fulfilment of their ultimate potential. Herzberg's theory (1987) emphasises the importance of responsibility, advancement, recognition, growth and the nature of the work itself. Other researchers have translated these and similar motivation theories into the characteristics of jobs which will motivate people to perform well. Such characteristics include variety, autonomy, responsibility, challenge, interaction with others, task significance and clear goals and feedback.

Further research into motivation by Vroom (1964) and Lawler and Porter (1968) indicates that, although there is still much value in the theories outlined above, the picture is much more complex in reality. Whereas previous theories sought to find the answer to the question 'What motivates people?', this more recent work acknowledges the importance of individual differences and concentrates on the conscious or unconscious thought processes that individuals go through to determine the effort they will put into their work. The questions that individuals ask themselves are

- 'If I try hard, will I succeed? (Have I got the right skills, knowledge, support and so on?)'
- 'If I succeed, will I get the reward I expect/have been promised (for example, promotion, more responsibility, a business trip abroad, a bonus and so on?)'
- 'Do I really want the reward? (Would I value something else more – such as more holiday, working less hours, learning different skills, and so on?)'

See Nadler and Lawler (1977) for a diagramatic representation of this process. These expectancy/valency/instrumentality theories explain why some of the job-design schemes based on a motivational approach have not succeeded. Practical examples of schemes are described later in this chapter. For a recent comparison of the different perspectives on motivation and the implications these have for job design, see Kakabadse et al. (1988).

The mechanistic approach

This approach is based on the scientific study of jobs, as exemplified by the scientific management approach of Taylor (1911). The work needed to be done is studied in detail to determine how each element of the work can be done most efficiently, in order to increase productivity. Work study is based closely on this approach. Currie (1963, p. 16) describes the objectives of work study as to achieve

- the most effective use of plant and equipment,
- the most effective use of human effort, and
- the evaluation of human effort.

Detailed analyses are produced of job activities (to the level of which hand is doing which activity) using stopwatches and timings down to seconds. Summary charts, string diagrams, multiple activity charts, flow process charts and so on are produced so that decisions about job design may be made on the basis of objective data. Decisions usually involve work being split into highly specialised jobs, with simplified tasks, minimum idle time and minimum training required.

The human factors approach

This approach concentrates on the equipment that an individual uses in his or her job. The objective is to arrange and design the equipment so that the attention and concentration that it requires do not exceed the ability of the least able person likely to be appointed to the job. This approach had a very high profile in the 1970s and 1980s and was often centred on the design of the individual workstation when computer terminals were arriving on desks. Lighting levels and positioning, office furniture design and positioning, equipment design and layout of dials and instruments were all seen as key in reducing fatigue and stress. User-friendly design was seen as reducing error and maximising performance.

The biological approach

This approach emphasises the importance of the interaction between the job-holder and the environment. It is aimed at reducing unnecessary physical demands and minimising injuries and discomfort. Included in this might be design of seating and desks, as in the human factors approach above, and Pearce (1987) comments that well-chosen equipment and furniture can improve employee health and morale and the effectiveness of the organisation. Also included in this approach are many items of a broader nature. Rest breaks, shift times, temperature and noise levels would all be addressed under this heading. Factors in the emotional as well as the physical environment could be included, for example to minimise the stress levels created by jobs.

Which approach?

It is clear that there is value in each of the above approaches, as all have something to offer when jobs are being designed or redesigned. Campion and Thayer (1989) argue that each has draw-backs too, and that job design involves trade-offs between all of these approaches. However, the motivational approach does offer more advantages over a wider range of jobs – from senior manager to car assembly worker – so we will look in more detail at how this approach can be put into practice.

Motivational job design

The main ways in which this approach has been put into practice are via job rotation, job enlargement, job enrichment and the setting-up of autonomous working groups. While each of these is described separately, there are clearly areas of overlap in schemes that are put in place.

Job rotation

This is the simplest and easiest method to implement. It involves employees moving from one job to another of a similar nature at predetermined intervals. There is most evidence of this being used in skilled or semi-skilled manual jobs, but increasingly it is used in clerical and associated work. An example of job rotation is where assembly workers move from assembling one product in week one, to a second product in week two, two a third in week three, and then back to the first product in week four. In some jobs the rotation would be over shorter periods; in others, such as clerical work, it would be longer. Job rotation in managerial work may come under the description of 'development', where managers are moved within their function (or without) over, say, three-year intervals, and without being promoted to a higher grade.

The advantage of job rotation for the individual is primarily in the variety it produces at all levels, and the development at some, but there may be disadvantages in the interference of the functioning of the work group. At lower levels the variety may be minimal, and workers may be swopping one boring task for another which is only slightly different. The advantage for the organisation is more broadly skilled employees who are more flexible for a low-cost outlay. Disadvantages may be the additional training required, difficulties at change-over times and maintaining accountability in tracing back the source of problems.

Job enlargement

Job enlargement involves adding additional tasks onto a job. These are usually of the same type and level as the original task, and are related to it in some way. The purpose is to reduce dependency on others which may control the pace of the job and restrict an individual organising a job to meet his or her own needs. A clerical job, before being enlarged, might involve processing travel-claims forms on the computer at a time when the computer was not being used by another person to confirm travel arrangements. An enlarged version would involve both tasks and thus a greater control over when the tasks were done.

The reactions to job enlargement have been mixed. Hackman and Lawler (1971) reported that workers with enlarged jobs were more satisfied and performed better, yet Kilbridge (1960) found that many workers preferred the pre-enlargement jobs. The disadvantage to some workers is that the routineness of routine jobs is attractive as it permits greater social interaction and daydreaming. The other disadvantage is for those workers who found the enlarged jobs more stimulating, as the effects of a larger job may soon wear off and the need for further enlargement arises. For management the disadvantages stem from greater training and often from investment in more equipment to facilitate job enlargement.

Job enrichment

There are two varieties of job enrichment: *horizontal job enrichment*, which is very like job enlargement described above, and *vertical job enrichment*, which we shall describe in this section.

Birchall (1975) comments that job enrichment is aimed at increasing the workers' involvement in the organisation and/or the job and is a method of giving an employee greater opportunity for achievement and recognition. Jobs are designed so that employees are allowed to do a 'whole' or a much larger part of a job, and there is some degree of task closure in that there is a clear end-point of a task. The implication of this is that in many cases tasks will be adopted that were previously considered as supervisory or management tasks.

An example of a clerical job enrichment scheme designed by Herzberg (1987) is shown in fig. 12.2. In management and professional work, Schumaher promotes a form of job design based on creating jobs which have within them a plan–control–do–evaluate cycle. This not only allows a whole job to exist but also generates feedback within the job so that the job-holder can monitor his or her own performance and take action to improve this. Job enrichment for manual workers may mean them taking on supervisory tasks and decisions as their role expands, and the abandonment of traditional systems such as conveyor belts. The cost implications of this often mean that job enrichment is easier to introduce in new plants rather than in established ones.

Autonomous working groups

The establishment of autonomous working groups aims to achieve the advantages of job enrichment at the same time as offering other advantages such as the greater satisfaction of social needs and greater control over the way in which the work is organised. The facility for self-organisation and self-regulation in these groups gives workers a sense of greater autonomy. These groups are sometimes called *self-managing work teams*.

Within the groups, there is the opportunity to use a greater range of skills, to be involved in management activities and decisions about working methods and to be involved in how the work is planned, scheduled and allocated to individuals. The group is given the responsibility for the achievement of an end-product or target or major work unit and is given substantial discretion to decide how this is achieved. Most of the examples of autonomous working are found in the manual work area – for example,

Figure 12.2
Techniques of clerical job enrichment

Principles of vertical job loading	
Principle	**Motivators involved**
A Removing some controls while retaining accountability	Responsibility and personal achievement
B Increasing the accountability of individuals for own work	Responsibility and recognition
C Giving a person a complete natural unit of work (module, division, area, and so on)	Responsibility, achievement, and recognition
D Granting additional authority to employees in their activity; job freedom	Responsibility, achievement, and recognition
E Making periodic reports directly available to the workers themselves rather than to supervisors	Internal recognition
F Introducing new and more difficult tasks not previously handled	Growth and learning
G Assigning individuals specific or specialized tasks, enabling them to become experts	Responsibility, growth, and advancement

(Herzberg, 1987)

Norstedt and Anguren (1973) report the group approach adopted by Saab–Scania for vehicle manufacture.

Flynn et al. (1990) relate that in practice the results of self-managing teams have been mixed, and some teams have been modified or entirely abandoned. They point out that this technique is not a panacea for the organisation of manual work, and that it is very dependent on the individuals in the work team being able both to work independently and simultaneously to contribute to group success. They argue that these groups are not always appropriate, and not all workers would perform well in this environment, as not all want decision-making responsibility or to be part of a team. Special consideration therefore needs to be given to the staffing of such teams, and Flynn et al. give a good example of the selection criteria and processes that can be used.

Study themes

1　Read Herzberg (1987) on motivation. What problems can you identify with his research approach and results?
2　Read chapter 5 on 'Motivation to work' in Kakabadse et al. (1988). Describe and analyse the role of the human resources manager in the Airways International example of a motivation problem. How acceptable would this role be in your organisation?
3　Identify and evaluate the approach used to design jobs which is described by Yeadle and Clark (1989).
4　How does the article by Buchanan (1987) on high-performance work design relate to and expand on the four perspectives of job design described in this chapter?
5　Read Robertson and Smith's (1985) analysis of the implications of the expectancy/valence/instrumentality theories. Extend these implications to your organisation and use them

　(a)　to account for current levels of job performance;
　(b)　to identify changes – including the required behaviour of managers – that could be made to improve job performance.

References

Birchall, D., 1975. *Job design: a planning and implementation guide for managers*, Gower, Aldershot.
Buchanan, D., 1987. Job enrichment is dead; long live high-performance work teams, *Personnel Management*, May, pp. 40–3.
Campion, M. A., and Thayer, P. W., 1989. How do you design a Job?, *Personnel Journal*, January, pp. 43–6.
Currie, R. M., 1963. *Work Study*, Pitman, London.
Davis, L. E., 1966. The design of jobs, *Industrial Relations*, vol. 6, pp. 21–5.
Flynn, R., McCombs, T., and Elloy, D., 1990. Staffing the self-managing

work team, *Leadership and Organization Development*, Vol. 11, no. 1, pp. 26–31.

Hackman, J. R., and Lawler, E. E., 1971. Employee reactions to job characteristics, *Journal of Applied Psychology*, vol. 55, pp. 259–86.

Hackman, J. R., Lawler, E. E., III, and Porter, L. W., 1977. *Perspectives on Behavior in Organizations*, McGraw-Hill, New York.

Herzberg, F., 1987. One more time: how do you motivate employees?, expanded reprint of a 1968 article, *Harvard Business Review*, September–October, vol. 87, no. 5, pp. 109–20.

Kakabadse, A., Ludlow, R., and Vinnicombe, S., 1988. *Working in Organisations*, Penguin, Harmondsworth.

Kilbridge, M. D., 1960. Reduced costs through job enlargement: a case, *Journal of Business*, vol. 33, pp. 357–62.

Lawler, E. E., and Porter, L. W., 1968. *Managerial Attitudes and Performance*, Irwin Dorsey, Chicago.

Maslow, A. H., 1943. A theory of human motivation, *Psychological Review*, vol. 50, pp. 370–96.

Nadler, D. A., and Lawler, E. E., III, 1977. Motivation: a diagnostic approach, in Hackman et al. (1977).

Norstedt, J. P., and Anguren, S., 1973. *The Saab–Scania Report*, Swedish Employers' Confederation, Stockholm.

Pearce, B., 1987. The human factor in office design, *Personnel Management*, October, pp. 56–8.

Robertson, I. T., and Smith, M. J., 1985. *Motivation and Job Design: theory, research and practice*, Institute of Personnel Management, London.

Taylor, F. W., 1911. *Scientific Management*, Harper & Row, New York.

Vroom, V. H., 1964. *Work and Motivation*, John Wiley, Chichester.

Yeadle, D., and Clarke, J., 1989. Personnel strategy for an automated plant, *Personnel Management*, June, pp. 51–5.

C
Employment

Chapter 13

Employment

Before an organisation decides to enter the process of recruitment and selection, there are a considerable number of legal considerations affecting any new employees which should be borne in mind. These include *contract requirements*, the *rights of full-time and part-time employees, pay requirements, holidays and time off work, age and hours requirements* and *union rights.*

Contract requirements

Rideout (1989) discusses the problems of defining the term 'employment' and the fact that the courts are increasingly ready to recognise forms of labour outside an employment relationship. An organisation must understand the legal differences between the terms 'contract of service' and 'contract for services'. Thomason (1988) remarks that the 'contract for services' is more akin to a commercial contract than an employment contract and, as yet, is not subject to the same degree of regulation as the contract of employment. The judicial requirements of defining the term 'employee', not only for the purposes of labour law but also for tax and social security purposes, have proved an extremely difficult task, and the increasing importance of varying patterns of work in the labour market has left the law far behind.

The contract of employment is based on the acceptance of mutual obligations, while recognising that the power of the employer is almost always stronger in the negotiation of the terms of the contract. The terms of a contract result from a complex mixture of sources, not all written but which could be deduced from any or all of the following:

1 *Information obtained from the selection process* – for example, information contained in the job advertisement, statements

163

made at a selection interview or in a letter of offer of appointment, although these terms cannot override those expressly
stated (Selwyn, 1988).

2 *Common-law duties (implied terms)*   Employer's duties include
the duty to pay the agreed remuneration and the duty to ensure
the employee's safety. The employee's duties include the duty
to obey all reasonable instructions and to work honestly and
loyally.

3 *Custom and practice*   These may include practices which are
well-known to the industry concerned – for example, the dates
on which holidays are taken and the need for workmen to
provide their own tools.

4 *Acts of Parliament*   Various Acts deal with matters of importance to the contract – for example, the Employment Protection
Consolidation Act 1978 and the Wages Act 1986.

5 *Individual negotiation with employer* – for example, requesting
and receiving permission for attendance at an external training
course.

6 *Collective agreements*   Terms negotiated with a trade union for
a specified group of workers are normally applied to the individual contracts of those workers.

The terms of the contract do not have to be laid down in writing,
but all employers are obliged to give a written statement of main
terms and conditions of employment within 13 weeks of the start
of that employment (Part I, Employment Protection Consolidation Act 1978). This written statement is often wrongly described
as the contract of employment, because, as Justice Browne-
Wilkinson said in the case of *Systems Floors (UK) Ltd* v. *Daniel*,

> [the statement] provides very strong prima facie evidence of
> what were the terms of the contract between the parties but
> does not constitute a written contract between the parties.
> Nor are the statements of the terms finally conclusive; at
> most they place a heavy burden on the employer to show that
> the actual terms of the contract are different from those which
> he has set out in the statutory statement. [1982] ICR 54

The written statement must include

1 the identity of the parties;

2 the date the employment began and if any previous service counts as continuous with the present contract;

3 the job title;

4 the scale or rate of remuneration and the method of calculation;

5 the intervals at which the remuneration is paid;

6 terms and conditions of hours of work, including the normal hours of work;

7 details of holidays and holiday pay;

8 details of the sickness scheme and pay;

9 pension rights, including whether the organisation has contracted out of the government scheme;

10 notice periods to be given by employer and employee;

11 information about disciplinary procedures, the person to whom appeals can be made and how to institute the process – or the employee can be referred to a reasonably accessible document containing all this information. (Employers with fewer than 20 employees are no longer obliged to give their employees details of the disciplinary procedure.)

The rights of full-time and part-time employees

The present employment protection legislation distinguishes between the rights of full-time and part-time employees. Even though part-time employees represented 24.2 per cent of those employed in Britain in December 1989, part-timers are discriminated against by the employment protection legislation. Full rights are achieved only after five years' continuous service by those working 8–16 hours per week and not at all by those working fewer than 8 hours per week. The legislation separates the rights of full-time workers who work 16 hours or more, for example when claiming unfair dismissal or redundancy, which both have a qualifying period of two years for full-time workers, and part-time workers, who are identified as those working 8 hours or more, and who have a qualifying period for a claim of unfair dismissal of five years.

In June 1990 the European Commission published controversial draft directives (EC 1990) which aim to bring part-time workers the same rights and benefits, *pro rata*, as those enjoyed by their full-time colleagues – for example, in relation to such matters as National Insurance contributions by employers, holidays, training and maternity leave. They are also intended to apply to temporary workers. If these directives are adopted by the Community, member states will have to implement them by 31 December 1992. While these proposals received overall support from the Trades Union Congress, the Equal Opportunities Commission and the Institute of Personnel Management, they are strongly opposed by the employers' organisations.

Pay requirements

In those industries which are still covered by a Wages Council, the pay rate which is stated in advertisements and in letters of offer must comply with the adult hourly rate given in the most recent Wages Order, if employing a person of 21 or over.

The Equal Pay legislation contains an implication that the contracts of employment of all women are considered to include an equality clause which operates in the following circumstances:

- where the woman is doing like work to a man,
- where she is doing work which is rated as equivalent to that of a man, or
- where her work is of equal value to that of a man's.

This consideration of equality applies both to pay and to conditions of employment. A detailed discussion of this topic is given in chapter 19.

An employer is obliged to give all employees an itemised pay statement which details their gross pay, all deductions from that pay and the net amount of wages or salary payable. The payment of wages no longer has to be made in 'coins of the realm', and under the Wages Act 1986 it is lawful to pay employees by another method to be agreed between the parties.

A guarantee payment must be made to any employees who, available for work on a day when they were contracted to work, were not provided with any employment for the whole day, due to problems which were not the result of an industrial dispute involving employees of their employer. An employee must have been employed continuously for one month to qualify for such a payment, and the statutory minimum payments are made for a maximum of five working days in any period of three months.

Holidays and time off work

Workers have no automatic right to receive an annual holiday with pay. Although this is usually covered by the terms of the contract of employment and/or union agreement, there are no general statutory obligations concerning minimum holiday entitlements. There is, however, a legal right to a paid holiday on bank and public holidays (or on a substituted day), which are listed in the Banking and Financial Dealings Act 1971.

An employee who is sick is entitled to receive Statutory Sick Pay, which is paid by his or her employer on behalf of the government for up to 28 weeks of absence, before the employee can claim State Sickness Benefit. Entitlement to Statutory Sick Pay (SSP) is limited to those who

1 pay National Insurance contributions
2 are employed for longer than three months, *and*
3 are not involved in a trade dispute.

The employer can deduct the amount paid out in SSP from the total amount of employers' and employees' Class 1 National Insurance contributions that have been collected, together with an extra amount to compensate for the employers' National Insurance contributions paid on SSP. The government has proposed that, from 6 April 1991, an employer will be able to recoup only 80 per cent of the SSP payments, and there is to be no compensation paid to employers, but at the time of writing this was being contested in Parliament.

The terms and conditions of the employee's employment may, of course, provide for more generous pay arrangements for periods of illness.

An employee who is pregnant and has an appointment to attend for ante-natal care must be allowed to do so and be paid at the appropriate hourly rate. A pregnant employee who has worked full-time for the employer for two years has the right to inform the employer of her wish to return to work up to 29 weeks after the birth of her baby, and the employer must not refuse to allow her to return – though the procedure for this is extremely complicated. On behalf of the government, the employer administers the Statutory Maternity Pay scheme for a period of up to 18 weeks starting from the eleventh week before the expected week of confinement. The government has no plans to amend this scheme in the same way as it proposes to amend the SSP scheme.

Age and hours requirements

The minimum age at which a child can be employed at all is 13, and there are restrictions on the location of that employment. Normally children will start full-time employment only at or after the age of 16.

Most of the hours restrictions on female employees were removed by the Sex Discrimination Act 1986.

It is now illegal to discriminate between the normal age of retirement required for men and that required for women – for example, to make the retirement age for men 65, while insisting that women retire at 60.

Union rights

The right to join and the right not to join a trade union are both available to all employees. An employee cannot be prevented or deterred from joining an independent trade union, nor from taking part in union activities at appropriate times; nor can an employee be pressurised into joining a trade union. It is now unlawful to refuse a person employment on the grounds that that person is a member of a trade union, is not a member of a trade union, will not agree to become a member of a trade union or will not cease to be a member (Employment Act 1990).

Discrimination inhibitors

As Seear and Pearn (1983) observe, all selection involves discrimination. What the legislation in this field attempts to do is to abolish discrimination on grounds which have no bearing on suitability for the job. The legislation prohibits discrimination on the grounds of sex or race in the areas of recruitment, selection, pay and terms and conditions of employment, *inter alia*, and allows positive action in limited areas. There is also legislation with limited impact for disabled people and ex-offenders.

Both the Race Relations Act 1976 (RRA) and the Sex Discrimination Acts 1975 and 1986 (SDA) lay down that it is unlawful not only to discriminate in the arrangements for determining who should be offered employment, and in the terms on which employment is offered, but also to discriminate by refusing or deliberately omitting to offer employment.

Discrimination can be either 'direct' or 'indirect'. Certain conditions for selection may constitute a form of indirect discrimination – for example, a height requirement, minimum levels of educational qualification, or certain written selection tests – unless they can be justified as being essential to the performance of the job. A limited number of occupations, where it is necessary to employ a person of a particular sex or a person of a certain racial background, fall into the exempt category of 'genuine occupational qualifications' (GOQs). All advertisements must be free of discrimination on grounds of sex, race or marriage. This is discussed in further detail in the next chapter on pages 178 and 179.

It is questionable whether an organisation can justify the inclusion in its application form of questions concerning colour or ethnic origin, unless it is made clear that this information is required for monitoring purposes only. The same applies to questions on marital status and number of dependants. It is not discriminatory to ask for that information, but it is important to explain to all applicants the use that the organisation makes of the information.

The current quota scheme for disabled people is based on the Disabled Persons (Employment) Acts of 1944 and 1958, which impose a duty on employers with 20 or more employees to employ a minimum of 3 per cent registered disabled people. If an employer is below this quota, it is a criminal offence to recruit anyone other than a registered disabled person without obtaining a permit to do so.

Unless specifically asked, a job applicant is under no legal duty to disclose information about any previous criminal convictions. Where a question on this is included in an application form or at an interview, an ex-offender is governed by the terms of the Rehabilitation of Offenders Act 1974. If a conviction is 'spent', an ex-offender is not obliged to disclose it, unless applying for a job in the list of excepted professions or excepted classes of occupation.

Vacancy determination

Before embarking on the expensive and time-consuming process of recruitment and selection, it is valuable for the employing organisation to consider what the nature of the vacancy(ies) is, and whether there is a necessity to employ additional workers for that or any other position. It is important for there to be a centrally placed authority to review such matters on behalf of the organisation.

It is crucial to look at the context in which a vacancy arises and to see, preferably through the medium of a monitoring procedure, if it involves retirement, resignation or dismissal, or if it is the result of promotion, transfer, new orders or additional work requiring previously unavailable skills. By assessing this information, the organisation will know, for example, if it needs to amend the job or person specification in order to attract employees. For example, an alteration of shift times could make a position more convenient, especially for married women; widening the area of responsibility could make a tedious job more attractive.

By referring to the organisation's manpower plans, a decision can be reached on whether there is to be external recruitment to that position and, if so, in view of external determinants such as demographic problems and pay comparisons with other organisations, whether the best approach to the recruitment problem would involve encouraging applications from older workers or married women returners or offering job-sharing or part-time positions – although selection must be based on merit.

Organisations may feel that the best course for them at that time is to forgo recruitment and to redesign the available positions by, for example, installing new capital equipment, increasing the amount of overtime available or altering shift times. The possibility of contracting work out to subcontractors and the relative merits of the alternative options (chapter 3) cannot be excluded from this decision.

Study themes

1 What are the features of the Employment Protection Consolidation Act 1978 and the Wages Act 1986 that an employer has to remember when drawing up contracts of employment?
2 In what ways do part-time employees in your organisation have more limited legal rights in their employment than full-time employees?
3 How do Seear and Pearn (1983) suggest that discrimination in selection decisions will be unlawful?

References

Bowers, J., 1990. *Bowers on Employment Law*, Blackstone, London.
EC, 1990. Draft directives on part-time and temporary work, *Equal Opportunity Review*, no. 33, September/October, pp. 32–5.
Rideout, R., 1989. *Rideout's Principles of Labour Law*, 5th edn, Sweet & Maxwell, London.
Seear, N., and Pearn, M., 1983. *Selection Within the Law*, in Ungerson, B., ed., *Recruitment Handbook*, 3rd edn, Gower, Aldershot.
Selwyn, N., 1988. *Selwyn's Law of Employment*, 6th edn, Butterworth, London.
Thomason, G., 1988. *A Textbook of Human Resource Management*, Institute of Personnel Management, London.

Chapter 14

Recruitment

Recruitment . . . is the creation of a pool of labour from which a selection will be made. (Thomason 1988, p. 284)

A good recruitment system is crucial to the organisation, not least because the recruitment of suitable employees will improve retention and morale among the existing workforce by accentuating to those both inside and outside the organisation the importance it attaches to people. Any organisation which recruits people who are incompetent, or who will leave voluntarily through dissatisfaction, will find the exercise expensive and inefficient. The process of recruitment can also be time-consuming for managers, who are required to filter the applications and interview the candidates; for clerical staff, who provide the administrative backup; and for supervisors and trainers, who induct and train new employees. Therefore it is worthwhile to operate a thorough recruitment process – though within the constraints of what is appropriate to the needs of the organisation concerned. The recruitment process must also take account of external factors, such as the availability of particular categories of employee and the market for specialised skills, and must operate within a long-term plan, rather than dealing only with short-term needs.

Increased awareness in firms . . . of the importance of adequately skilled and trained labour has drawn attention to the planning of recruitment and this, in turn, demands a better understanding of the operation of the labour market and the mobility of labour. (Atkinson and Purkiss 1983, p. 10)

The available talent thus identified is unlikely to match precisely the requirements of the organisation, which may then decide if it wishes to redesign the jobs available or offer relevant training to secure sufficient labour for the organisation's needs.

ACAS's advisory booklet on *Recruitment and Selection* states that a recruitment system should be

> effective – producing enough suitable candidates and distinguishing accurately between the suitable and the unsuitable

> efficient – using the most cost-effective advertising and recruitment sources and methods

> fair – maintaining the company's good name with existing employees and potential recruits alike by dealing fairly, honestly and courteously with all applicants. (ACAS 1983)

It is crucial for the organisation to realise that the process of recruitment and selection is not a one-way system, in which the company decides who is to be 'honoured' with the offer of employment. Recruitment is now recognised as a two-way process: candidates often need to be convinced that the organisation, the position being offered, the remuneration and any additional perquisites and the future prospects fit in with their individual career plans. The recruitment process is as much a marketing exercise as the selling of the company's products, and should therefore be equally well organised.

> The final employment decision is made by the prospective employee. He decides whether to accept or reject the offer of employment he receives. (Torrington and Chapman 1983, p. 70)

Who should be responsible within the organisation for the operation of its recruitment system? This is one of the traditional roles of the personnel department, in consultation with line management:

> The process is usually initiated by line management and administered by the personnel specialists, with, however, the line managers having the final decision as to who is selected. (Thomason 1988, p. 284)

The undertaking of recruitment by a central function gains from the ability of that department to collate all the organisation's vacancies, to be aware of the long-term requirements of the organisation and to have developed expertise in assessing the labour markets and choosing the correct media for the vacant positions. The personnel department can also undertake a most important monitoring role, which will be referred to again later in the chapter.

The first task of the recruiting department on being notified of a vacancy is to assess whether a new employee is in fact required. This is dealt with in chapter 13. Assuming that this task has been undertaken, and after referring to any relevant information from the exit interview of the previous job-holder, if appropriate, the next step for the recruiting department is to collect together all available information about the position to be filled. If the organisation is small, it may be possible for one person to consider the job's important aspects and the requirements of the job-holder. In larger organisations, the use of a job description and person specification is more common. In order to compile a job description, it is necessary to carry out a job analysis. In some organisations, copies of job descriptions of the major company positions may already be available and used for job evaluation, training or manpower planning purposes. Existing copies of job descriptions should be checked to ensure that they are still current.

Watson (1989) has drawn together from various personnel texts the items to be covered in the job description, and they include job title, job location, reporting relationships, the main purpose of the job, its key tasks and its main contacts both internal and external to the organisation. In compiling a job description, it is important to use only 'action verbs' to describe the main tasks.

The job description then provides the basic data from which to compile the person specification. A person specification is a process by which both the essential qualities necessary to undertake the job and the desirable qualities of the ideal candidate for the job are described. To be especially useful, note should be made of any factors which will limit the recruitment sources, such as unusual working hours, difficult working conditions or areas from which relocation would be financially unacceptable. It is important to ensure that the standards set as essential for any position are not made more stringent than necessary, as this may cause them to discriminate unfairly against a particular racial group or sex.

The specification can be then used as a comparator in the selection process. As ACAS explains (1983), it is not a scientific method but it can remind the interviewer 'to be realistic and systematic', rather than using an unsubstantiated impression of the candidate which could be coloured by the interviewer's prejudices. In the UK, the two most popular formats for this are the Seven Point Plan (Rodger, 1970) and the Five Fold Framework (Fraser, 1978).

After compiling the job description and the person specification, it is then necessary to consider the remuneration which will be offered. This consists of not only the pay rate to be offered but also, to a greater extent than ever, the benefit package to accompany it. In many cases, the rate to be offered is related to existing agreements, Wages Council orders or a current job evaluation system. It is, however, important to be aware of the current market forces, by checking the rates offered by competitors or by participating in a survey of the going rates in the marketplace.

It is now time to consider how to encourage suitable candidates to apply for the available vacancies. There are numerous channels for informing prospective candidates of an organisation's vacancies, but they would never all be used at the same time.

The first decision is whether it is to be the established policy of the organisation to search for suitable internal candidates and/or to advertise all vacancies internally. In some large organisations, it is accepted that all vacancies up to a certain level of seniority will always be internally advertised or that a search will be undertaken to see if there are any suitable existing employees before any other methods of recruitment are employed. By doing so, the organisation allows all those who feel that they are capable of filling the position to express an interest; it allows internal applicants the opportunity to map out their own career paths. It also provides an opportunity for existing employees to inform their friends and relatives of forthcoming vacancies. If an internal candidate is appointed, there is a much shorter change-over period, and less need for induction and initial training. There are, however, disadvantages to this approach – there may not be appropriately qualified existing employees or enough members of the organisation interested in the position, and advertising only internally does not allow internal candidates' qualifications and experience to be compared with those available in the labour market.

It is useful to maintain a register of people who approach the organisation for positions at a time when there are no suitable vacancies. These casual enquirers and all unsolicited requests for employment can provide a worthwhile data bank which should be consulted at appropriate times. One major advantage of these applicants is that they have already expressed an interest in working for the organisation, though the value of that information will depend on the time lapse since the applications were originally made.

Organisations which have a regular requirement for certain groups of employees, such as school-leavers or graduates, can ensure a steady flow of applications by promoting contacts with schools and universities, and by attending career conferences and participating in the 'Milk Round' – though the latter process is both time-consuming and extremely tiring for the recruiting staff.

Vacancies can be brought to the attention of a wider audience by placing information on external notice-boards, though the amount of relevant information about the positions available which can be put there will be highly limited – possibly just the job titles and a telephone number.

A further method of recruitment is to make the vacancy known to the Department of Employment, to be advertised in Job Centres or to those on the Professional and Executive Register (PER). While this ensures that the vacancy is given a wide audience in a relatively short period, it is suitable for only a limited number of positions in the organisation. Other agencies may also be able to supply candidates for particular categories of vacancy – for example, secretarial and computer staff.

In addition, the organisation can advertise its vacancies or it can employ consultants to recruit or headhunt on its behalf or to place advertising in the appropriate media. Advertising is a popular method of recruitment, which is often considered in advance of many others.

The process of recruitment is usually one which proceeds in stages, each dependent on the success of the preceding one. The object of the recruitment system is to choose suitable channels which will produce a sufficient number of qualified applicants without the recruiters being overwhelmed with responses. A decision on which channels are most suitable would depend on the scarcity of candidates of the required calibre, the time-scale that is being allowed and the budget. If an organisation is faced with a shortage of suitable applicants, it will have no alternatives but to use progressively more expensive channels of recruitment, to widen the geographical area over which the organisation is search-ing or to lower its entry requirements. The time-scale allowed is also important to the decision on the channel of recruitment, for some methods are extremely slow to reach their conclusion – for example, if recruitment consultants are appointed, the process will take a considerable time. Obviously, the budget available for the recruitment has to be used effectively and efficiently – in order to make the best use of available resources, and providing for the costs of administration, the candidates' travel expenses and, perhaps, the successful applicant's relocation expenses.

Advertising

While advertising can be a very expensive form of recruitment, it is very popular as a way of bringing vacancies to the attention of the widest audience while also, if an advertisement is well planned, providing useful public relations for the organisation. Advertising is normally considered to be limited to newspaper advertising, though in this category there is an extensive range of possibilities, including daily papers, weekly editions and monthly journals.

The decision on where to place an advertisement depends on a number of factors. The national papers, as well as being very prestigious, will be appropriate if the vacancy is for a senior position requiring candidates from a large geographical area. In most cases, however, recruitment takes place locally in the first instance, and the local papers can provide a useful and inexpensive channel with a quick lead-in time. If a particular professional qualification is required, then the journal of that profession will be read by appropriately qualified people, though the time till publication will be the longest of all periodicals.

Other media in which one can advertise if a large budget is available include local radio, television information networks such as Prestel, cinema, posters, videos and exhibitions. When assessing which is the most suitable means of publicising vacancies, the organisation must remember what section of the population the advertisement is intended to attract.

An examination of a particular newspaper's advertisement pages should provide a guide to its suitability for the organisation's vacancies. If a certain publication is known to have a particular supplement of interest to the category of person the organisation seeks, such as the *Education Guardian*, then advertising in that supplement could be productive. If advertising on local radio, then one should choose popular times for listening.

An advertisement should deal with the following subjects:

1 basic information about the organisation,
2 location of the job,
3 any changes or developments which will affect the job,
4 summary of the main activities of the job-holder,
5 qualifications and experience required,
6 pay and benefits,
7 how to respond.

It is important that the advertisement makes clear what method of response should be used – telephone for more details or for an application form, write giving particulars or to request an application form, submit a curriculum vitae, attend in person at the organisation's premises or at an informal gathering.

It has become less usual to state an age range in the advertisement. While this is not illegal in the UK, there are not many circumstances in which it is essential to limit the target audience by naming age disqualifications. It is also not advantageous to the organisation to place the advertisement anonymously, with response to a box number. In most cases, applicants prefer to know to which organisation they are responding, and the reputation of the organisation is often a factor in favour of applying for a position in that company.

Advertisements should be pleasing to the eye and include an effective presentation and artwork and a fluent style of writing. They should omit jargon known only to organisation members and state clearly all requirements and responsibilities. A catchy title will draw the reader's attention, and if the organisation has a logo which is well-known, that can add to the pleasing effect.

When composing job advertisements, the writer should be aware of the requirements of the Sex Discrimination Acts 1975 and 1986 and the Race Relations Act 1976. An advertisement must not discriminate either directly or indirectly on the grounds of sex or race. Job titles should not be used which could imply discrimination, and if a position such as 'waiter' is advertised, the text should make clear that the job is available to both sexes. This 'indication to the contrary' is required even when neutral job titles such as 'applicants' or 'candidates' are used. An advertisement for a job which has been done mainly by men or women in the past must not indicate a continued preference for that sex, and care must be taken about the use of the terms 'he' and 'she'. Any pictures must also not give a biased impression. An advertisement must not contain an unjustifiable requirement or condition which could be considered as indirect discrimination, such as requiring all candidates to have attended Eton or to be six feet tall! However, there are certain circumstances where there are 'genuine occupational qualifications' (GOQs) which allow for the advertising of jobs and recruitment to be limited to one sex or race. Under the Sex Discrimination Act and the Race Relations Act, employers are allowed to specifically encourage one sex or one racial group to train for or apply to do a particular job. This positive discrimination is dependent on the situation existing that, in the previous twelve months, no person of that sex or race was doing that kind of work, or that the numbers involved were comparatively small. Although in such cases one can advertise encouraging one sex or racial grouping to apply for or train for certain jobs, one cannot discriminate by sex or race when it comes to selecting who should be appointed from among the applicants.

An effective and efficient recruitment system depends on good administrative techniques. It is important to respond within a reasonable period to all letters received following the placement of an advertisement, and to be sure to have staff available to answer telephone queries. Also, managers must have set aside dates for the selection process to begin. A monitoring exercise, which assesses the recruitment channels chosen, the costs incurred, the response rates and any difficulties encountered, is essential to provide background data for future decisions.

Study themes

1 How does Thomason (1988, pp. 277–84) explain and justify the distribution of decision-making responsibility in recruitment between line and personnel managers?
2 Read Pearn and Kandola (1988) and decide how you would use their 'do-it-yourself JTR method' in your organisation.

3 What are the advantages and disadvantages of a policy of advertising job vacancies within the organisation before external advertising? Which policy would you recommend in your organisation?

4 Read Section 5 of the Race Relations Act and Section 7 of the Sex Discrimination Act concerning genuine occupational qualifications. Which of the following vacancies do you think could be limited to a person of a specific sex or racial background:

(a) teaching English to schoolchildren whose mother tongue is not English,
(b) housemaster/housemistress in a single-sex boarding school,
(c) waiting and bar staff in a French restaurant,
(d) sales representative working mainly in Muslim countries,
(e) fashion models,
(f) photographic models,
(g) social worker working mainly among people with limited English and from an ethnic minority background.

References

ACAS, 1983., *Recruitment and Selection*, Advisory booklet no. 6, Advisory, Conciliation and Arbitration Service, London.

Atkinson, G., and Purkiss, C., 1983. Recruitment and Mobility of Labour, in Ungerson, B., (ed.), *Recruitment Handbook*, 3rd edn, Gower, Aldershot.

Courtis, J., 1976. *Cost Effective Recruitment*, Institute of Personnel Management, London.

Courtis, J., 1989. *Recruiting for Profit*, Institute of Personnel Management, London.

EOC, 1990. *The Sex Discrimination Act and Advertising*, Equal Opportunities Commission, Manchester.

Fowler, A., 1990. How to write a job advertisement, *Personnel Management Plus*, October.

Fraser, J. M., 1978. *Employment Interviewing*, 5th edn, Macdonald and Evans, London.

Pearn, M., and Kandola, R., 1988. *Job Analysis: a Practical Guide for Managers*, Institute of Personnel Management, London.

Plumbley, P. R., 1985. *Recruitment and Selection*, Institute of Personnel Management, London.

Plumbley, P., and Williams, R., 1981. *The Person for the Job*, 2nd edn, Kogan Page, London.

Ray, M., 1980. *Recruitment Advertising*, Institute of Personnel Management, London.

Rodger, A., 1970. *The Seven Point Plan*, 3rd edn, National Institute of Industrial Psychology, London.

Thomason, G., 1988. *A Textbook of Human Resource Management*, Institute of Personnel Management, London.

Torrington, D., and Chapman, J., 1983. *Personnel Management*, 2nd edn, Prentice-Hall, Hemel Hempstead.

Watson, T., 1989. Recruitment and Selection, in Sisson, K., (ed.), 1989. *Personnel Management in Britain*, Blackwell, Oxford.

Windolf, P., and Wood, S., 1988. *Recruitment and Selection in the Labour Market*, Gower, Aldershot.

Chapter 15

Selection

As the most important resources of an organisation are its people, ensuring that the right people are selected to be employed is vital to the organisation's success. The selection process enables *both* the organisation to decide which people best fit its needs and individuals to decide to what extent the organisation fits their needs.

There is no one best method of selecting people. In fact no selection tools have very high success rates, but the decisions made will have the best chance of success if a combination of methods is chosen appropriate to the job on offer, if there is thorough preparation and if the selectors are clear about the selection criteria.

What are we selecting for?

Unless the selectors are clear about what they are looking for, there is very little chance of them finding it and knowing when they have found it. Preparing selection criteria is usually the part of the selection process which is given least attention, and yet it is of critical importance. Lewis (1985) defines selection criteria at three different levels: organisational, functional/departmental and individual job criteria. Most attention is normally focused on the job in hand, as in the need to have a certain typing speed and accuracy when selecting for a secretary. Sometimes, however, organisational criteria are also critical, as when the organisation is undergoing a culture move from being purely task-centred to being equally people- and task-centred. In those circumstances, people management and other people skills would be important in every management job.

In order to diagnose job-related criteria, selectors need to start with a clear understanding of the job that is needed to be done.

This may be described in terms of tasks and/or accountabilities. Incomes Data Services (IDS 1985) report that this stage of job analysis is often neglected. From this, the skills, knowledge, experience and other characteristics that are required for someone to perform this job in a competent manner can be defined. This information is often written up in the form of a person specification, and a variety of standard formats have been suggested, the two most notable being Alec Rodger's Seven Point Plan (1970) and Fraser's Five Fold Specification (1978). These frameworks are shown in fig. 15.1. More recently, job criteria in the form of competency statements are being used. These statements describe the behaviour that is required of the job-holder in certain key areas, such as in the areas of influencing others, managing people, negotiating and so on. An example of the behaviour required in the commercial area for a representative's job is shown in fig. 15.2.

A further set of criteria that may be important in the selection process is those related to potential. What potential do we need/desire the selected person to have for further development within the organisation? This needs to be carefully considered if it is

Figure 15.1

Two traditional approaches to person specification

(a) **Rodger's seven point plan**

    Physical make-up
    Attainment
    General intelligence
    Special aptitudes
    Interests
    Disposition
    Circumstances

(b) **Fraser's five fold grading**

    Impact on others
    Qualifications/acquired knowledge
    Innate abilities
    Motivation
    Adjustment/emotional balance

Employee Resourcing

Figure 15.2

Competency profile for a representative

Competency	Example of a behavioural indicator
Proactivity	Takes calculated risks
Results orientation	Sets and communicates goals for self
Seeking critical information	Uses an appropriate variety of sources
Adaptability	Effective when dealing with variety (e.g. level, background) of people
Self-confidence	Prepared to act on own judgement
Self-control	Works effectively under time pressure
Thoroughness	Checks to ensure tasks completed
Determination	Demonstrates repeated efforts to solve a problem
Interpersonal awareness	Sees things from the other person's perspective
Concern for impact	Actions preserve the dignity of others
Communication	Asks appropriate questions to aid understanding
Negotiation	Identifies and builds on common ground
Influencing	Identifies key players and their impact
Conceptualisation	Connects isolated events
Originality	Generates new ideas
Analytical thinking	Considers all possible implications before acting
Rational persuasion	Uses data to back-up point of view

thought to be a requirement. Too many organisations select for potential growth, employing the very best qualified person, without really considering how long he or she would be content to do the job on offer and what real opportunities they can provide for growth in the future.

The criteria that are developed for selection are fundamental in the decision of which selection tools to use and in communicating to job candidates what the job would demand of the successful applicant.

The selection process

Decisions need to be made not only about the selection methods that will be used but also about the order in which they will be employed and the weightings that will be attached to the results of each tool. Careful consideration needs to be given to who will be involved at each stage of the process and with whom the final selection decision will rest. The selectors need to ask themselves 'How much information can we give potential candidates in advance, and how much pre-work would it be helpful to ask them to do?'

Decisions also need to be made about coordinating the selection for very similar jobs where there would be almost the same pool of applicants. Detailed planning is important to ensure that every member of the organisation who is involved knows exactly what his or her role is, and arrangements need to be made in advance for how all the collected information is to be shared as quickly as possible. Candidates require sufficient information so that they know what to expect when they arrive to be assessed on the appointed day. A good check for a selection process, before it is finalised, is to consider what it will feel like from the candidates' point of view. Will it make sense to them? Will it be too long a day? What will they get out of it? Selection needs to be recognised as a two-way process, as candidates will be making judgements about the organisation and assessing whether the organisation and the job would meet their needs. An emphasis on user-friendly selection processes, as described by Herriot and Fletcher (1990), can only assist the organisation in this respect. Cosentino et al. (1990) describe a selection process used by Toyota which was not only rigorous but also user-friendly and supplied candidates with plenty of information about what to expect from the organisation.

Choice of selection methods

There is a wide variety of selection tools available, and the choices made will depend on factors such as type and level of job, abilities of the managers involved, time required, accuracy demanded and cost. (See Torrington and Hall 1991.)

Although interviews are the most commonly used method of assessment, there is evidence to suggest that these offer little better than chance prediction of job performance. Tests offer a more accurate assessment, and assessment centres better still. Figure 15.3, produced by Smith (in Rees 1989), shows how the different methods compare in terms of predicting job performance.

Later in this chapter we look in more detail at interviews, tests, application forms and assessment centres. Other, less frequently used, methods include graphology, phrenology and physiognomy, and these are described in more detail by Fowler (1990). Palmistry, astrology and body language are also used. Telephone screening is a more conventional method, but is used only to a small extent. Self-assessment is inspiring increasing interest; it is dependent on giving the applicants more detailed job information and a realistic job preview so that they are much better equipped to decide whether to pursue their application or not (see Anderson and Shackleton 1990). Less attention is centred on references these days, and these are best used as a factual check immediately before offering a position, rather than as a character reference which influences the selection decision.

Whichever methods are used, the feedback to be received by candidates needs to be agreed. When will they be informed of the decision? Will reasons be given? Will 'objective assessment' data be given to them? How will they be debriefed? These questions should be asked for both successful and unsuccessful candidates. The importance of how data is fed back to the individual is demonstrated by Elliott (1990) when he describes the reactions of two different individuals to their test results.

Figure 15.3
Selection methods and job performance

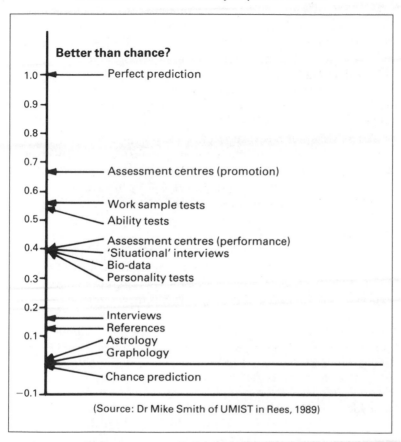

(Source: Dr Mike Smith of UMIST in Rees, 1989)

Application forms and CVs

Traditionally, application forms were designed to capture individual data which would then form the basis of the employee's
personnel record. At the same time they were often used as a
screening device to help the decision about whom to interview.
Forms are now increasingly designed as a selection tool, and the
basic record data such as National Insurance number are eliminated and asked for at a later stage when the person is employed.

Allan (1990) argues that forms could be designed in an even more user-friendly way – for example, by personalising them or by adding introductory paragraphs explaining why certain information is sought. Not only is the form a preliminary screening device for the employer, the potential candidates also use this in their selection process. Forms that are unduly long, badly printed or ask for seemingly irrelevant information are less likely to be filled in, and the most appropriate candidates may screen themselves out of the selection process because they do not wish to work for what appears to be an unprofessional organisation.

For more senior posts, curricula vitae are an acceptable alternative to application forms. Sometimes guidelines are given specifying the areas of information that are required; other organisations leave it to the individual. The way that CVs are constructed can supply additional information against selection criteria for the organisation to use.

A current extension of the use of application forms is weighting or biodata. For this, the form is used to supply historical and verifiable pieces of information about the individual in a selection context (such as number of jobs held over a number of years and length of full-time education). This data is then compared with the characteristics of successful job-holders. This is a very simplistic approach, however, and it is difficult for many applicants to believe that success in a position depends on being, amongst other things, the eldest member of the family.

Interviews

As we have said, interviews do not have a high predictive ability, and some very perceptive criticism of the interview can be found in Webster (1964). He concluded that interviewers decided whether to accept or reject a candidate within four minutes, and then looked for evidence to justify this; that they seldom changed their initial judgement and that their behaviour indicated this judgement to the candidate. However many problems are associated with interviews, though, they are still an essential part of the selection process, and the face validity of a face-to-face conversation is high. The skill is in carrying them out so that the problems are minimised and the benefits are maximised. At their best, interviews are excellent vehicles for collecting information about candidates, and for enabling candidates to collect information about the organisation. They cannot be surpassed as a method of allowing the candidate and the employer to 'tune in' to each other and to establish whether they could develop an effective working relationship.

Interview strategy

The interview can be approached in a variety of ways, the most common being a frank and friendly style which allows initial information in the application form to be explored in more detail by the interviewer and the job and organisation to be explored by the candidate. The interviewer strives to maintain rapport at all times, and hopefully candidates go away feeling that they have had a challenging, but not unpleasant, experience and that they have been fairly treated.

A version of this approach includes problem-solving situations based on hypothetical questions, such as 'What would you do if you turned up to run a training course and found that the room had been double-booked?' The disadvantage here is that answers reveal only what the candidates *think* they would do, and there is no knowing whether this would happen in reality. To get around this difficulty, behavioural events can be included – individuals are questioned about things that did actually happen in the past. They are asked to describe the situation and what they did, what their thought processes were and what happened as a result. This is a useful approach when the person specification is expressed in terms of competencies.

Other approaches include a stress strategy, often used on the premise that organisation life is stressful, with a desire to see how the individual copes. There is little to recommend this approach, which has the problem that unsuccessful interviewees will leave the premises with a less than positive image of the organisation. An alternative version of this is the sweet-and-sour strategy, described by Hackett (1978), where there are two interviewers, one adopting the stress strategy and the other playing the nice guy. The expectation is that, having been grilled by the first interviewer, the candidate will open up and tell all to the second.

The remainder of this section is written with the frank and friendly strategy in mind.

How many interviews and interviewers?

There are two schools of thought relating to this aspect of the interview process. One view is that a full and frank interview can take place only on a one-to-one basis, as this is the only forum in which the required level of rapport can be developed. The other view is that justice needs to be seen to be done, and that the candidate needs to be judged by a panel of interviewers who meet the interviewee at the same time. There are a number of options between these extremes.

The advantages of the individual interview can be gained by a series of individual interviews, which can also bring a variety of different views to bear on the employment decision. So, for example, a candidate may be interviewed by the potential immediate manager, by the head of department and by a representative from the personnel function. The more senior the post, the greater the number of interviews that are likely. The advantage to the candidates is that they are able to meet more of the people they will potentially work with and get a broader view of the organisation. The potential disadvantage with this process is that candidates are asked the same questions by each of the interviewers and are bored and weary by the end of the day, with a poor view of the organisation. Coordination of interviewers is key here, so that each covers only the area agreed and areas of overlap are known and can be explained to the candidate.

Interviews in tandem are another alternative, whereby the candidate is interviewed by two members of the organisation. The usual combination is the line manager and a representative of the personnel function. Often less daunting than a panel interview, it is still more difficult to maintain rapport and the flow of the conversation than in one-to-one interviews.

Panel interviews have the advantage that they save the interviewee time and allow for a quick decision, and Muir (1988) argues that, among other advantages, they minimise personal bias. The drawbacks lie in the tribunal nature of the interview and the tendency for judgement rather than encouraging a two-way exploratory conversation.

Interview structure

It is vital that the interviewer has planned the structure of the interview and is thoroughly briefed about each candidate. The structure helps set the candidate at ease, helps ensure that all areas are covered, looks professional, can be used as an *aide-mémoire* and makes it easier to compare candidates.

A broad structure that is useful is to see the interview in three parts: beginning, middle and end. In the beginning, the purpose and structure of the interview can be discussed and agreed and time be given to develop rapport. The end is clearly important in allowing for a summary of what has been covered and said, checking that the candidate has all the information he or she needs and explaining what is going to happen next and in what time-span.

There is much more scope for how the middle of the interview can be structured. Some interviewers work through the application form; others adopt a biographical approach. If pre-work has been requested – for example, in describing behavioural events – then this could provide the structure, with more general questions at the beginning or the end. Other interviewers prefer to work through key areas such as education, work experience, job on offer, interests and so on.

The structure can be a broad framework or more tightly defined. In targeted selection, for example, the structure is planned in detail in advance, with the preparation of lists of precise questions that must be asked. Questions from the candidate can be incorporated in steps throughout the interview or be requested at the beginning and/or the end.

Interview skills

From what has been said, planning and preparation for the interview are clearly vital to its success. A structure that makes it clear to the candidate that this is a two-way rather than a one-way process is central. In collecting information, interviewers need to be skilled not only in asking the most effective questions but also in listening. It is tempting for interviewers to spend too much of the time talking themselves and to allow insufficient time for the candidate. It is recommended that interviewers talk for no more than 30 per cent of the time – if that.

The most valuable questions are those which do not lead the candidate to an answer, or make assumptions, but are open questions (starting with what, who, why, when, where, how). When precise data are needed, closed questions (requiring a yes or no) can be useful, as can comparative questions ('Would you prefer this or that, and why?').

Other interview skills include checking that you have understood what the candidate has said and summarising not only at the end but at key points throughout before leading on to the next topic of conversation.

Testing

The use of testing in selection is increasing, and tests are available which cover such aspects as intelligence, personality, trainability, ability, aptitude and values. Rees (1989) discovered more than 600 different ones in use in the UK. In 1984, Torrington and Hall (1991) found that two-thirds of their survey respondents were using tests, and Wills (1990) found a similar percentage of county councils using them, with another 31 per cent considering their use. Yet there remain strong views against as well as for testing in this context. Fletcher et al. (1989) comment that, in spite of increasing use, the level of knowledge about tests lags behind.

Those in favour of the use of tests quote such advantages as increased quality of selection resulting in increased productivity, higher-quality work, reduced turnover of staff and so on, and decreased costs for processing large numbers of applications (see, for example, Toplis et al. 1987). Other sources see testing as a method of collecting data about individuals that could otherwise not be obtained (as described in IDS 1985). An example of this would be in hard-to-fill technical vacancies where candidates without any relevant educational or work experience were being considered. Testing also provides clean data which can easily be used in a comparative way across all candidates.

The alternative view stresses different cultural characteristics which affect the way in which tests are completed. Some races, groups of people or individuals are more used to filling out test forms and working to deadlines, and these will do comparatively better than those without such experiences. Concerns may also be expressed over the way in which tests are validated against job performance, arguing that the rating of subsequent job performance is subjective rather than objective.

How tests are used

It is the *way* in which tests are used in the selection context that is critical. All those who administer tests need to be fully qualified to interpret them, and this will involve attending a training course run by the supplier.

Decisions also need to be made as to how test results are interpreted in conjunction with the results of other selection tools. Some employers use tests as a screening device and process applications further only if the results of the test are favourable. Others see the test as a part of the whole process and make no decisions based on tests scores alone: test data are considered only alongside other selection data in order to get a rounded picture of the applicant.

Reputable tests have been validated against the population as a whole, and also provide validation figures against certain groups in the population. It is, however, important for test users to validate test scores *within* the organisation, against specific jobs. Every organisation is different, and an individual who does well in one organisation can do badly in another even though the job itself is very similar.

Testers also need to consider how they will provide feedback on test scores and interpretation to those who have been tested. Although some organisations currently do nothing, this is an area in which organisations can enhance their reputation in the community and nationally. Also, by giving detailed feedback, there is the opportunity to gain the applicants' views on their scores and interpretation, and this usually enhances the data collected from the test. Used in this way, tests are seen less as secretive judgemental techniques but more as an objective basis for further discussion. Clearly this demands considerable skills on the part of the tester.

Types of test

The choice of which test to use is dependent on the type of

information that is sought. If an inappropriate type of test is chosen, the data collected will be misleading or at best meaningless.

Aptitude tests give a measure of the *potential* of the individual to develop in specific or more general ways. Clearly a high level of aptitude will not necessarily result in high-level performance, as other factors such as motivation will contribute to this. Attainments tests differ in that they measure *current* skills and abilities. These tests can be paper-based but are often practical demonstrations of what the individual can do – such as typing, presenting or electrical wiring. Such tests are often designed by the employer to match the immediate demands of the job.

Trainability tests are another practical test often designed by the employer. They involve individuals attempting tasks they have not done before but that they have just been shown how to do. The tests measure performance improvement, response to training and, in part, potential rather than current ability.

Intelligence tests give an overall indication of mental capacity, and this has been correlated with ability to retain new knowledge, pass examinations and succeed at work. These tests would need, however, to be carefully validated in terms of the specific job for which the individual was applying.

Personality tests cause more concern than other types of tests, partly because there is a view that personality cannot be measured and because there are very different views of how personality is constructed. These tests depend on individuals being honest when they complete the test, although there is a temptation to mark the socially acceptable answer. Many articles (such as Harrison 1979 and Wills 1984) stress the importance of personality for management jobs, and yet Swinburne (1985) argues that few personality tests lend themselves to occupational use.

Assessment centres

Assessment centres are being increasingly used as selection devices, particularly for management jobs and for the selection of graduates. They involve a group of comparable individuals who are being assessed at the same time for appointment to the same or similar jobs. When used internally, they may also be used as development exercises, so that individuals are thoroughly de briefed and an individual development plan is agreed with the individual and his or her manager which takes account of performance in the assessment centre.

Assessment centres have the advantage that they cover a wide variety of aspects of individual performance in both formal and informal settings. Some assessment centres would last one day, but many would be two full days, with overnight residence being compulsory.

The types of activity that could be included are interviews, tests, individual exercises, presentations, group discussions and exercises, role plays and informal conversations over dinner. Individual exercises might, for example, require a trainer to devise within 45 minutes an approach to analysing the training needs of a particular group, or give a sales executive an in-tray to be cleared within 45 minutes before going abroad for six months. Group exercises might involve discussing the results of individual exercises so that the group agrees on the best course of action to take. Other group exercises might involve individual presentations (sometimes prepared before the event), the purpose of which is to persuade the group to take a certain stance. The presenter not only puts forward a point of view but also has to take questions and lead the discussion. Team exercises might involve the group being split into two or more teams and competing against each other in a game such as parachuting eggs or making boats to race.

Assessment centres therefore offer considerable opportunity to observe the behaviour of individuals in situations similar to those found in the work environment. The way that individuals interact with others, influence them, lead them and support them can be seen rather than reported, and these aspects are perhaps often more important in management roles than scores in an intelligence test (above an agreed minimum).

Assessment centres are costly to set up, and involve a number of managers for considerable spells of time. Not only do managers have to devote time to the actual assessment, they also need to be trained in how to analyse individual and group behaviour and how to give feedback to the candidates. Assessment centres are also costly in terms of design, hotel residence and the fees of the consultants who are often involved because of the complex nature of the process. Identification of many of the issues involved in assessment centres – such as definitions, organisational policy statements, assessor training, rights of participants, informed participation and validation – is found in a paper produced by the Task Force on Assessment Center Guidelines (1989).

In spite of the disadvantages, performance in assessment centres does generally correlate more highly with eventual job performance than does performance in other selection methods.

Selection decisions

Selection decisions need to be firmly based on the selection criteria defined at the beginning of the process, and should be made as soon as possible after the last candidate has been seen. All those involved in the decision need to be clear about the agreed weightings for each part of the process if more than one tool was used and if they were judged to be of differing value to the decision.

One method of collating all the relevant information that the selector(s) has amassed is to produce a matrix with all the candidates across the top and all of the selection criteria down the side. The boxes in the matrix can then be filled in with the data collected. When the matrix has been completed, the results can be summarised against each candidate in a simple fashion, such as:

A – exceeds all criteria;
B – meets all criteria and exceeds some;
C – meets all criteria;
D – meets most criteria;
E – meets few criteria.

If the criteria are of differing importance – which in reality they often are – then notes can be added about which criteria are exceeded/met/not met. The most appropriate person to appoint might not, of course, be in category A or B!

It is not suggested that the technique above is followed in a mechanical way: its value is in ensuring that all relevant data are taken into consideration, and in the discussion it stimulates when a group of selectors are making a decision. If the matrix is properly completed, it also ensures that the decision is made using hard data and specific examples rather than vague feelings that a candidate is good at xyz.

The value of having more than one selector is often demonstrated in these discussions. One of the authors was involved in some selection training and observed the group of selectors filling in the matrix at the end of the day. It was fascinating to watch the astounded expressions of some selectors as others revealed factual data and specific examples about a candidate that they had no inkling of! Indeed, it often sounded as though they were talking about different candidates.

Where selectors reach an impasse, it is important that a process to resolve this has been agreed in advance. It is even more important that all selectors understand why their views are different, and to check whether additional criteria are being added at decision time.

Validation

Most organisations invest large sums of money in their selection of employees, but not so many validate, in any formal way, how effective this investment has been. Validation can be a complex statistical process, but it can also be a simple tool. It depends on selection data being retained which show differentials between those appointed, at the time of appointment. A grading system similar to the above can be used, but perhaps with slightly more grades. If more than one selection tool has been used, it is important to retain separately data from each. The performance of each candidate who was employed is then assessed at a point in the future, using criteria such as appraisal results, salary increases, promotions, one-off assessments or whatever criteria are relevant to the organisation and the job. The initial rating on each selection tool can then be compared with the ultimate job performance and the results can be correlated to show to what extent selection assessments predict job performance.

Checking for bias

Our legal framework demands that selection decisions should discriminate fairly, and not unfairly in regard to different racial groups or sex. This aspect is covered in more detail in chapter 19, but some key issues are worth raising here:

- If some questions *could* be construed as discriminatory – such as 'Do you have any children?' – it is important that they are asked of all candidates.
- Consider why you are asking the question. Is it relevant to the person's capability to do the job? What inferences are you making from it, and what assumptions have you made? An incorrect assumption could lose you the best candidate. For example, why should a woman with small children be unable to spend 20 per cent of her time away from home?
- It is vital to cover the above issues in detail in any management training on recruitment and selection.
- Keep detailed notes of those candidates that were not selected, with reasons why.
- Monitor what is happening to women and ethnic minorities in the selection process. For each ethnic or sex or disability group, analyse the numbers applying, the numbers interviewed/tested and the numbers appointed. Compare the trends for each group.

Letters of offer and contracts of employment

Letters of offer are best sent as quickly as possible after the decision to appoint has been made, even if the offer is subject to satisfactory references. The letter could be preceded by a telephone call to ensure that the preferred candidate is still interested in the position. Speed is essential, as the best candidates may have offers or interests elsewhere, and too much elapsed time may mean that they are lost. Speed of reply and response is also important in enabling the employer to approach another candidate if the preferred candidate declines the offer but there is an alternative who is considered to be employable.

Letters of offer need not contain masses of information – title of position and salary offered are clearly the key matters of concern to potential appointees at this stage. Other matters, such as hours of work and holidays, will have been discussed during the interview, and these and other additional job details can be confirmed in the contract of employment.

Full-time employees and those working 16 hours per week or more are legally entitled to a contract of employment (or a written statement of main principles of employment), and this has to be produced by the employer within 13 weeks of their beginning work. Useful guidance in this area can be located in *Employing People* (ACAS 1985) and in *Written Statement of Main Terms and Conditions of Employment* (DoE 1979).

Study themes

1 Collinson (1987) gives evidence to show that, although personnel professionals had the skills to offer the organisation effective and efficient selection practices, in reality they were unable to guarantee such practices. Read Collinson's article and analyse what happens in your organisation, using similar criteria.

2 In what ways can the personnel function influence selection practices in the organisation to a greater extent, both in a short-term tactical way and in a long-term strategic way?

3 To what extent does your organisation use self-selection in the selection process? What are the advantages of using self-selection to a greater extent? Design a practical self-selection procedure for a defined job in your organisation.

4 Read Boyatsis' book (1982) describing competencies. Competencies are best defined using a very thorough research process. Where this is not yet possible, a 'halfway house' approach can be used. List the skills/knowledge required for a defined personnel position in your organisation. Group the skills/knowledge into four groups – technical/professional (such as employment legislation), personal (such as presentation and influencing), managerial (such as coaching and assessment/appraisal) and business (such as understanding business performance) – and describe them in terms of *behavioural outcomes/observable performance*.

5 There are two widely used approaches to personality testing: ipsative and normative tests. Read the article by Fletcher et al (1989) which compares the two. What are the key differences between these approaches and what is *your* verdict of the best approach to be used, and why?

6 Design an assessment centre to be used to select an appointee for the personnel post described in Study Theme 4, or another personnel post for which you have a full personnel specification. List and describe the activities to be included and show how they could be used to test for all the skill/knowledge areas or competencies that have been identified.

References

ACAS, 1985. *Employing People*, Advisory, Conciliation and Arbitration Service, London.

Allan, J., 1990. How to recruit the best people, *Management Accounting*, February.

Anderson, N., and Shackleton, V., 1990. Staff selection decision-making into the 1990s, *Management Decision*, vol. 28, no. 1, pp. 5–8.

Boyatsis, R. E., 1982. *The Competent Manager*, Wiley, New York.

Collinson, D., 1987. Who controls selection? *Personnel Management*, May, pp. 32–5.

Cosentino, C., Allen, J., and Wellins, R., 1990. Choosing the right people, *HR Magazine*, March, pp. 66–70.

DoE, 1979. *Written Statement of Main Terms and Conditions of Employment*, Department of Employment, London.

Elliot, B., 1990. Psychology and the selection process, *Accountancy*, March, p. 122.

Fletcher, C., Johnson, C., and Saville, P., 1989. A test by any other name, *Personnel Management*, March, pp. 46–51.

Fowler, A., 1990. The writing on the wall, *Local Government Chronicle*, 26 January, pp. 20–3.

Fraser, J. M., 1978. *Employment Interviewing*, 5th edn, Macdonald and Evans, London.

Hackett, P., 1978. *Interview Skills Training: Role Play Exercises*, Institute of Personnel Management, London.

Harrison, R. G., 1979. New personnel practice: life goals planning and interpersonal skills development: a programme for middle managers in the British Civil Service, *Personnel Review*, vol. 8, no. 1.

Herriot, P., and Fletcher, C., 1990. Candidate-friendly selection for the 1990s, *Personnel Management*, February, pp. 32–5.

IDS, 1985. *Psychological Assessment*, Study 341, Incomes Data Services, London.

Lewis, C., 1985. *Employee Selection*, Hutchinson, London.

Muir, J., 1988. Recruitment and selection, *Management Services*, November, pp. 12–15.

Rees, R., 1989. Can you improve your selection methods? *Works Management*, February, pp. 42–7.

Rodger, A., 1970. *The Seven Point Plan*, 3rd edn, National Institute of Industrial Psychology, London.

Swinburne, P., 1985. A comparison of the OPQ and 16PF in relation to their occupational application, *Personnel Review*, vol. 14, no. 4, pp. 29–33.

Task Force on Assessment Center Guidelines, 1989. Guidelines and ethical considerations for assessment center operation (endorsed by the 17th International Congress on the Assessment Center Method), *Journal of Business and Psychology*, vol. 4, no. 2, Winter.

Toplis, J., Dulewicz, V., and Fletcher, C., 1987. *Psychological Testing: a Practical Guide for Managers*, Institute of Personnel Management, London.

Torrington, D. P., and Hall, L. A., 1991. *Personnel Management: a New Approach*, Prentice-Hall, Hemel Hempstead.

Webster, E. C., 1964. *Decision-making in the Employment Interview*, Industrial Relations Centre, McGill University, Canada.

Wills, Q., 1984. Managerial research and management development, *Journal of Management Development*, vol. 3, no. 1.

Chapter 16

Performance Appraisal

Few aspects of personnel work arouse such extremes of reaction as performance appraisal. The following extracts are from answers written by students of the Institute of Personnel Management, taking professional examinations in the summer of 1989:

> Our scheme has been abandoned because of a lot of paperwork to be completed by the manager and the time-consuming nature of the preparation by both appraiser and appraisee. Assessment dragged on from week to week without any tangible outcome, there was no follow-up and few people understood the process. The interview was spent with managers talking generalities and appraisees having nothing to say. (from a large engineering company)

> We have had approximately one new scheme per year over the last six years. These have ranged from a blank piece of paper to multi-form exercises, complete with tick boxes and a sentence of near death if they were not complete by a specified date. (from an international motor manufacturer)

> Our scheme is not objective and has become a meaningless ritual. It is not a system of annual appraisal; it is an annual handicap. (from a public corporation)

Despite the problems and widespread management frustration about its operation, the potential advantages of appraisal are considerable and appraisals can produce spectacular results. Here is another extract from the same set of examination answers:

> I have had annual appraisal for three years. Each time it has been a searching discussion of my objectives and my results. Each interview has set me new challenges and opened up fresh opportunities. Appraisal has given me a sense of achievement and purpose that I had never previously experienced in my working life. (from an insurance company)

It is such possibilities that make appraisal one of the most valuable of all personnel initiatives. It is valueless unless the general experience of it is satisfactory. Appraisees have to find some value in the appraisal process itself and have to see tangible outcomes in follow-up. Appraisers have to find the appraisal process not too arduous and have to see contructive responses from appraisees. When the general experience of appraisal is satisfactory, it becomes an integral part of managing the organisation and modifies the management process. What makes it one of the most difficult of all personnel initiatives is the variety of purposes to which it can be put, for example:

- checking achievement against agreed objectives,
- agreeing individual objectives for the future,
- assessing training and development needs,
- making promotions,
- settling annual salary reviews, or
- appraising performance to see if it can be improved.

This chapter deals with the last of those purposes, for which one finds two contrasted approaches: the control approach and the development approach.

Contrasted approaches to appraisal

Few appraisal schemes are at one extreme or the other, but making the contrast enables us to understand the schemes we find. Of those currently in use, a majority are towards the control end of the spectrum, but the development approach is gaining in popularity.

The *control approach* has the starting point of a view expressed by someone 'up there' – representing the view of controlling, responsible authority – in saying:

> We must stimulate effective performance and develop potential, set targets to be achieved, reward above-average achievement and ensure that promotion is based on sound criteria.

At first glance, few people would argue with that perfectly

reasonable statement. In practice it is feared and almost always resisted by people acting collectively, either by representation through union machinery or through passive resistance and grudging participation. This is because people whose performance will be appraised construe the message in a way that is not usually intended by the controlling authorities, like this:

> This will put pressure on poor performers so that they improve or leave. That would be all right except that appraisal depends so much on subjective judgements by individual managers, which will put us all at risk. We will be less secure and tied down more tightly, and will lose a bit more control over our own careers.

We are always apprehensive about judgements that will be made about us by other people, however good their intentions. Nervousness about selection interviews is the most common manifestation, but if you 'fail' a selection interview you can walk away, massage your ego and try another application with a clean slate. The anxiety about 'failing' in appraisal is that you remain in the situation where your performance (perhaps) has been criticised.

The control approach is likely to produce the following:

- Negotiated modifications to schemes. In order to ease the apprehension of people who feel vulnerable, alterations are introduced to make the scheme more acceptable. These frequently make the schemes ineffective, either because they become bland and pointless or because the concession confirms that there was – and therefore probably still is – something to be worried about.
- Them and us attitudes within the organisation, including resistance by managers both to the formality that is introduced into the working relationship between themselves and their close colleagues and to the amount of administrative work involved in the process.
- Tight bureaucratic controls to try to ensure consistency and fairness of reported judgements.
- Bland, safe statements in the appraisal process.
- Little impact on the actual performance of most people appraised. The exceptions are that the small number of self-assured high achievers probably make the most of the oppor-

tunity to squeeze out some constructive criticism that they can build on, and the even smaller number of lazy incompetents may be sorted out.

This approach works best when there are clear and specific targets for people to reach, within an organisational culture that emphasises competition. There are considerable problems, like who sets the standards and who makes the judgements? How are the judgements, by different appraisers of different appraisees, made consistent? Despite its drawbacks, this approach is still potentially useful as a system of keeping records and providing a relatively impersonal framework for career development in large, bureaucratic organisations.

The *development approach* to appraisal starts with a philosophy that is trying to respond to a different question, coming from a different direction: not from the position of those in charge but from an uncertainty in the mind of the individual job-holder:

> I am not sure whether or not I am doing a good job. I would like to find ways of doing the job better, if I can, and I would like to clarify and improve my career prospects.

The essential difference of this approach is that the question is addressed by job-holders *to themselves*. Not 'Will someone tell me what to do and pat me on the head or boot me up the backside?' but, 'Where can I find someone to talk through with me my progress, my hopes, my fears. Who can help me come to terms with my limitations and understand my mistakes? Where can I find someone with the experience and wisdom to discuss my performance with me so that I can shape it, building on my strengths to improve the fit between what I can contribute and what the organisation needs from me?'

There is again a specious attraction in this. One would assume that those in charge would readily support a scheme based on such a premise. There tends, however, to be a slightly different construction put on this approach, which is something like:

> This could lead to people doing what they want to do rather than what they should be doing. There is no coordination, no comparison and no satisfactory management control.

This approach to appraisal:

- can develop cooperative behaviour between appraisers and appraisees, encouraging self-discipline and the acceptance of autonomous responsibility;
- makes it easier to confront issues and to resolve problems;
- does not work well with bureaucratic control;
- produces searching analysis directly affecting performance;
- requires high trust, candour from the appraisee and considerable skill and integrity from the appraiser.

This approach works best with people who are professionally self-assured, so that they can generate constructive criticism in discussion with a peer, and in protégé/mentor situations where there is high mutual respect. There is great reliance on the appraisal interview and less emphasis on filling in the forms properly. For that reason it can be more attractive than the control approach, as managers frequently begrudge time spent talking to people but most of them dislike even more spending time filling in forms.

Despite the attractions of this approach, there are two problems: first is the lack of the *systematic* reporting that is needed for attempts at management control of, and information about, the process; second is the problem of finding appraisers with the ability and willingness to carry out a highly skilled and sensitive task.

Reasons for appraising performance

The different participants in the appraisal process have a range of potential interests in making it succeed. Among the reasons why managers may wish to appraise their staff are the following:

- *Human resources development* – to ensure that staff abilities and energies are being used effectively and that skills or aptitudes are not being neglected if there is scope for their better use.
- *Training* – to identify training needs so that individual contributions may be developed.

- *Human resource planning* – to identify skill shortages, skill stocks and succession needs.
- *Promotion* – appraisal can assist decision-making in promotion, although direct links between appraisal and promotion are rare and difficult to create except under a control approach.
- *Authority* – appraisal sustains the hierarchy of authority by confirming the dependence of subordinates on those who carry out the appraisals.

There are also a range of reasons why all of us may wish to be appraised:

- *Performance* – one's ability to do the job may be enhanced by a process which identifies and emphasises one's strengths and develops an understanding of what changes are needed to overcome any problems, so that there is a greater sense of control over what one is doing and confidence in achievement.
- *Motivation* – reassurance that one is coping and clarification of how one could do better can increase the level of enthusiasm and commitment to the job.
- *Career* – developing one's understanding of personal strengths and the quality of one's contribution can help in the process of planning career moves and direction.

Problems with appraisal

The remarks at the opening of this chapter indicated some of the problems that appraisal produces. Any scheme has to anticipate these and attempt to avoid them. Among the difficulties for the appraiser are the following:

Prejudice The appraiser may be prejudiced in favour of or against the appraisee, which could bias the appraisal process. Equally, the appraiser might be biased through over-anxiety not to be prejudiced. Not only is there a risk that the appraiser's judgement could be distorted, there is also the possibility that the appraisee could 'play to' the assumed prejudice.

Insufficient knowledge of the appraisee Nearly always appraisal schemes require that the appraiser is senior to the appraisee. This can produce the problem of the appraiser carrying out the appraisal because of being at an appropriate position in the hierarchy rather than because of having a good understanding of what the appraisee is doing.

The 'halo effect'   If an appraisee is generally likeable or generally keen, loyal and exhibiting acceptable behaviour, those qualities may be read into the whole of the performance when the appraisal takes place, with the appraiser blinded to any faults because of the shining light of the halo. Those who are generally *disliked* will have difficulty in getting their good-quality performance recognised.

Distinguishing performance from its context   It can be difficult to distinguish what a person has achieved from the circumstances in which the achievement has been produced, especially when there is an element of comparison with other appraisees. One sales representative may be handling a product with serious delivery and quality problems, while another is promoting a product with few problems. If the second produces better results than the first, is that due to having an easier task?

Some problems concern both the appraiser and the appraisee – for example:

Paperwork   Those responsible for schemes try hard to make sure that judgements are consistent and fair. Those carrying out appraisals frequently ask for help and guidance because of apprehension about what they have to do. The combination of these drives can easily result in a level of documentation that is very cumbersome, and resented by those involved – even though it is for their benefit and partly at their request.

Formality   Most meetings and discussions at work are relatively informal, and managers usually try to reduce status barriers (not, of course, status symbols) between themselves and their immediate colleagues. Like selection, the appraisal process inevitably introduces a degree of formality as the two participants are cast in starkly contrasted roles, both knowing that they will have to deliver something to the other when the process is concluded.

Then there are the problems that can often cause appraisal schemes to fail:

Lack of action   Both parties to the appraisal have to deliver afterwards. The appraisee has to deliver some modification of performance, and will be strongly motivated to do so. The appraiser probably has to do something as well, to facilitate the modification of performance – arranging for attendance on a specific training course, making time available for the appraisee, organising some change of duties or similar action. When the appraiser fails to deliver, the appraisee feels let down and begins to resent the time given to appraisal and to regret the degree to which he or she had been frank, admitting areas that needed improvement and seeking assistance. Sometimes appraisers fail to deliver because their motivation is not as strong as that of the appraisee (it is not their career at stake), but more often they find after the interview that the course of action discussed at the interview cannot be delivered, for reasons that had not been foreseen.

Everyone is 'just above average'   Fletcher and Williams (1985, p. 11) refer to an organisation where the overall performance ratings were:

Outstanding	4.0%
Very good	50.5%
Good	39.0%
Fair	6.5%
Not quite adequate	0.5%
Unsatisfactory	0.0%

Appraisees are looking for reassurance that all is well, and the easiest way for appraisers to deal with this is by a statement or inference that the appraiser is doing at least as well as most others, and better than a good many. It is much harder to face someone with the opinion that he or she is average. Most of us are, but who wants to be? Appraisers also shy away from the extremes of 'outstanding' or 'unsatisfactory'. Each of those gradings presents problems to the appraiser. The outstanding person will look for promotion or some other reward, and the person who is unsatisfactory will either dispute the judgement or cringe – either way, he or she will not like the appraiser, and who likes being unpopular? Terms like 'good' or 'average' are taboo among the designers of appraisal schemes, for the very reasons suggested here, but appraisees will be looking for reassurance and will either squeeze it out of the appraiser or infer it from the most innocent, non-committal remark.

Appraising the wrong features   Sometimes behaviours other than the real work are evaluated – such as time-keeping, looking busy and being pleasant – because they are easier to see. This is not the same as the halo effect but a review of what is easy to assess rather than what needs to be assessed.

Who should the appraiser be?

There are a number of different approaches to the question of who the appraiser should be.

- *The immediate superior*   We have already seen that the appraiser is most often a person of superior rank, and this is probably essential in schemes of the control orientation, as outlined at the beginning of the chapter. The advantage of appraisal by the immediate superior is that this person usually has the most detailed and up-to-date knowledge of what the appraisee has been doing. When there is a good working relationship between the two, the annual appraisal can be an admirable summary and review of the continuing comment and feedback that should have taken place during the preceding year.
- *The 'grandparent'*   The person next up the hierarchy above the immediate superior may be the appraiser when there is particular interest in making comparisons between people in order to identify potential for promotion. The advantage of this is that it distances the appraisal process from the everyday working relationship. The 'grandparent' may also be used in a different

way: to vet the 'parent's' appraisal in order to confirm that it has been done properly.

- *The 'foster parent'* Someone of senior rank, but in a different line – like a management development officer – can be used when, because appraisees spend time in a number of different teams or projects, there is no 'parent' with a continuing knowledge of the work being done and a stake in the appraisee's future. This is a method that has both the benefits and the problems of detachment.
- *One's peers* Appraisal by one's colleagues of equal rank is rarely found, despite the advantage of one's peers probably having an excellent all-round appreciation of what one does. The main problem seems to be the reluctance of people to be tough with a colleague.
- *One's subordinates* Appraisal by subordinates is even less common. Mainly this is due to the reluctance of most people to be judged in this way. Another reason is the belief that subordinates have only a limited knowledge of the work that is done.
- *Oneself* A relatively recent development is for the total appraisal process to include an element of self-appraisal. Initially it is difficult to believe that this will be unbiased, but, as long as they are not asked to compare themselves with others, appraisees are frequently perceptive and constructively critical of their own performance (Meyer 1980). Fletcher (1984) suggests that the most useful approach is to ask appraisees to rate the various aspects of their performance against each other, rather than compare themselves with other people. Taylor et al. (1989) suggest an approach whereby the appraisees carry out a review of their development and improvement strategies, which is followed six months later by the formal appraisal with the immediate superior.
- *Assessment centres* A specialised form of appraisal is the use of an assessment centre, in which a number of people are assessed (or appraised) by a variety of means over several days. This is appraisal not for the purpose of improving performance but to determine suitability for promotion or for appointment to a position calling for qualities that have not previously been exercised in that person's career. These centres are probably the most effective means of assessing potential, mainly due to

the variety of techniques that are deployed, such as psychological tests, in-tray exercises, discussion groups and simulations.

The appraisal interview

The heart of the appraisal process in management is the interview.
The problem-solving approach is the most effective in the appraisal interview, although it is a mode that requires skill and openness
in both the appraiser and the appraisee. This is not the only type
of appraisal interview, however: Norman Maier (1976) identified
two main alternatives:

- *Tell and sell* is where the appraiser acts as judge, using the
  interview to tell the appraisee the result of the appraisal and
  what needs to be done to improve. This is sometimes known as
  the 'ski instructor' approach and can be very appropriate when
  the appraisees have little working experience and have not yet
  developed enough self-confidence to analyse their own performance: they are dependent on a mentor to guide them closely
  and readily acknowledge that dependence.
- *Tell and listen* still casts the appraiser in the role of judge,
  passing on the outcome of an appraisal that has already been
  completed, but adding the step of listening to reactions. These
  could sometimes modify the appraisal that has been made, but
  also enable the participants to have a reasonably frank exchange.

Maier's three types have shaped the thinking of personnel
managers since they were first propounded in the late 1950s, with
the problem-solving approach being the accepted orthodoxy.
Recently, however, that has been taken a stage further by the idea
of the *contingency approach*. Advocates suggest that concentrating
on the personal interaction is important but insufficient: the style
of the interview must also be consistent with the general culture
of the organisation in which the appraisal takes place – the activity
cannot be separated from its context:

> investment in a system must involve statements about certain
> desired organisational characteristics and about the treatment
> of people in an organisation. It is mistaken . . . to regard

appraisal as merely a technique or a discrete process with an easily definable boundary. (George 1986, p. 33)

For appraisal to succeed and survive, it needs to reflect wider values of the organisation, and it can even be used to symbolise and sustain a particular type of culture. A further consideration is that the appraisal style must not only be consistent with organisational culture: it must also be consistent with the appraiser's normal management style (Pryor 1985). The tough, uncompromising autocrat who turned on a smiling, honeyed performance for a 60 minute appraisal interview would bewilder any appraisee.

Conducting the interview

The first step is to brief the appraisee about the form the interview will take – possibly asking for a self appraisal form to be completed in readiness. To some extent this is establishing rapport in advance, with the same objectives, and makes the opening of the eventual interview easier.

Self-appraisal can form a useful preliminary to the interview, as it gives the appraisee some initiative and ensures that the discussion can begin by covering matters which the appraisee can handle and has thought about.

The appraiser needs to review all the available evidence on the appraisee's performance, including reports, records or other material regarding the period under review. Most important will be the previous appraisal and its outcomes.

The interview – like any other – begins with the appraiser establishing rapport. This can be difficult, because it is attempting to smooth the interaction between two people who probably have an easy social relationship but who now find themselves ill at ease because they are embarking on the sort of conversation they are not used to having with each other, so they have to test each other out and find a way of engaging with each other.

A useful development from initial rapport can be a review of the main points about the performance in the period under review. This will probably include the outcome of the previous appraisal, but it is useful to limit this phase of the discussion to a review of clear facts, without recourse to judgements about the facts, serving as a reminder to both participants.

The next step is for the appraiser to offer positive reinforcement to the appraisee, isolating those aspects of performance that have been disclosed which are clearly the most impressive or at least satisfactory. If these are singled out for favourable comments that carry conviction, those comments will provide the foundation of reassurance that the appraisee needs in order to avoid being defensive. Ideally this is not simply a stage in which the appraiser offers positive strokes to the appraisee, but one in which both parties single out the encouraging features by mutual discovery, even though the appraiser is leading the way. The appraiser is looking for and pointing out evidence that is there for them both to see, and their joint appraisal of that evidence brings them together and builds the confidence of the appraisee to handle any less satisfactory features that may come later. The points are clear and specific.

Then the appraiser asks the appraisee to comment on things that are not as good as they might be in the performance – areas of possible improvement and how these might be addressed, including features where the appraisee feels there is a need for management action to provide greater support, opportunity or training. The appraisee will offer this type of comment only if there has been effective positive reinforcement earlier. We can acknowledge and face up to inadequacies in our performance only when we are reasonably sure of ourselves. Having acquired such sureness, the appraisee is able and willing to examine areas of dissatisfaction by the process of discussing them with the appraiser, knowing that the discussion will be worth having because of the appraiser's expertise, information and 'helicopter' view. This stage in the interview is not easy for the appraiser:

> some employees prefer to be told rather than invited to participate . . . the manager receives extra pay and status for making decisions, so why should the manager expect them to do his or her job as well? (Wright and Taylor 1984, p. 110)

That is probably becoming a rare and blinkered view, and most people welcome the opportunity to participate in shaping their own destiny, but managers should not underestimate the delicacy

of enabling someone to analyse critically his or her own performance.

If the appraiser has succeeded in getting the appraisee to analyse
what has been happening in the recent past, the time has now
come for the appraiser to apply his perspective by raising opportunities for improvement that the appraisee cannot, or will not,
see. If they are brought in at this point in the interview, there is
the best chance that they will be understood and accepted, leading
to action. The appraiser may not succeed, finding that the suggestions are resisted because the appraisee finds them unreasonable.
What can be even worse is that the appraisee accepts the suggestions glumly but is unable to deal with them because the fragile
edifice of self-confidence that has been constructed collapses under
the weight of what seems like demoralising criticism. Although it
is not possible to guarantee success, this is the time to try to
discuss improvements, as the appraisee has developed a basis of
reassurance and has come to terms with some shortcomings that
he or she had already recognised.

The appraiser has to assess whether any further issues can be
raised and, if so, how many. None of us can cope with confronting
all our shortcomings all at the same time, and the appraiser's
underlying management responsibility is that the appraisee is not
made less competent by the appraisal interview. There is also a
fundamental social responsibility not to use a position of organisational power to damage the self-esteem and personal adjustment
of another human being.

The final stage of the interview is to agree what happens next,
with both parties probably needing to take some action.

Following-up appraisal interviews

Except in the most relaxed and informal schemes, the appraiser
will keep some record of what has taken place. This might be a
personal note for future reference; it might be a formal record
agreed with the appraisee, signed by a 'grandparent' and incorporated in the appraisee's employment file; or it might be at some
point between those two extremes. If the record is to be seen by
anyone other than the appraiser, there is then the question of
whether the scheme is open or closed.

In the rapidly declining number of closed schemes, the person appraised does not see what has been written. This may enable the appraiser to be less restrained in the evaluation, but it takes away some of the appraisee's motivation to take action, through not really knowing what the assessment was.

In open schemes, the account of what the interview dealt with is shared by both parties and the action required is clear.

If there are things the appraiser has to do in follow-up, it is essential that those steps are taken; otherwise the appraisee feels let down and construes the appraisal process as something that does not really matter. Furthermore, the conclusion of the interview and its report are not only the winding-up of the current appraisal: they are also the foundation for the next.

Making appraisal work

Finally, here are some key points in making sure that appraisal succeeds

- *Make the purpose clear*   Make sure that all involved are clear about what the purpose of the scheme is and – more importantly – what the scheme is not for. For example, does it have a bearing on promotion or not? Does it affect merit pay or not?
- *Get ownership of the scheme clear*   The scheme must be owned by the appraisers and the appraisees: not by the personnel department.
- *Go for openness and participation*   Appraisees will assume the ownership referred to above if they are able to be active (probably through their self-appraisal input) rather than passive and if there is full and frank feedback of the appraisal and how it is being viewed by others.
- *Go for as much objectivity as possible*   Incorporate as many features as you can that can be assessed by objective criteria. The subjective view of the appraiser remains central and crucial, but it is both informed and legitimised when it stems from a basis of factual evidence that is impervious to subjective judgement.
- *Train*   Both appraisers and appraisees need training so that they understand what the scheme is for and how they can make

it a success. That feature of training is probably more important than social-skills training, although trainers frequently have that as the main component.

- *Bash bureaucracy* Keep form-filling to the minimum and build up interpersonal analytical discussion, understanding and confidence-building to the maximum.
- *Emphasise action* Make sure that participants (especially appraisers) see the appraisal interview as the centrepiece but not the end of the appraisal process: the road to Hell is paved with good intentions.

Study themes

1 To what extent can the benefits of both the control approach and the development approach to appraisal be created in a single scheme?
2 Think of jobs where it is difficult to disentangle the performance of the individual from the context of the work. How would you focus on the individual's performance in these situations?
3 Latham and Wexley (1981) argue in favour of peer appraisal. Read their argument and consider its relevance to your own working situation.
4 Randell et al. (1984) believe there are three broad categories of appraisal – reward reviews, potential reviews and performance reviews – and that any appraisal system should attempt to deal with only one of these categories. What is their reasoning and how convincing do you find it?
5 In the second of two national surveys of performance appraisal practice, Long (1986) notes that there has recently been a substantial increase in performance reviews for non-managerial staff. Why has there been an increase? Why was performance review for non-managerial staff previously less common?
6 In the light of the points raised in this chapter, how convincing do you find the arguments of Taylor et al. (1989) in favour of their system of self-appraisal?
7 Kane and Freeman (1986 and 1987) say management by objectives and performance appraisal don't mix. Why?
8 How do the approaches of Maier (1976) and Dainow (1988) to the appraisal interview differ?

9 Tom Peters (1989) quotes an American colleague as saying that 'performance appraisal is the number one American management problem . . . it takes the average employee (manager or non-manager) six months to recover from it' (p. 495). Having read this chapter and Peters's comments (pp. 495–8), how can the problem be lessened?

References

Dainow, S., 1988. Goal oriented appraisal, *Training Officer*, January, Vol. 24, No. 1, pp. 6–8.

Fletcher, C., 1984. What's new in performance appraisal? *Personnel Management*, February, pp. 20–22.

Fletcher, C. A. and Williams, R., 1985. *Performance Appraisal and Career Development*, Hutchinson, London.

George, J., 1986. Appraisal in the public sector: dispensing with the big stick, *Personnel Management*, May, pp. 32–5.

Kane, J. S., and Freeman, K. A., 1986 and 1987. MBO and performance appraisal: a mixture that's not a solution, Parts 1 and 2, *Personnel*, December and February, vol. 63, no. 12 and vol. 64, no. 2, pp. 26–36, 26–32.

Latham, G. P., and Wexley, K. N., 1981. *Increasing Productivity Through Performance Appraisal*, Addison-Wesley, Wokingham.

Long, P., 1986. *Performance Appraisal Revisited*, Institute of Personnel Management, London.

Maier, N. R. F., 1976. *The Appraisal Interview: Three Basic Approaches*, University Associates, La Jolla, California.

Meyer, H. H., 1980. Self appraisal of job performance, *Personnel Psychology*, vol. 33, pp. 291–5.

Peters, T., 1989. *Thriving on Chaos*, Pan Books, London.

Pryor, R., 1985. A fresh approach to performance appraisal, *Personnel Management*, June, pp. 37–9.

Randell, G. A., Packard, P., and Slater, J., 1984. *Performance Appraisal*, Institute of Personnel Management, London.

Taylor, G. S., Lehman, C. M., and Forde, C. M., 1989. How employee self-appraisals can help, *Supervisory Management*, August, pp. 32–41.

Wright, P. L., and Taylor, D. S., 1984. *Improving Leadership Performance*, Prentice-Hall, Hemel Hempstead.

Chapter 17

Discipline

Discipline is regulating human activity to produce a controlled performance. In the work situation there are three types. In *managerial discipline* everything depends on the person in charge; a group of subordinates do what someone directs them to do. In *team discipline* the performance comes from the mutual commitment of each member of a group; they succeed or fail together. With *self-discipline*, an individual is absolutely dependent on having training, expertise and self-control; there is no one else on whom to depend.

The poor performer

Everyone's work is sometimes unsatisfactory. Often it is for reasons out of his or her control – poor organisation, poor working conditions, carelessness by other people or lack of suitable equipment. Also, few of us are equally good at everything we have to do. Where there are *specific difficulties* within an overall excellent performance, these are often easiest to remedy, as the rest of the team will be willing to compensate, or will try to help overcome the shortcoming. The poor performer of whom we all complain most is the individual with a long-term history of not working as well as is normal in the particular setting.

Sometimes this type of poor performance is due to someone not being able to keep up with the changes, like the chief clerk who was keeping detailed records of departmental expenditure by entering the same figures in three different books, while the brand-new computer sat untouched on the desk in front of her. People in this category can be most frustrating to their colleagues but bring out sympathy from those less involved. Moving 'downwards' to a less demanding position could assist many people who find themselves in this situation, although it remains a rare solution unless it is accompanied by some face-saver like simultaneously moving to part-time hours.

Some poor performers are suffering from being *overpromoted* to posts they cannot handle, or are struggling with jobs for which they no longer feel any enthusiasm. Others struggle for a variety of personal reasons.

Before anything can be done about poor performance, it is important to *establish a gap* between required performance and actual performance. For every job there are criteria of what is expected, and it is important to check all the criteria, rather than decide that everything is unsatisfactory because of problems on a single criterion. Having established a gap between actual and required performance, the next step is to identify reasons for the gap through discussion with the person concerned and then move on to agree reasonable, joint goals and a date to review the performance.

It can be helpful to categorise reasons under three headings, for example:

1 *Personal reasons* outside the firm's control:

- Intellectual capacity
- Physical ability
- Emotional stability
- Domestic/family circumstances
- Health

2 *Organisational reasons* outside the individual's control:

- Current job
- Job changes
- Pay
- Poor training
- Lack of investment in equipment
- Poor physical conditions
- Lack of planning
- Poor management
- Location and transport difficulties

3 *Individual reasons* arising from a mismatch with the organisation/job:

- Poor understanding of the job
- Feeling of unfair treatment
- Lack of motivation
- Personality clashes within the group or with superiors
- Lack/excess of confidence
- Training programme misunderstood

If you are the manager responsible for a poor performer, there is little you can do about problems in the first category – although understanding that the problems exist will be a great help. You could do something about the second category, and could help the poor performer deal with the matters in category 3.

Rules

Every workplace has rules. Some come from statutes, like the tachograph requirement for HGV drivers, but most are worked out to meet the particular situation of the organisation in which they apply. Rules should be clear, so that the people affected can understand and remember them, and there should be enough to cover all usual disciplinary matters. There is a better chance of rules being both understood and obeyed if they are jointly determined, where that is feasible, and if there is training to help people both understand and remember what governs their behaviour. A sample disciplinary procedure is shown in Figure 17.1.

The Department of Employment (1973) put rules into six categories, relating to different types of employee behaviour. This remains a most helpful categorisation.

- *Negligence* is failure to do the job properly by someone who is capable of doing it. In contrast, the incompetent employee is not able to do the job properly and is not deliberately breaking the rules.
- *Unreliability* covers behaviours such as lateness or unexpected absence.

Figure 17.1
Sample Disciplinary Procedure

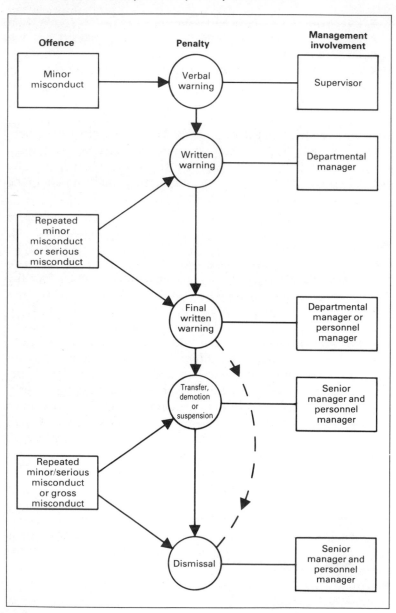

- *Insubordination* is refusal to obey instructions from someone in a position of authority or deliberate disrespect to such a person.
- *Interfering with the rights of others* covers a range of socially unacceptable behaviours, such as fighting or intimidation. Sexual harassment or racial taunts both come in this category.
- *Theft* is clear-cut when it is from another employee, but theft from the organisation should be supported by very explicit rules, as taking company property for one's own use is regarded by some as one of the perks of the job.
- *Safety offences* are those behaviours that can cause a hazard.

The Institute of Personnel Management conducted a survey (IPM 1979) of disciplinary practice in nearly 300 organisations and found that the three main reasons for disciplinary action were poor timekeeping, unauthorised absence and poor standards of work. On that basis, the rules most frequently invoked by managers were those relating to negligence and unreliability.

The main purpose of rules is not, however, to justify penalties, but to provide guidance on what people *should* do. If people know the rules, the majority will comply and will put pressure on the deviants to comply as well.

Compliance

Everyone has to *know* what the rules are and why they should be obeyed: it is not sufficient simply to tell people.

Induction provides an excellent opportunity to make rules coherent and to explain why they should be obeyed. This can be reinforced by placing a new employee with a working team that has high standards of compliance.

Training throughout employment is central to compliance. There are always new working procedures or new equipment being introduced, and training will reduce the risk of safety offences, negligence or unreliability by developing confidence in the new routines.

Penalties are an inescapable feature of the organisational justice framework, including a clear understanding of what penalties can be imposed, by whom and for what. The following are typical forms of penalty.

- The *rebuke* is the simple 'Don't do that', or 'You can't bring food in here.' This is often all that is needed, because someone has forgotten, not realised a rule was to be taken seriously or did not understand.
- Great care is required with *warnings*, as unfair-dismissal legislation with its associated code of practice has made the system of warnings an integral part of disciplinary practice, which has to be followed if the employer is to succeed in defending a tribunal claim of unfair dismissal. For the employer to show procedural fairness there should normally be a formal oral warning, or a written warning, specifying the offence and the likely outcome if it is repeated. Further misconduct could then justify a final written warning that further repetition would lead to a penalty such as suspension or dismissal. All written warnings should be dated, signed and kept on record for an agreed period. Details must be given to the employee and to his or her representative, if desired. The means of appeal should also be pointed out.
- *Disciplinary transfer* is moving the employee to less attractive work. The seriousness of this is that the employee's colleagues know the reason. *Demotion* is less common because it is so humiliating. Those demoted either leave or carry on (probably because they cannot leave) with considerable resentment, and having lost so much confidence that their performance remains unsatisfactory.
- A tactic that is serious without the disadvantage of being long-lasting, like demotion, is *suspension*. This is usually for a few days with pay, either as a punishment or while an alleged offence is being investigated. An employee can only be suspended without pay if the contract of employment explicitly permits it.

The disciplinary interview

The manager conducting the interview will prepare by *collecting evidence*. This will be information about the aspects of the working performance that are unsatisfactory and why, with as much factual corroboration as possible, including details of earlier warnings, cautions or penalties that have been invoked. There may be witnesses, especially if the problem centres round an allegation of some misdemeanour that is denied.

Conducting the interview

The interview is taking place only because of management dissatisfaction with what the employee has been doing, so the start is a *statement of the facts*, not moral outrage, about that dissatisfaction. It has yet to be established whether or not the employee is blameworthy.

After setting out the nature of the management dissatisfaction, the manager then asks the employee to say what the reasons are and hears the situation described from a different point of view. This stage of the interview presents a number of difficulties – for example, the person who cannot understand that there is a problem at all, or someone who is not willing to talk about the matter at all, or angry defiance from someone who feels the situation is simply unjust.

Now is the time to move towards a solution. Simply clarifying the problem and talking it through may produce the solution, but, if the employee will not respond, there are at least three further possibilities:

- The first is to persuade the person that he or she will not achieve his or her objectives without a change in behaviour. ('You have to have a good attendance record if you want to get a job as a PA.')
- The second is to suggest that some people disapprove of what he or she is doing. ('Other people in the department feel you are not pulling your weight.')
- The third possibility is to use penalties, such as a warning, suspension, demotion or dismissal.

The closing of the interview has to make the return to the workplace as positive as possible. The manager who sends the person away feeling humbled and demoralised may have won 'the match' but undermined future performance. In disciplinary situ-

Employee Resourcing

ations it is essential to put the matter right; simply proving that you are right and the other person wrong is of no value.

Following up the interview

A record has to be kept, not only to have a note of what should happen, but also for procedural reasons:

> After the disciplinary interview is over, it is essential to record both the fact that it has taken place and a synopsis of what transpired. Thus if the interviewee has been officially reminded during the interview that the consequences of further offences will have to be considered in terms of the further stages of a disciplinary procedure . . . he should be given a copy of a permanent record of the fact that this was said.' (Hackett 1981, p. 154)

Sometime after the interview, the matter has to be reviewed to see what has changed. If everything is satisfactory, it may be necessary to review any formal warnings the employee may have received, as procedure often includes provisions for 'cleaning the slate' of an employee who manages to put matters right after a trouble-free period. It is also necessary to consider disciplinary problems in aggregate. If some problems are frequent, there is need for further investigation.

Study themes

1 The book *Managing the Poor Performer*, by Valerie and Andrew Stewart (1982) is one of very few thorough treatments of the topic. Read the book and consider how you would use it (a) to help you manage poor performers better and (b) to manage your own performance better.

2 In the ACAS advisory booklet *Absence* (1983) is the passage:

> Where disciplinary action is invoked, employees and their representatives will have an interest in seeing that their colleagues' cases are well presented and given proper consideration by management; *they will also have an interest in seeing that management takes appropriate action against the very few who try to exploit the disciplinary . . . provisions . . . at the expense of the majority.* (p. 13)

Do you agree with the end of that passage, in italic type? Are there exceptions, in your experience? In what type of circumstance will employees generally resist management rules?

3 In the booklet *I'd Like to Have a Word With You* (1987), Tina Tietjen identifies ten categories of difficult respondent in disciplinary interviews. One of these is 'the compulsive confessor':

> he will own up to everything, and as a result never get ticked off for anything. The 'yes I know it's my fault I've been coming in late, not working as hard as I might, and haven't cleared up the swarf, etc.' is a clever ploy. All this person is trying to do is to beat you at your own game (p. 23).

What is wrong with being beaten at your own game, if the result is what is needed? Remember the final paragraph above in the section 'Conducting the interview'.

4 If you can, watch the video that accompanies Tietjen's book and consider how you would have handled the situations portrayed.

5 Can you recall any disciplinary incidents at work where you feel that the outcome was clearly wrong because the manager responsible rushed the proceedings, either backing away from action that was unpleasant but necessary or moving to a penalty that was too harsh? Could this have been avoided if there had been a systematic approach to the interview?

6 A well-known discussion of discipline is in the article by John Huberman, 'Discipline without punishment' (1964). Read the article and decide how realistic his suggested approach is.

7 Read the ACAS Code of Practice no. 1, *Disciplinary Practice and Procedures in Employment* (1977). What do you think of the comments in section 15(c) on criminal offences outside employment.

Check-list for dealing with disciplinary matters

1 How do those working with you know what you expect them to do?

2 What opportunity is there for them to discuss with you whether the work you expect is possible? Include formal and informal opportunities.

3 What records do you keep about the work of those you are responsible for? How could these help you in dealing with disciplinary problems? Who has access to them?
4 Do you have someone working for you at the moment who you regard as a poor performer?

- Have you talked to him or her about it?
- Have you established a gap between expected and actual performance?
- Are the reasons personal, organisational or individual, or a mixture?
- Try setting joint goals and a review date together.

5 Are there any aspects of your work which you know you are doing less well than you ought? Why do you think this might be? What might help you to resolve these problems?

References

ACAS, 1977. *Disciplinary Practice and Procedures in Employment*, Advisory, Conciliation and Arbitration Service, London.
ACAS, 1983. *Absence*, Advisory booklet no. 5, Advisory, Conciliation and Arbitration Service, London.
Department of Employment, 1973. *In Working Order: a Study of Industrial Discipline*, HMSO.
Hackett, P., 1981. *Interview Skills Training*, 2nd edn, Institute of Personnel Management, London.
Huberman, J., 1964. Discipline without punishment, *Harvard Business Review*, August.
IPM, 1979. *Disciplinary Procedures and Practice*. Institute of Personnel Management, London.
Salamon, M. W., 1987. *Industrial Relations: Theory and Practice*, Prentice-Hall, Hemel Hempstead.
Stewart, V. and A., 1982. *Managing the Poor Performer*, Gower, Aldershot.
Tietjen, T., 1987. *I'd Like a Word with You*, Video Arts Ltd, London.

Chapter 18

The Use of External Agencies

The last decade has seen increasing use of specialist agencies and consultancies by the personnel function. It is most important that the user department is clear about its rationale for using one type of agency rather than another, as these external bodies offer a wide range of different services, which may not be apparent at first sight, and their costs vary tremendously.

The majority of agency use is in connection with recruitment, and in this chapter we cover temp agencies, employment and file-search agencies, JobCentres and the Professional and Executive Register (PER), advertising agencies, selection consultants and headhunters. We also discuss suppliers of accredited tests, whose use may also be connected with development, and individual self-employed consultants who may be engaged in any area of personnel activity.

The key to getting value for money from any agency that is used is to agree a detailed remit and to brief the agency in depth about the organisation, its requirements and, in particular, the identified success criteria for that assignment. The personnel department also needs to continue to manage the agent, rather than washing its hands of any responsibility for the outcome of the assignment. Adshead (1990) talks about treating the consultant as a full member of the personnel team (temporarily at least), and Fowler (1991) sees the consultant–user relationship as a working partnership.

Temp agencies

Temp agencies deal with a variety of staff vacancies, from manual (for example, production workers and drivers) through to executive (for example, computer staff and training centre or other administrators). Agencies covering executive staff are less common, and the group of staff most often covered in this way are secretarial/clerical/copy-typing.

The advantage of such agencies is that they can respond to immediate and unplanned needs – for example, when a senior secretary falls sick and it is essential to cover absence longer than perhaps two days. In these circumstances, payment would usually be made to the agency on an hour-by-hour basis and, given agreed time sheets, the agency would then pay the temporary worker at a lower rate.

Some agencies would also offer staff on a longer-term contract, say three months to a year. There are advantages for some employers here, as, depending on the accounting procedures, temporary staff would not be included in headcount. This means that, where headcount is restricted but some choices remain about spending, using such staff may be the only way to increase staffing to meet work needs.

Employment/file-search agencies

These agencies cover a similar range of staff to the agencies described above, although there is likely to be a greater emphasis on the executive and administrative levels. For some areas – particularly accountancy – more senior jobs are dealt with in this way.

These agencies operate on the basis of having a register, or file, of individuals who are job-seeking in a certain area. When an employer contacts them with a job to fill, they are able to supply, fairly quickly, a list of potential candidates to be considered. They will also advertise the post in question if this is required. Paper details of individuals are supplied, and the organisation takes over the responsibility from there, paying the agency a fee for the introduction, (which is usually a percentage of the salary, ranging from around 10 to 17 per cent) when an individual is appointed.

From an individual's point of view, he or she has the opportunity of walking into an agency and asking about appropriate jobs that are currently placed with the agency. If there are jobs of interest where the individual appears to meet employer needs, the agency will often contact the employer immediately by telephone and try to arrange an interview.

JobCentres and PER

JobCentres and the Professional and Executive Register now operate as separate organisations and tend to cover different, but sometimes overlapping, areas of the labour market. JobCentres have the advantage of being very responsive in advertising a vacancy, by displaying a card in the Centre itself. Details required are organisation name, telephone number, hours, wage and a brief job description – and these may be given by telephone. Where required, these details can be distributed to other Job-Centres by computer. The JobCentre will contact the employer immediately there is an interested party, and an interview can be arranged immediately by telephone.

JobCentres also offer a wider range of services, and can advertise through Oracle on television, can advertise the vacancy anonymously and can offer initial screening for appropriate vacancies by asking candidates to fill out an application form and involving them in an initial discussion. The JobCentres are keen to expand the type of jobs that they deal with and are increasingly taking on more professional posts, and jobs with salaries up to around £15 000 p.a.

PER operates in a very different way, and its initial contact will often be to arrange for a consultant to go and meet the employer to explain the range of services available and the best options in a given situation. Its fees, as with independent agencies, depend on the type of service that is given, and it offers interviewing services, initial selection and search.

Advertising agencies

Advertising agencies offer a wide range of services, from designing the layout of a text advertisement (for which their fees would come via commission from the advertising media used, rather than from the employer) to planning and implementing a major campaign with supporting literature, where fees can soar to tens of thousands of pounds.

In selecting an agency for either major or minor work, the usual practice is for the agency to make a presentation about itself to the potential customer, the organisation. To get more out of this presentation, the organisation can ask the agency to offer its suggested approach(es) to a particular assignment. The organisation also needs to ensure that it meets the particular consultant who will have its account, who may not have been included in the initial image-forming presentation.

Wheeler (1988) stresses the importance of choosing the most appropriate agency, as recruitment advertising cannot be divorced from corporate advertising, and therefore the organisation's image is at stake. He suggests checking on such things as previous work, current clients, experience with different media, presence of regional offices and examples of the agency's work to a brief. Membership of the IPA (Institute of Practitioners in Advertising) is a good indicator, as this should ensure that the agency is committed to The Advertising Standards Authority's and the Independent Broadcasting Authority's codes of practice and standards, including that all advertising should be legal, decent and honest.

Selection consultants

Selection consultants are involved in advertising for an initial selection of potential candidates. One of the advantages of using such an agency is that the employer can remain anonymous, if this is important for recruitment in a sensitive area, and can trade on the reputation of the agency. Agencies can also be helpful in that they often specialise in a particular area of the labour market and can bring their experience to bear on the vacancy in question if the employer's experience is limited.

Additional advantages are seen in time-saving. Curricula vitae can be sent direct to the consultancy, the short list of individuals to be interviewed can be selected, and first interviews can be conducted without any heavy time demands on the employer. Some consultancies also offer candidates from their data bank of individuals seeking jobs, although these are often built up in a more selective and sensitive way than for the standard file-search agencies.

Fees will be around 15 to 25 per cent of the first year's salary, and are usually paid in instalments at stages of the assignment. Advertising and testing will involve supplements to the basic fee.

These consultancies will often offer additional services either associated with recruitment or in the more general human resources area. For example, they could be involved in the analysis of the job, in supplying professional human resources staff on a temporary basis, in recruitment and selection training or in career counselling.

Executive search/headhunters

Executive search is a more specialised activity. It is offered by some of the selection consultants as an alternative approach, and is also offered by specialist headhunters. An excellent guide to the services offered by the various consultancies is *The Executive Grapevine* (Baird 1990).

The use of this approach is usually reserved for the most sensitive organisational vacancies, highly specialised positions or those vacancies where it is anticipated that there will be some problem with recruitment. Positions are rarely advertised, and the headhunter proceeds with the assignment via a network of contacts which it has built up. There are usually agreements that, when a headhunter has placed an individual with a client organisation, it will not poach from that organisation for a specified time period, often around 18 months.

Headhunters will target possible candidates from their network, which is continually expanding, and usually make initial contact by telephone. If there is some interest and match of needs, the next step would be for an informal meeting. Eventually the headhunter will present a choice of candidates to the client in line with the number and criteria agreed.

In selecting a headhunter, it is important to seek one which specialises either in the specialism or in the commercial sector where the vacancy exists. Other factors would be checking on the salary level that the consultants most often headhunt, and on their past/present clients. It is vital to obtain a written proposal from the headhunter, which could be asked about the competencies it would expect to seek (given a thorough briefing on the organisation and on the position to be recruited) and the way it intended to tackle the search.

The cost of headhunters is greater than any other consultancy approach – usually around 30 per cent of initial salary, plus expenses incurred during the search. Payment is normally in three equal stages, and some headhunters offer guarantees in the form of further support if the appointment does not work out.

Individual self-employed consultants

Individual self-employed consultants are rarely used for full recruitment assignments but, in connection with recruitment activity, they may be called in to run recruitment and selection training, to administer tests and interpret and feed results back to candidates and to take part as assessors when assessment centres are used. They may also be involved in assessor training and in the design of assessment days.

Other activities that self-employed consultants would be used for would centre around running and designing training events, carrying out career counselling, carrying out job evaluation, and organisational analysis and design.

Most often these consultants are paid on a day rate, ranging from about £300 to £700, and they are therefore sometimes as expensive as employing the larger companies. Individual consultants are often engaged through a network of contacts rather than through advertising, and they have usually been associated with the organisation before, perhaps by working for it before declaring independence. Their prior understanding of the organisation is often a great asset.

Suppliers of accredited tests

Before using any supplier of accredited tests, it is vital that the user is clear about the remit and the competencies required for the vacancy in question. Only from this data can the user decide what to measure and, from there, which test would be most appropriate to measure this. To help with some of this process, some test suppliers, for example Saville and Holdsworth (1990), can provide materials to help the user identify the most appropriate test. There is also the possibility of tests being tailored to meet specific needs.

In choosing a test supplier, criteria would be the supplier's stated adherence to the guidelines of the BPS (British Psychological Society) and the IPM, adequate validity data supporting each test, the quality of training provided and the costs involved. Suppliers will supply only to users who have attended the appropriate training – usually provided by themselves – and who have subsequently registered their use with themselves. The costs of using a test vary from around £2 to £12 per administration, plus the costs of time and the costs of initial training, which range from around £2000 to £5000.

Study themes

1 Write a brief for a self-employed consultant who is to run a two-day recruitment and selection course for you on six occasions throughout the year.
2 Scan *The Executive Grapevine* (Baird, 1990) and, from the information presented, select a short list of five selection agencies for a job you have specified in your organisation. Justify your short list on the basis of the criteria you consider to be important.
3 Interview five personnel managers and obtain their views on the use of agencies as opposed to carrying out activities in-house, summarising

   (a) the benefits to the organisation,
   (b) the disadvantages to the organisation,
   (c) the cost justification for the agencies' services.

4 Read Fowler's (1991) article on executive search and Adshead's (1990) article on headhunters. Write a report:

   (a) supporting the use of that type of agency for filling a specified vacancy in your organisation, and
   (b) describing the process you would use to select the most appropriate headhunter for this task.

5 Read the IPA's literature which explains its role, services and standards. From this, describe what service you would expect

from an IPA-registered advertising agency. What controls are there to ensure that registered agencies act as you would expect?

References

Adshead, J., 1990. Headhunting without tears, *Personnel Management*, October, pp. 56–7.

Baird, R. B., 1990. *The Executive Grapevine 1990: the corporate directory of executive recruitment consultants 1990/91*, Executive Grapevine Ltd, London.

Fowler, A., 1991. How to use executive search, *Personnel Plus*, January, pp. 20–1.

Saville and Holdsworth, 1990. *Occupational Tests 1991*, Saville and Holdsworth, Esher.

Wheeler, D., 1988. How to recruit a recruitment agency, *Personnel Management*, April, pp. 63–8.

Chapter 19

Equality of Opportunity

Discrimination in our society has been acknowledged as unjust and as adversely affecting the rights of various categories of people, especially in relation to employment, education and housing. The practice of discrimination is, however, still widespread. The discussion in this chapter will be limited to the area of employment.

The existence of discrimination in society in general exacerbates problems which are seen in the work situation. As Wedderburn (1986, p. 447) writes:

> Many workers bring to their subordinate status as employees additional disadvantages that derive from discrimination against them in the wider society.

The prejudices which are held are not necessarily overt, and many managers might deny their existence. However, the results of years of discrimination can be measured in terms of comparative unemployment figures, levels of employment, pay and conditions and opportunities for training and promotion for the disadvantaged groups.

Why should any employing organisation want to prevent discrimination from operating within it?

Firstly, there is the question of 'natural justice'. In our society, the part played by work – or the lack of it – is significant to everyone's lives, both inside and outside the place of work, as Braham et al. (1981, p. 11) explain:

> The kinds of jobs done by workers in terms of pay levels, skills, status, levels of autonomy and involvement, physical conditions, fringe benefits - the whole pattern of extrinsic and intrinsic rewards from work – are a fundamental part of, and fundamental to, their whole experience of life as well as that of their dependants.

That experience should involve equal opportunities for all to exercise their rights and should impose an obligation on society to support them in doing so.

Secondly, it is in the interests of any employing organisation to make the best use of all the resources available to it, including the human resources. It is in the interests of the organisation to recruit and select those who will best fulfil its requirements, and then to train and promote them as appropriate to their talents. If the employing organisation recruits those best able to achieve the tasks required of them, it will establish a workforce whose culture allows and encourages the advancement of those who deserve to receive it, which will be motivating for all employees.

From a totally practical viewpoint, much discussion has taken place in the literature on the effect of demographic changes in the working population for the 1990s. The reduced numbers of young people available for employment is expected to cause enlightened employers to widen their options and find new sources of recruitment. These sources will of necessity be from the presently disadvantaged groups. Ninety per cent of the projected 1 million growth in the British labour force by the year 2000 will be women (DoE 1989), and the whole workforce will be getting older. It is estimated that by 2000, one-third of the workforce will be over 45. Discrimination against disadvantaged groups will therefore be an even greater liability to the future needs of employing organisations than it is now.

Disadvantaged groups

The main groups experiencing discrimination and for whose benefit anti-discrimination legislation has been introduced are women and different racial groupings. Other categories who feel that their opportunities are limited through prejudice include disabled people, ex-offenders and older people seeking employment.

Women

According to the New Earnings Survey of 1986, 42 per cent of the labour force were women; by 1989 this had risen to 43 per cent (*The Times* 1 November 1989). Although women constitute such a large section of the workforce, only 3 per cent of companies have female chairpersons and only 6 per cent of senior managers are women. A majority of women are still working in certain labour-intensive sectors of the labour market – often those which are low paid and least unionised – and in traditional women's occupations. Women also form the largest proportion of the part-time labour force.

> Overall employment continues to be highly gender segregated, both vertically, within hierarchies and horizontally, across occupations. (Dickens 1989, p. 169)

This segregation is even more complete on a 'micro' level (Dickens 1989), where it has been shown that 63 per cent of the women in the *Women and Employment Survey* (DoE and OPCS 1984) worked only with other women, and 83 per cent of the men worked only with other men. This separation of the sexes may partly be related to employers' attempts to circumvent the effects of the Equal Pay Act, which was intended to bring the relative wages of men and women into closer alignment. After a large rise in the average gross hourly earnings of women as a percentage of men's from 63 per cent in 1970 to 75.5 per cent in 1977, women's average hourly earnings as a proportion of those of men did not show any increase until 1989, when the figure was 76.4 per cent, and 1990, when it was 76.9 per cent. (Lewis 1990) Even though these figures represent some advance as far as women's relative earnings are concerned, in terms of total weekly payments women are still far behind, as men have more access to premium pay opportunities, including overtime payments.

The introduction of legislation against sex discrimination in the UK began with the Equal Pay Act, which was enacted in 1970 but not brought into operation until 1975, and which dealt only with matters of pay and terms and conditions of employment. This law was amended by the Equal Value (Amendment) Regulations 1983. The Sex Discrimination Acts 1975 and 1986 extended the legislation to discrimination in employment, education, housing and the provision of goods, facilities and services.

Race

The largest migration of people into the UK came between the 1950s and the 1970s as a result of the British Nationality Act of 1948. In 1982, an official estimate of the numbers of the population originating from the new Commonwealth was 2.2 million – that is, 4 per cent of the then total population. The racial minorities are concentrated in lower-status and lower-paid jobs, and are subject to significantly higher levels of unemployment than the rest of the workforce. While 42 per cent of the white population is under 30, it is estimated by the Commission for Racial Equality that the ethnic-minority population is on average younger, with 60 per cent of the West Indian community and 70 per cent of the Asian community in that category.

The Race Relations Act 1976 introduced legislative measures into the fight against discrimination on the grounds of race in employment. The Commission for Racial Equality has noted that there is no European Community-wide legislation against racial discrimination and it has recently called for European legislation to counter racial discrimination.

Disabled people

Research published in 1990 estimated that 3.1 per cent of the total working-age population were eligible to register under the Disabled Persons (Employment) Act (EOC 1990c, p. 24) whereas approximately 1 per cent of the working-age population are currently registered. This research also estimated that 22 per cent of the total number of disabled people are unemployed, while the 1989 EC Labour Force Survey estimated a figure of 20.5 per cent unemployment among disabled people. This compares with 5.4 per cent unemployment for the same period in relation to the general population. It has also been found in the research that

> people with disabilities in work are also likely to be found disproportionately in lower level jobs. (EOC 1990c, p. 24)

While it is acknowledged that disabled people may be limited in the activities that they can undertake, 'this is unlikely to be the only reason' (EOC 1990c, p. 24).

The current legislative framework is based on the 1944 and 1958 Acts. It relates to a quota system, which imposes a duty on employers with 20 or more employees to employ a minimum of 3 per cent of registered disabled people. It is not illegal to be below quota, but, if an employer is below quota, it is a criminal offence to engage someone other than a registered disabled person unless the employer has received a permit to do so. What is notable about the quota system is how few employers are complying with its requirements. In a study carried out by IFF Research covering 1026 employers (Morrell 1990), only 32 per cent of the sample were knowledgeable on the subject, and this lack of awareness explains to some extent why the scheme is so poorly implemented. There is also little enforcement of the scheme.

A company employing more than 250 employees is also subject to the provisions of the Companies Act 1985, which requires the directors in their report to shareholders to describe the policy which the company has operated, in the previous financial year, towards the recruitment, training, career development and promotion of people with disabilities and the retention of newly disabled employees. There is, however, no legal sanction to ensure that policy is put into practice.

In October 1984, the government issued a *Code of Good Practice on the Employment of Disabled People* (MSC 1984), but its existence is not widely known. While the government has considered the introduction of other measures to combat discrimination against disabled people, including anti-discrimination legislation in this field, it has concluded that

> anti-discrimination law would be complex to draft and uncertain in its application (EOC 1990c, p. 26)

Ex-offenders

It is estimated by the Apex Trust (1990), a pressure group which looks after the interests of ex-offenders, that over 5 million people in the United Kingdom – that is, 20 per cent of the working population – have a criminal record. However, it has been found that most crime is committed by a small percentage of offenders, while

Most offenders are of the non–recidivist type; they offend once or twice usually during adolescence, and then settle down to lead honest lives leaving the system of criminal justice behind them. (EOC 1990d)

The legislation relating to ex-offenders is the Rehabilitation of Offenders Act 1974. This law states that, unless specifically asked, a job applicant is not under any legal obligation to disclose information about previous convictions. If an employer discovers the information about the convictions at a later time and dismisses the employee as a result, that person is covered by the unfair dismissal sections of the employment legislation, provided that the employee has worked for that employer for two years. While most employers will, at some stage of the recruitment process, question an applicant about criminal convictions, there are circumstances where an ex-offender can answer in the negative without doing wrong. This applies when a conviction is 'spent' – that is, the rehabilitation period for that offence has passed. The length of the rehabilitation period depends on the nature and duration of the punishment. There are, however, a large number of occupations which are excepted from the provisions of this Act, and these include teachers, social workers, doctors and solicitors.

Older people

Within a society which has a greater proportion of economically active older workers and a predicted shortage of young prospective employees,

it is a business imperative for employers to review their personnel policies, practices and procedures to prevent the inappropriate use of age and age related criteria in all employment decision-making. (IPM 1991)

For a recent Institute of Manpower Studies report, Metcalf and Thompson (1990) surveyed 20 major organisations with a total workforce of over 650 000 and found that older workers are still subject to prejudice concerning their abilities to cope with 'physically demanding', 'time-pressured' and technology-based positions. There are also procedural difficulties facing older workers, including the decreasing but still existent practice of including specific age ranges in advertisements, and problems of entering company pension schemes and training courses.

Ways of countering discrimination

While there has been an increasing amount of legislation relating to discrimination against certain disadvantaged groups – particularly women and racial groups – attempts to combat discrimination have also been made through encouraging changes of practice. These have included national and international campaigns, such as the Year of the Disabled, and also promoting equal opportunities policies both in industry and in the wider community.

Equal pay

The Equal Pay Act was put on the statute book in 1970 and brought into effect on 29 December 1975. It has been amended by the Sex Discrimination Acts 1975 and 1986 and by the Equal Pay (Amendment) Regulations of 1983.

The Equal Pay Act brought into being the idea of a clause on 'equality' which would be implied as existing in every woman's contract of employment where such a clause did not actually exist. This clause allows for the alteration of a contract of a woman where any terms of it are less favourable than that of a man, in the following situations:

1 Where the woman is doing *like work* to a man.
   The definition of like work is considered in two stages: firstly, the woman's work and the man's are of the same or of a broadly similar nature; secondly, the differences between the tasks undertaken in the two jobs are not of practical importance in relation to the performance of the job.
2 Where the woman's work is *rated as equivalent* to work done by a man.
   Where a woman's work is rated as equivalent to that of a man on the basis of a job evaluation scheme, they must be considered to be equal. This does not require employers to introduce a job evaluation scheme, but it does mean that any existing job evaluation scheme must be impartial and non-discriminatory.

3 Where the woman's work is *of equal value* to that done by a man.

This classification was introduced following a complaint that the Equal Pay Act did not comply with EEC Directive 75/117, and legislation was brought into effect by the Equal Value (Amendment) Regulations. These deal with the situation where the work of a woman is of equal value to that of a man in terms of the demands made on her under headings such as skills and knowledge, responsibilities, mental demands, physical demands and working conditions. This claim of equivalence can be made with respect to a male co-worker at the same establishment or at a different establishment of the same employer, if they are covered by common conditions of employment.

The fact that, by any of the three means above, a woman may establish that she is employed on work which is equal to that of a man does not bring an automatic outcome in favour of the woman. The employer can argue that the difference in the contract terms of the woman and of her male comparator is due to a 'material factor' which is not the difference of sex. In the cases of like work and work rated as equivalent, such a defence of 'material factor' *must* be a material difference between the woman's and the man's cases – that is, factors such as length of service or level of experience. In equal value claims, the defence of material factor may be raised at the initial hearing and *may* be a material difference, such as those cited above, but can also include

> factors which were not directly attributable to the individuals themselves, such as market forces. (IDS 1990, p. 7)

In practice, the distinction between the terms *must* and *may* has become blurred – by the fact that in a like work claim (*Rainey* v. *Greater Glasgow Health Board* [1987] ICR 129) the House of Lords allowed a defence based on market forces. The material factor, which must be the genuine cause of the pay differential, must not itself be a discriminatory element – for example, separate pay structures which cause the pay difference but are the result of discriminatory practices.

Claims for equal pay are heard by the industrial tribunals procedure. In the case of an equal-value claim, an initial hearing will consider elements of the case, including any defence of 'genuine material factor', after which it will adjourn its proceedings and refer the question to a member of a panel of independent experts appointed by ACAS, who will prepare a report. This report is not always accepted by the tribunal, and there is one case in which a new report was then commissioned.

A number of administrative and legal problems have arisen, especially in relation to equal value claims. The large number of applications – including a considerable number of multiple applications on equal-value claims – together with the adjournment to await the expert's report, have made the whole system cumbersome and lengthy, with the average time taken by an equal value claim estimated at 17 months (EOC 1990b, p. 11), especially as cases are considered in relation to an individual and not to a group. The costs incurred are tremendous, and legal aid is not available during the tribunal hearing; so, in practice, cases can only be brought if supported by a trade union or the Equal Opportunities Commission. The case law resulting from each completed case is complex and adds to the nuances of the law.

Discrimination

As the laws concerning discrimination on the grounds of sex and race have been referred to in a number of chapters, only a short summary of the law will be included here. In both sex and racial discrimination, there are two main categories of discriminatory practices: *direct* and *indirect*.

The term 'direct discrimination' refers to a situation where a person is treated less favourably than others – either on the grounds of race, or where a person of one sex is treated less favourably than a person of the other sex or a married person less favourably than a single person (or vice versa).

'Indirect discrimination' exists when the requirement or condition applied to a position by an employer has a discriminatory effect because it is difficult for persons of a particular racial group, sex or marital status to comply with it. If it can be shown that the proportion of persons of that racial group, sex or marital status that cannot fulfil that requirement or condition is significantly larger than the equivalent proportion of the rest of the population, and if there is no justification for that requirement or condition and its effect is detrimental to that group, then it is classified as indirect discrimination.

The main exceptions to the laws on discrimination arise in relation to 'genuine occupational qualifications', and where positive discrimination is allowed.

Enforcement

The legislation which outlaws discrimination establishes statutory bodies – the Commission for Racial Equality (CRE) and the Equal Opportunities Commission (EOC). They have powers to hold formal investigations and issue non-discrimination notices, and they may apply for an injunction in certain cases. These bodies have also issued codes of practice which can be used as guidance by an industrial tribunal. Within these codes, they recommend the use of ethnic and sex monitoring of the workforce.

Study themes

1 The present equal pay laws have been described as 'paradise for lawyers, hell for women' (*The Times*, 16 November 1990). Read EOC (1989) and EOC (1990a) – do you agree with the quotation?
2 Read Crofts (1984) and consider the arguments for and against the monitoring of the ethnic origins and sexual composition of your workforce.
3 Using your own experience and a reading of Braham et al. (1981), list as many reasons as you can for equalising employment opportunity being in the *management* interest.
4 The average hourly earnings for women are approximately three-quarters of the average hourly earnings for men.

   (a) Do you feel that that is fair? If so, why? If not, why not?
   (b) Read the equal pay legislation. Is there an amendment that would narrow the gap between male and female earnings?

5 Imagine that a management colleague says to you, 'Don't send me anyone with a criminal record, no matter how trivial the

offence and no matter how long ago. I don't trust them. Once a thief, always a thief!' IIow would you respond?

References

Apex Trust, 1990. *Evidence to House of Commons Employment Committee Enquiry into Recruitment Practices*, Apex Trust, London.
Braham, P., Rhodes, E., and Pearn, M., (eds.), 1981. *Discrimination and Disadvantage in Employment*, Harper and Row/Open University, London.
Crofts, P., 1984. Counting on monitoring for racial equality, *Personnel Management*, March.
Dickens, L., 1989. Women – A Rediscovered Resource? *Industrial Relations Journal*, Autumn Editorial, vol. 20, no. 3, Basil Blackwell, Oxford, pp. 167–75.
DoE, 1989. Labour force outlook to the year 2000, *Employment Gazette*, April, vol. 97, no. 4, HMSO, London, pp. 159–72.
DoE and OPCS, 1984. *Women and Employment*, HMSO, London.
EOC, 1989. *Equal Pay – Making it work*, Equal Opportunities Commission, Manchester.
EOC, 1990a. *Equal Pay for Men and Women – Strengthening the Acts*, Equal Opportunities Commission, Manchester.,
EOC, 1990b. Equal value update, *Equal Opportunities Review*, no. 32, July/August, Equal Opportunities Commission, Manchester, pp. 11–25.
EOC, 1990c. Equal opportunities for people with disabilities: proposals for reform, *Equal Opportunities Review*, no. 33, September/October, Equal Opportunities Commission, Manchester, pp. 24–7.
EOC, 1990d. Wiping the slate clean: equal opportunities for ex-offenders, *Equal Opportunities Review*, no. 34, November/December, Equal Opportunities Commission, Manchester, pp. 18–24.
IDS, 1990. *Equal Pay – Material Factors*, IDS Brief 414, February, Incomes Data Services, London.
IPM, 1991. *Age and Employment: an IPM Statement*, Institute of Personnel Management, London.
Lewis, C., 1990. Pay in Great Britain: Results of the 1990 New Earnings Survey, *Employment Gazette*, November, vol. 98, no. 11, HMSO, London, pp. 571–5.
Metcalf, H., and Thompson, M., 1990. *Older Workers: Employers' Attitudes and Practices*, IMS Report no. 194, Institute of Manpower Studies, Falmer.
Morrell, J., 1990. *The Employment of People with Disabilities*, IFF Research, Research Paper no. 77, DoE, London.
MSC, 1984. *Code of Good Practice on the Employment of Disabled People*, Manpower Services Commission, Sheffield.
PAC, 1987/8. *Employment Assistance to Disabled Adults*, 21st report of

the Public Accounts Committee, House of Commons.

Prescott-Clarke, P., 1990. *Employment and Handicap*, Social and Community Planning Research, London.

Wedderburn, Lord, 1986. *The Worker and the Law*, 3rd edn, Penguin, Harmondsworth.

Chapter 20

Termination

There can be a number of reasons for the termination of the contract between an employer and an employee – sometimes the departing employee retires or resigns at his or her own wish, and in some cases the employee's decision to resign is a source of surprise to the employer. In the cases to be considered in this chapter, the effect of the employer terminating the contract of the employee without that employee's consent is analysed.

Notice periods

The termination of a contract of employment is subject to the legal requirements which give both the employer and the employee a right to a minimum *period of notice*. An employee is required to give his or her employer at least one week's notice, regardless of the employee's length of service. An employer's notice to an employee must take account of the employee's length of continuous employment in excess of one month, which is the basic qualification period for this right, and the notice periods are calculated on a sliding scale from one week up to a maximum of twelve weeks, depending on length of service. Conditions stated within a contract may improve these terms, but will not be legal if they attempt to diminish them. Either party can waive its right to notice, and an employee can accept payment in lieu of notice. It is nonetheless legal to terminate a contract without notice if the conduct of the other party justifies it. Whether that conduct was justified depends on individual circumstances and, if disputed, would be decided by the courts.

Written statement of reasons for dismissal

A departing employee, with the necessary qualifying period of employment, is also legally entitled to request a *written statement of reasons for dismissal* from his or her previous employer. It is important to note that an employee who has been dismissed has no right to receive such a written statement unless he or she requests one. The request can be made orally or in writing. The information contained in this written statement may prove valuable to an employee for the purposes of bringing a case of unfair dismissal, especially if it is necessary to contest the reasons quoted by the employer as part of its defence.

Exit interviews

The practice of conducting *exit interviews* is time-consuming but of immense value to the company. Apart from the obvious need to complete all the formal documentation, such as the P45, it is a vital opportunity to collect information on problem areas identified by the departing employee, such as poor salaries compared with competitors, lack of promotion, transport difficulties or inadequate supervision. Data on turnover, when compiled, can provide much needed information for manpower planning purposes, and can identify particular difficulties in relation to one group of employees.

Early retirement

Some organisations – particularly large ones – have permanent or temporary schemes which encourage early retirement in return for a financial reward. This type of scheme can be introduced on a temporary basis to ease an organisation's compulsory redundancy quota by rewarding voluntary selection for termination. It can also be available on a more permanent basis to reduce bottlenecks for promotion. What such schemes cannot guarantee is that the employees whom the company would find difficult to replace are not those who apply for the benefits of the scheme.

Redundancy

An employer can dismiss employees if the work done by those employees no longer exists. In a redundancy situation, the employee is entitled to receive a notice period relating to the redundancy, dependent on the length of service, or payment in lieu (as mentioned above), and also redundancy payments based on the employee's age, length of service and current salary.

Unfair dismissal

There are circumstances where employees who are dismissed without notice or who leave after a period of notice claim that they have been *unfairly dismissed*. They may also claim constructive dismissal (where an employee resigns because of the conduct of his or her employer) or that they have been refused permission to return to work after the birth of a baby. Since June 1985, the use of the unfair dismissal legislation has been limited to those with two years' service or more.

Before the introduction of the unfair dismissal legislation, in 1971, the only action available to an employee who had been dismissed summarily, or who had been given insufficient contractual notice, was an action in the civil courts for *wrongful dismissal* – a remedy, even though an inadequate one, which remains open to those with less than two years' service and which may prove more attractive to those with generous contract terms compared with the compensation available from the industrial tribunals. The drawback of the wrongful dismissal approach is that the only compensation payable is for loss of payment: there is no possibility of any damages or of reinstatement or re-engagement.

Since 1971, the unfair dismissal legislation has become a major element of statutory employee protection. As Anderman (1985, p. 1) explains, it has had a sizeable influence on the clarification of management practice and procedures, with voluntary disciplinary procedures abounding as a result of the law. The existence of a third party to whom contentious cases could be referred has improved labour relations, because there is no longer a tendency to strike in support of a dismissed employee. Also, the threat of unfair dismissal proceedings has often been sufficient to persuade a recalcitrant employer to deal fairly, at least in financial terms, with the employee.

Though the most recent statistics of industrial tribunal cases, for 1988–9, show a fall in the number of unfair dismissal cases taken to the tribunal and in the percentage of tribunal cases which dealt with unfair dismissal (down from 73 per cent in 1987–8 to 61 per cent in 1988–9), there were still 17 870 cases. Of those, 39 per cent (6935) were resolved by ACAS, 27 per cent (4879) were withdrawn for other reasons and just 32 per cent (5786) proceeded to the tribunal hearing. Of those which went to a tribunal hearing, 37.5 per cent (2166) were successful – a mere 12.1 per cent of all applications (DoE 1990). Of the 2166 successful cases, 58 resulted in reinstatement or re-engagement; in 797 cases the remedy was left to the agreement of the parties; and at 1272 hearings an award of compensation was made. It is pointed out that, while reinstatement and re-engagement are the first and second remedies considered by the tribunal if requested by an applicant claiming to have been unfairly dismissed, in only 3 per cent of the cases which were won by the applicant did the tribunal order the employer to re-engage or reinstate the employee. In many cases the applicant may have found another position, or the relations between employer and employee may have deteriorated to such an extent that 'it would be impracticable to expect them to resume a normal working relationship' (DoE 1990, p. 214).

Where there is no order for re-engagement or reinstatement, compensation for unfair dismissal consists of a basic award and a compensatory award. The basic award is calculated in a manner similar to that for redundancy payments, and is related to pay, length of service and age. The maximum number of years taken into consideration is 20, and the maximum weekly pay is £184 (from 1 April 1990). The maximum basic award payable is £5520. The compensatory award is a payment to compensate for loss of earnings and an estimate of future loss, including benefits such as pension rights. The maximum figure for this award is £8925. The average (median) award for unfair dismissal cases in 1988–9 was £1732. If an employer is ordered to reinstate or re-engage an applicant and refuses to comply, the tribunal cannot force this matter but can order the payment of an additional award of between 13 and 26 weeks' pay up to a maximum of £184 per week. Appeals on matters of law are referred to the Employment Appeal

Tribunal (EAT).

An ex-employee who considers that he or she has been unfairly treated in losing a position in a company must complete a form IT1 not more than three months after the 'effective date of termination' and return it to the Central Office of the Industrial Tribunals. The applicant must state, before the outcome of the case is discussed, whether he or she would prefer to return to work for the employer or to receive compensation. Copies of the completed application form are then forwarded to the employer, who must respond (on form IT3), and to a conciliation officer from ACAS. Conciliation will be attempted if either party requests it or if the conciliation officer thinks there is any reasonable chance of success. If this stage proves to be unsuccessful, a pre-hearing assessment may follow at the request of either party or on the initiative of the tribunal. This consists of a short hearing before a full tribunal. Of 517 pre-hearing assessments undertaken in 1988–9, a warning that the applicant might be liable for costs if he or she proceeded was issued in 244 cases. Only 42 continued with their claims to a full hearing, of which 37 lost their cases and 13 had costs awarded against them. As a result of the view that pre-hearing assessments have not proved effective in filtering out the cases without sufficient grounds, the Employment Act 1989 introduced a formal stage called a pre-hearing review (which will be conducted by only a tribunal chairman) and the possibility of requiring a £150 deposit from either party as a condition of proceeding further.

Tribunal procedure

A tribunal consists of three people: a chairman with legal knowledge and two lay members who may come from a wide cross-section of industry, commerce and public service but who usually have some practical experience of industrial relations in the workplace. It is usual for one to have a union background and the other to be from an employers' organisation.

It is not necessary for any party to an industrial tribunal to have any legal representation, though the parties are free to do so if they choose. Statistics (DoE 1990) show that applicants may be marginally more successful if they are represented, although this representation may be by their trade union, a friend, or a law centre as well as by a solicitor.

Stages of a dismissal case

A claim for unfair dismissal is considered in the following stages:

1 the qualifications for making a claim of unfair dismissal,
2 proof of dismissal,
3 reasons for dismissal.

1 The qualifications

(a) The applicant must be an 'employee'. Although an employer may consider the applicant to be self-employed and therefore excluded from the legislation, the tribunal has the right to examine and decide on the true nature of the relationship between the parties, as part of its deliberations.
(b) The applicant must not be in a category specifically excluded from the legislation – for example, share fishermen and members of the police or armed services.
(c) The application must have been presented within three months of the 'effective date of termination'.
(d) At the 'effective date of termination', the applicant must have worked for the employer for at least two years if he or she worked for 16 hours or more per week, or for five years if he or she worked more than 8 but less than 16 hours per week.
(e) The applicant must not have reached the normal retiring age, provided that this is the same for men and women, even if it is not 65.
(f) The applicant must not have a fixed-term contract in which he or she, in writing, waived his or her rights relating to dismissal.

2 Proof of dismissal

This is the second stage of a tribunal's deliberations and is considered before there is any discussion on the fairness or otherwise of a dismissal. It deals with the existence of proof that dismissal actually took place – for example, that the employer terminated the employee's contract with or without notice, that the employer terminated a fixed-term contract without renewal, or that the employee terminated his or her own contract because of the conduct of the employer (constructive dismissal). Examples of situations in which constructive dismissal can be considered to have taken place include the unilateral reduction by management of the employee's basic rates of pay, refusal to pay overtime for overtime hours as stated in a contract of employment, and major alterations in responsibilities.

3 Reasons for dismissal

Once an employee has successfully passed the previous two stages by proving that he or she is qualified to make a complaint and by showing that he or she has actually been 'dismissed', the tribunal must then consider whether the dismissal was fair or unfair in the circumstances. This stage is also dealt with in sections:

(i) The employer's reason for dismissal is identified and the tribunal considers whether it was a reason which justified dismissal (a decision on whether the dismissal was *potentially fair*). The onus of proof for this stage lies with the employer.

The dismissal must come into one of five categories, discussed below:

(a) lack of capability or qualifications,
(b) misconduct,
(c) redundancy,
(d) statutory bar,
(e) some other substantial reason.

The test of reasonableness in applying these categories is considered at the next stage, and detailed examination of each of these categories follows a discussion on the matter of reasonableness.

(ii) If the reason for dismissal is considered by the tribunal to be potentially fair, then the tribunal proceeds to the next stage. This stage tests the *reasonableness* of the employer's decision in relation to the reason identified in the earlier stage. It is determined in accordance with 'equity and the substantial merits of the case', and taking account of 'the size and administrative resources of the employer's undertaking' (a decision whether the dismissal is *actu-*

ally fair in the circumstances). The onus of proof for this stage is placed neutrally,

> in the sense that the tribunal must look at the evidence and weigh and decide without any guidelines as to what it should do if the evidence is evenly balanced. Of course this does not remove a burden on the employer to come forward with evidence for any of his assertions, and in particular that he acted reasonably. (Anderman 1985, p. 107)

The tribunal will examine whether the employer acted reasonably or unreasonably in treating the reason for the dismissal as a sufficient reason for dismissing the employee.

In its deliberations, the tribunal will take into account any case law which is relevant and also the ACAS *Code of Practice on Disciplinary Practice and Procedures in Employment* (ACAS 1977). According to the Code, the basic elements of a disciplinary procedure are that the employer should conduct an investigation to establish the facts, conduct a hearing to allow the employee to put his or her case, and make a decision on the outcome dependent on all the circumstances known at that time to the employer.

It is suggested by the ACAS Code that the disciplinary procedures should

(a) be in writing;
(b) specify to whom they apply;
(c) provide for matters to be dealt with quickly;
(d) indicate the disciplinary actions which may be taken;
(e) specify the levels of management which have the authority to take the various forms of disciplinary action, ensuring that immediate superiors do not normally have the power to dismiss without reference to senior management;
(f) provide for individuals to be informed of complaints against them and to be given an opportunity to state their case before a decision is reached;
(g) give individuals the right to be accompanied by a trade union representative or by a fellow employee of their choice;
(h) ensure that, except for gross misconduct, no employees are dismissed for a first breach of discipline;
(i) ensure that disciplinary action is not taken until the case has been carefully investigated;

(j) ensure that individuals are given an explanation for any penalty imposed;

(k) provide a right of appeal and specify the procedure to be followed.

A decision in the Employment Appeal Tribunal in 1979 in the case of *British Labour Pump Ltd* v. *Byrne* added great confusion to the argument about the reasonableness of the employer's decision. In that case, it was argued that if an employer adopts an unfair procedure in dismissing an employee, but it is shown on the balance of probabilities that the result would have been the same if the employer had adopted a correct procedure according to the Code – that is, the employee would still have been dismissed – then the dismissal is considered to be fair. This was known as the 'no difference' rule. This precedent applied until the Polkey decision (*Polkey* v. *A. E. Dayton Services Ltd*) in the House of Lords in 1987.

The Polkey decision referred to a case where five of the six drivers in a company were to be made redundant. The employer did not consult them, but called in five of the drivers and dismissed them one by one. The tribunal which considered the case of one of the drivers, Mr Polkey, held that the employer had breached the correct procedure but that the result would have been the same if the procedure had been followed. The House of Lords unanimously condemned this approach, which was referred to as 'the British Labour Pump principle'. It stated that the tribunal does not have the right to argue that if the employer had acted differently he would still have dismissed the employee. As the Lord Chancellor said during this case:

> It is what the employer did that is to be judged, not what he might have done. ([1987] IRLR 503)

The effects of this judgment are twofold. Firstly, the employer who does not operate a fair system of discipline can no longer argue that following a correct procedure would have produced the same result and would therefore have made 'no difference' to the outcome. That question is considered to be irrelevant in applying the test of reasonableness, though it is still a relevant factor in the matter of the compensation awarded. Secondly, any procedural irregularity will be considered as a matter of importance by a tribunal considering an unfair dismissal case.

Lord Bridge, in the Polkey case, itemised the procedural steps needed in the majority of cases, 'if an employer is to be considered to have acted reasonably in dismissing:

> in a case of incapacity, giving an employee fair warning and a chance to improve

> in a case of misconduct, investigating fully and fairly and hearing what the employee wants to say in explanation or mitigation

> in a case of redundancy, warning and consulting affected employees, adopting a fair basis for selection and taking reasonable steps to redeploy affected employees' (IDS 1989)

Although the provisions of the ACAS Code of Practice are not legally binding, the Code is admissible as evidence before a tribunal.

The exception to this rule applies in the matter of 'utterly useless' cases – where, it was argued by the House of Lords in the same judgment, a reasonable employer could have concluded that to have followed a proper procedure would have been 'utterly useless'. This is a matter for a tribunal to consider in relation to all the circumstances known to the employer at the time of the dismissal. In the Polkey case, the employer argued that his dismissal came within this category, but a ruling on this was never given, as the employer withdrew.

Although the 'no difference' rule can be used only in exceptional circumstances to decide the fairness or otherwise of a case, the rule can still be applied in the matter of *compensation*.

> Where a tribunal have found a dismissal unfair on 'procedural' grounds they must reflect in their award the percentage chance – estimated on the balance of probabilities – that dismissal would have ensued even if a fair procedure had been followed. (IDS 1989)

The consequent reduction in compensation would be additional to any reduction brought about by the contribution of the employee to the dismissal situation.

The possible reasons for dismissal are now considered in relation to the reasonable conduct required by the employer.

(a) Lack of capability and qualifications

It may be appropriate to dismiss an employee if he or she is incompetent, although normally it is expected that a suitable warning or warnings and an opportunity to improve would be given, in accordance with the company disciplinary procedure. It is expected that adequate training will have been given and that there is proof of the employee's incompetence to show to the tribunal. If a position were offered to an employee on the understanding that he or she study to reach a particular qualification but that employee subsequently failed to achieve the qualification after a reasonable number of opportunities, it might be appropriate to dismiss that employee.

Dismissal of an employee on the grounds of ill-health can be upsetting to all parties but can be appropriate as far as the law is concerned if handled in a correct and sympathetic manner. It is expected that a company procedure for dealing with such matters will be followed, and this will include consultation with the employee as to the length of the absence and his or her wishes in relation to returning to work. If the employee may be able to undertake another, less strenuous, job, then the company must make every effort to find one, though it may not be successful. Medical evidence will be sought, either from the employee's doctor or from a medical examination provided by the company's nominated medical representative. The position of the employee within the company is also an important consideration – if that person's role is crucial to the operation of the company, then it may be impossible to hold the position open for an extensive period.

(b) Misconduct

In cases of misconduct – such as disobedience, insubordination, criminal action or absence – the test laid down in *British Home Stores* v. *Burchell* ([1978] IRLR 379) is considered to be the approach that tribunals should take in such cases. It has three points:

1 The employer must show that there was a genuine belief that the employee was guilty of the misconduct in question.
2 The employer must have reasonable grounds for maintaining that belief.
3 The employer must have carried out such an investigation into the case as was reasonable in the circumstances.

An employer is expected to follow a fair disciplinary procedure, including gathering all evidence that is available at the time and carrying out the investigation as soon as possible after the incident, after allowing for the collecting of all relevant information.

Not all cases of misconduct will lead to dismissal, as the case must be considered in its context. For example, a person whose conduct has previously been good should not be dismissed for a minor insubordination or an initial period of absenteeism. A well-thought-out disciplinary procedure should include other lesser punishments, such as warnings or suspension, although suspension without pay should be used only if the contract of employment allows for this.

In cases of gross misconduct, which is normally where the conduct of the employee justifies summary dismissal by the employer, the offence may be the first one committed by that employee. Though the employee may be speedily removed from a position in the company because of the gravity of the accusation, the proper disciplinary and appeal procedure should still be carried out.

> This is because in cases of dismissal for misconduct the key question for tribunals is whether the employer acted reasonably in treating the employee's conduct as a reason for dismissal. Tribunals are not concerned in this context with whether the dismissal was with or without notice – they are only concerned with whether the dismissal was a reasonable response to the employee's conduct. (IDS 1990)

Though disciplinary rules will normally provide examples of misconduct for which the penalty will be summary dismissal, the list cannot be exhaustive nor can all circumstances be dealt with. However, it is well known, for example, that carrying matches down a coalmine is a case of gross misconduct in that working environment.

Conviction for an offence committed outside the working situation can result in dismissal only if the employee cannot continue to work, or if the nature of the offence is such that the employee cannot continue in his or her position.

(c) Redundancy

A person who is made redundant according to a correct procedure will have been fairly dismissed. The argument of unfair dismissal in the matter of redundancy relates to such matters as the existence or otherwise of a true situation of redundancy, fair selection criteria and application of those criteria, consultation with trade unions and allowing time off to look for alternative work.

(d) Statutory bar

Dismissal in this category arises from situations such as a person whose work involves driving losing his or her licence and therefore being unable to drive. The test of reasonableness would apply to the question of whether the person could continue to fulfil his or her duties without the use of a car, whether alternate work was considered and if warnings were given if this was appropriate.

(e) Some other substantial reason

This category covers all the remaining substantial reasons which do not fall into any of the above categories. It deals, for example, with the dismissal of a temporary replacement for an employee who is on leave on medical or maternity grounds – this dismissal would be considered to be fair if, at the start of the employment, the replacement had been informed in writing of its temporary nature. It also includes cases where the employer considers that there could be a breach of confidentiality of commercial information – when, for example, the partner of an employee starts employment in a rival firm, or if he or she sets up a business in competition. This category also includes the dismissal of people whose personal characteristics are thought to be 'socially unacceptable'.

Study themes

1 Read chapter 3 of Anderman (1985) and then say how you understand the following terms:

   (a) constructive dismissal,
   (b) wrongful dismissal,
   (c) waiver clause under a fixed-term contract.

2 Hilary, who is 29, has been employed by XYZ Ltd for six years as a stock-checker. Due to difficult trading circumstances, the management has decided to reduce the staffing in her section as it believes the staffing level to be too high. Hilary is told she has been selected for redundancy as everyone else in the section has longer service. She is offered two weeks' pay as compensation.

   (a) Are the reasons for her redundancy fair?
   (b) Is the financial compensation correct?

3 Consider the advantages and disadvantages to your organisation of conducting exit interviews for all leavers.

References

ACAS, 1977. *Code of Practice on Disciplinary Practice and Procedures in Employment*, Advisory, Conciliation and Arbitration Service, London.

ACAS, 1987. *Discipline at Work*, Advisory, Conciliation and Arbitration Service, London.

Anderman, S., 1985. *The Law of Unfair Dismissal*, 2nd edn, Butterworth, London.

Banerji, N., Smart, D., and Stevens, M., 1990. Unfair dismissal cases in 1985–86 – impact on parties, *Employment Gazette*, November.

Bowers, J., 1990. *Bowers on Employment Law*, Blackstone, London.

Dickens, L., Jones, M., Weekes, B., and Hart, M., 1985. *Dismissed*, Blackwell, Oxford.

DoE, 1990. Industrial tribunal statistics, *Employment Gazette*, Department of Employment, April, pp. 213–18.

IDS, 1989. *Unfair dismissal since Polkey*, IDS Brief 406, October, Incomes Data Services, London.

IDS, 1990. *Disciplinary proceedings and appeals,* IDS Brief 418, April, Incomes Data Services, London.

Rideout, R., 1989. *Rideout's Principles of Labour Law*, 5th edn, Sweet & Maxwell, London.

D

Pay and Employment Conditions

Chapter 21

Payment

There are many different terms used to define payment, which rewards the employee for making available to the employer 'time, skill, experience, brainpower and effort which employees bring forward in differing proportions' (Smith 1983, p. 9). These terms include 'compensation', 'reward', 'income' and 'remuneration', and the payment is expressed in the form of wages, salaries or pay. While the method of payment for manual workers was previously known solely as 'wages' – a method involving cash payments on a weekly basis – 'salaries' were paid to those of white-collar or management status and often consisted of direct payments into banks or building societies on a monthly basis. It was also considered normal for conditions of employment to differ between those on wages and those to whom salaries were paid. Moves towards the harmonisation of terms and conditions of employment between manual and staff employees, together with the removal of the legislative right to payment in cash and the problems of security for doing so, have helped to blur the distinctions which delineated payment methods according to terminology.

The system of payment for employees can include direct elements – dependent on performance or time spent – and indirect elements – that is, fringe benefits. The latter are increasing in popularity, though difficult to quantify in terms of the financial benefit derived from them. The direct elements of pay can be fixed or variable and may include basic pay, which does not vary; incentive payments, which are related to the performance of the individual or team; overtime payments, where work over the standard hours is paid at premium rates in accordance with contract terms; and additional payments for such things as increased responsibility or working in difficult conditions or unsocial hours. Allowances may also be paid, for such things as travelling to and from work, when undergoing training, for meals and lodgings when working away from home base and for supplying one's own tools and overalls.

Thomason (1988, pp. 359–60) classifies the 'reward package' into three categories:

> direct financial benefit . . . focuses on two elements of re-muneration which are directly related to performance: a) the basic rate . . . and b) any additional bonus which is paid for individual or group performance above this standard . . .
>
> indirect financial benefit . . . consists of those regular or intermittent payments (not related directly to performance) made for a variety of contributions (such as suggestions for improvement of production) or employee loyalty or commit-ment (such as high base rates, . . . pensions schemes . . . company cars or educational support plans).
>
> non-financial benefit . . . schemes which will increase the morale of employees . . . such experiments as job enlarge-ment, job enrichment, quality circles, . . . and various partici-pation arrangements.

This definition identifies a notion of reward far wider than the normal direct and indirect payments, and acknowledges the moti-vational effects of other types of 'reward'.

According to the New Earnings Survey 1990 (DoE 1990), the premium elements – that is, overtime, shift pay and bonus pay-ments – accounted for 18 per cent of the gross average weekly earnings of all employees in the manufacturing sector and 9 per cent of those in the service sector. The difference in the compos-ition of pay packages was also very marked between males and females. While the gross average weekly earnings of all males in manual occupations included a premium element of 26 per cent, the equivalent figure for females in manual occupations was 15 per cent. However, for non-manual workers, the premium elements were 8 per cent for males and 5 per cent for females.

Payment systems in certain industries, such as engineering, used to be built up from three levels of negotiation: industry, company and plant negotiations. While the minimum rates were decided nationally, complicated systems of bonus and additional payments were negotiated at the further two levels. With the withdrawal of major companies from the national negotiations, there has been more scope for companywide agreements.

There is often a variety of payment systems within one employing organisation, each system being appropriate to a particular group of employees. It would be comforting to assume that these systems have all come into being as part of a conscious management strategy, but this is often not the case. In many circumstances, the proliferation of payment systems has arisen in order to deal in an ad-hoc manner with problems such as labour relations or scarcity of particular skills. Once established, systems are hard to eliminate.

In order to devise a strategy on pay, an employing organisation has to be aware of its objectives in relation to the use of pay as a control mechanism, the constraints which apply to its choices, the financial objectives of its employees and their representatives, and the relationship of the payment system or systems to the total personnel policy of the organisation.

Any employer hopes and plans that its payment system will be attractive to employees in both the short and the long term, that it will assist the recruitment of the required talent and the retention of employees, and that it will reward those who perform their duties well. The employer aims to build an internal pay structure which differentiates rewards within the organisation according to value to the organisation, while also taking account of external pay pressures. This structure should allow for the inclusion of new positions in the organisation and reward the acquisition of additional qualifications and skills in operating new technology. It should recognise the importance to employees of pay as a motivating force in relation to the performance of their responsibilities.

The payment system should also contain stages through which the employees can proceed and be rewarded for such elements as long service or additional responsibility or as a result of promotion. While achieving this necessary flexibility, the organisation will wish to limit the complexity of its scheme, in order to reduce the opportunities for abusing the system and for confusing its participants. An ineffective system will not control labour costs – one of the major costs of production – and problems with payment systems are the cause of many disputes, especially in the area of labour relations.

Bowey and Thorpe (1986) laid down some ground rules for the implementation of a successful payment system:

- *Early consultation*   There is no point introducing a payment system without consulting the appropriate employee representatives and giving an opportunity to gather reactions and opinions on the proposals.
- *Stated objectives*   All parties should be aware of the objectives against which the system will be measured, and there should be no 'hidden agenda' (Duncan 1989, p. 221).
- *Effective communication*   Effective communication systems, together with adequate training of all managers and foremen and forewarning of problem areas and how to deal with them, will help to ensure smooth installation of the payment system. A manual should be issued to all employees.
- *A monitoring procedure*   Any payment system must be monitored to see if discrepancies or anomalies arise and to check that the system is operating in accordance with its objectives.
- *Sufficient lead-in time*   It takes a considerable time to bring a payment system up to an acceptable standard, and it is tempting to scrap a system without taking sufficient time to sort out the initial problems.

In perceiving whether payment levels are acceptable, employees may take into account some or all of the following important factors. These are described by Salamon (1987, p. 457).

- That they will receive a living wage – to maintain their standard of living in relation to the rate of inflation. This will be of particular importance in times of rising prices. The percentage rise in pay is compared to the percentage increase in the Retail Prices Index.
- That those who do similar work will receive the same pay (the rate for the job). This view, which is the basis of trade union beliefs in promoting the group interest, is often extended beyond the organisation and can be related to the status of the work concerned within society.
- That their rates of pay are comparable with those that can be commanded in the marketplace (the going rate). Employees will be aware of the rates of pay which they could obtain from other employers, even if they are not actually likely to move. The trade union representative will argue about the relative position of the organisation in relation to others in that market-

place. This is particularly so for skills that are in short supply.
- That additional or sustained effort will produce extra reward. Systems which, at least in part, reward additional or sustained effort are becoming increasingly popular among UK companies, and the opportunity to earn pay higher than the basic is considered to be a source of motivation for employees to continue to exert such effort.
- That the acceptance of responsibility will be rewarded. It is generally accepted that all employees of an organisation will not receive the same payment, and that the burden of responsibility and leadership will be rewarded with a differential payment.
- That other aspects of the position – such as the status, the satisfaction that is engendered or the conditions of employment – make the level of pay less important. One must be aware of situations where the employee is prepared to work for poor levels of pay or none at all, because of some other aspect of the position that is appealing.

The pressure which these factors will exert can depend on the strength of the trade union organisation of the employees, the level at which bargaining takes place, the shortages of the necessary skills and general economic conditions. The employer, in responding to arguments, may make reference to various factors such as the profitability of the company, the state of order books or the state of its financial resources – as appropriate to its case.

Payment systems, and even elements of them, can be divided into two main classifications:

1 *Systems based on time* Time-based systems are the simplest systems to operate, since the amount payable does not vary between payment periods. The merits of these payment systems are, according to Duncan (1989), that they are simple and cheap to operate and make forecasting labour costs simple, with few anomalies and labour disputes resulting. Yet the popularity of such schemes is reducing, even among non-manual employees. The problem lies in there being no element of reward for effort included in these systems.
2 *Systems based on performance* There are various forms of these systems, which are discussed in detail in chapter 25. These

include merit-related pay; performance-related pay; individual, group and plant-wide bonus systems; and profit-sharing schemes. For purposes of control of labour costs, the amount of weekly income which is derived from performance-related elements should be limited.

In order to be aware of how the organisation's payment values relate to those of other similar organisations, it is important to investigate the payment ranges available. Depending on the size of the organisation's workforce and its geographical spread, this information would be useful on a national or on an area basis, or where there is a particular shortage of labour, in relation to one skill specialisation. It is necessary to remember not to focus only on the payments made but to consider the value of the whole package, including benefits. There is also the problem of comparing similar positions, and identification by job titles is not always accurate enough. It may be necessary to write a concise form of the job description, in order to ensure that like is being compared with like.

Sources of comparative data include surveys which are published nationally, though these usually give information only on general trends and for limited professional occupations; information published in specialist journals, such as by Incomes Data Services; surveys carried out by special groups, such as Hay/MSL users (see chapter 22) or the local area of a trade association; or even special surveys commissioned by or carried out by one's own organisation. The use of regular sources of information, based on data collected in the same way, will add to the value of that information.

Having received all the necessary comparative data, the organisation will then have to decide at what point in the range of pay it wishes to place itself, and that decision will be related to policy and costs.

Study themes

1 In which situations is it advisable to operate a payment system based on time and when is it feasible to use a performance-

related system? Can elements of both be combined into one payment system? If so, how?

2 What information would you request from other companies if you were conducting your own salary survey concerning engineers?

3 A leading insurance company is quoted in *Personnel Management*, April 1990, as saying that its remuneration package is too 'cluttered', and that it is scrapping most fringe benefits. How important are fringe benefits as a method of remuneration in your organisation?

References

Armstrong, M., and Murlis, H., 1980. *A Handbook of Salary Administration*, Kogan Page, London.

Bowey, A. M., and Thorpe, R., 1986. *Payment Systems and Productivity*, Macmillan, London.

Duncan, C., 1989. Pay and Payment Systems, in Towers, B., (ed.), 1989. *Handbook of Industrial Relations Practice*, Kogan Page, London.

DoE, 1990. The New Earnings Survey 1990, *Employment Gazette*, November.

Husband, T. M., 1976. *Work Analysis and Pay Structure*, McGraw-Hill, Maidenhead.

Salamon, M., 1987. *Industrial Relations, Theory and Practice*, Prentice-Hall, Hemel Hempstead.

Smith, I., 1983. *The Management of Remuneration: Paying for Effectiveness*, IPM/Gower, Aldershot.

Thomason, G., 1988. *A Textbook of Human Resource Management*, Institute of Personnel Management, London.

Chapter 22

Payment Systems and Grading

One of the problems of payment systems is to establish a system of differentials and relativities which is seen by all employees to be fair, and which allows for the addition of new positions and reward for increased responsibility, while remaining competitive with other organisations.

Job evaluation

Job evaluation is a means of establishing the internal relativities of the positions in an organisation. Job evaluation does not usually consider pay rates, but establishes the relative values of positions and the increments between them, from which negotiation on basic pay levels associated with those values follows. Any system of job evaluation considers the positions in the organisation and what the responsibilities of those positions are. Job evaluation should not be concerned with the performance of the person holding that position.

Because some systems of job evaluation can be complex and concerned with figures and tables, it is often thought to be a precise technique with only one possible solution. In fact, all assessments are carried out by panels of evaluators, usually chosen by the management and trade unions.

> It is not possible to predict the outcome of a study, unless it is rigged, nor is it possible to prove that the results are correct. But the methodology of job evaluation is logical and it is based on a systematic analysis of the facts. (Armstrong and Murlis 1980, p. 29)

All systems of job evaluation depend on a detailed knowledge of the positions to be evaluated, either from the personal experience of the evaluators or by comprehensive job descriptions which have been drawn up based on observation of the job and question-naires or interviews with the job-holder and others.

There are two main classifications of job evaluation schemes: non-analytical and analytical.

Non-analytical schemes

These include job ranking (paired comparisons) and job classification.

Job ranking is a simple method of job evaluation. It either involves consideration of the whole position in relation to the others in the organisation or concentrates on one or a small number of elements of the position. Benchmark positions are established, and the other positions are ranked with those in mind and then divided into grades. The system of paired comparisons was developed in order to overcome the problems of comparing a large number of positions. Each position is compared with every other and given a points score, which is totalled to produce a ranking list.

Job classification also considers the whole job, but first establishes a defined grading structure before comparing the job description of the position to be evaluated with the grade definitions.

The non-analytical schemes are easy to administer and therefore cheap, but are really useful only in small organisations where the details of the positions are well known to the evaluators. These systems cannot cope with complicated jobs, and do not show the relative differences between grades and how the boundaries are decided.

Analytical schemes

These include points rating and factor comparison methods. As factor comparison is rarely used in the UK, it will not be considered further in this chapter.

Points rating schemes are based on a consideration of the factors which are common to all positions in the organisation, and these are listed and grouped, and given a range of points (called degrees) which are graded according to the importance of that factor to the position being evaluated. These factors are also weighted – that is, the maximum number of points which can be allocated to each factor is dependent on the organisation's view of that factor's relative importance. The job description is then considered relative to these factors, and the extent to which they are important is decided and degrees awarded. Thus a points rating for a position is built up and can then be compared with other points ratings.

There are a number of subjective elements of such a scheme. First the organisation has to select the appropriate factors, which must be carefully defined. It is not necessary to have a large number of factors, but they must represent all aspects of the position. Then weighting of the factors must be applied – and this can be based on another scheme, or on existing rankings, or on subjective views of their importance. Then levels or degrees must be given to each factor, and will depend on the amount of detail required.

Many organisations deal with these problems by buying in a ready-made points rating system, such as the Hay/MSL system, or by employing consultants to devise a unique scheme. A ready-made system such as Hay/MSL has the advantage that it gives its client companies comparable market rates based on their points rating system, so that it shows relative positions of companies as well as showing the overall movement in rates.

In general, job evaluation is a useful system for eliminating discrepancies in payment systems and establishing a method which is recognised by all to be based on well-informed judgements. It gives the organisation valuable information by creating detailed job descriptions, and it also provides for a system which can accommodate new posts and additional responsibilities. There are, however, certain circumstances where job evaluation would not be appropriate – for example, where there are few positions, where there are few resources available, when the job evaluation is used as an alternative to bargaining with trade unions, or where the results of the job evaluation exercise will not result in a new pay structure. It must also be borne in mind that some positions may not seem on analysis to be important or strategic to the organisation even though a great deal may depend on the abilities of the job-holder.

One interesting aspect of the application of job evaluation is related to the equal pay legislation and the 'equal value' amendments to it. Before the Equal Value (Amendment) Regulations 1983 came into force, in January 1984, a woman could claim equal pay only in two circumstances:

(a) when her pay was less than that of her comparator for 'like' work;
(b) when her pay was less than that of her comparator for work which was rated as equivalent under a job evaluation scheme.

This did not mean that the job evaluation scheme could be overtly discriminatory – 'setting different rates for men and women on the same demand' (Rubenstein 1984, p. 75) – but the law did not require the elimination from the scheme of factors which would discriminate on the grounds of sex. The introduction of the third category – that is, equal pay for work of equal value, in terms of the demands made by the woman's job and that of her comparator – has made a huge difference.

The 1983 Regulations allow the woman to challenge a firm's existing job evaluation scheme as discriminatory, and define the process of 'job evaluation' as a study evaluating the demands made on an employee under various headings (such as effort, skill and decision). The implications for systems of job evaluation seem to be immense – it would seem that only analytical schemes which evaluate jobs under various demand headings will fulfil the legal requirements, and the weightings applied to factors may also be considered to be sex-biased.

Payment levels and grades

The next stage, which follows and is separate from the job evaluation exercise, is to assign financial amounts to the values given to the positions in the organisation, while establishing a rational and logical system. The present payment levels can be plotted on a graph, together with the values established by the job evaluation system. This will produce a scattergram, through which a line of best fit can be drawn. It is important to compare the pay that will result from this system with the rates currently paid by other competitive employers.

Employees whose current pay falls below the line of best fit should have their pay increased substantially – though this may not be possible in a single step. Those whose pay is above the line of best fit will have their jobs 'red-circled' – it may not be appropriate to freeze these people's pay, but it is possible to limit that pay until the general rise in pay reaches this level, or to give increases to the present job-holder but bring the position into the system when that job-holder leaves.

It is also essential to develop a grading structure, with the midpoints of the grades along the line of best fit. The number of grades will depend on the requirements of the organisation, though too few grades will not allow sufficient opportunity for advancement and too many grades will add to the complications of the system. There should be ranges of pay (ladders) for each grade, with equal steps on either side of the midpoint, and a limited number of overlapping steps between grades.

Within any pay system, there must be a method of progression which rewards the employee for performance and/or for length of service. This can be through an incremental system, which rewards the employee with pre-determined increases at regular time intervals, or through a performance-related system, which is dependent entirely on performance (Armstrong and Murlis 1980, p. 101). In practice, in many organisations the progression of pay when looked at compared with age is a convex curve which rewards the employees who perform well in the early part of their careers (Husband 1976, p. 202).

Once established, after proper consultation with and explanation to all involved, all payment systems must be maintained and monitored, so that problems can quickly be identified and eliminated. An appeals procedure will help to channel any dissent and will provide a good method of dealing with queries and anomalies.

Study themes

1 What is meant by the following terms:

    (a) pay progression,
    (b) incremental schemes,
    (c) red circling,

(d) overlap,
(e) analytical job evaluation schemes?

2 Read EOC (1982) and chapter 6 of Rubenstein (1984). What effects have the 1983 changes to the equal pay legislation had on job evaluation schemes, and what advice would you give a personnel department concerning job evaluation as a result of this legislation?

3 What are the advantages and disadvantages of having

(a) overlapping bands in a pay structure,
(b) narrow-banded and broad-banded grades in a pay structure?

References

ACAS, 1984. *Job Evaluation*, Advisory, Conciliation and Arbitration Service, London.

Armstrong, M., and Murlis, H., 1980. *A Handbook of Salary Administration*, Kogan Page, London.

Armstrong, M., and Murlis, H., 1988. *Reward Management*, IPM/Kogan Page, London.

EOC, 1982. *Job Evaluation Schemes Free of Sex Bias*, Equal Opportunities Commission, Manchester.

Husband, T. M., 1976. *Work Analysis and Pay Structure*, McGraw Hill, Maidenhead.

IDS, 1985. *Blue Collar Job Evaluation*, IDS Study 348, Incomes Data Services, London.

Rubenstein, M., 1984. *Equal Pay for Work of Equal Value*, Macmillan, London.

Smith, I., 1983. *The Management of Remuneration: Paying for Effectiveness*, IPM/Gower, Aldershot.

Chapter 23

Merit and Incentive Features

Incentives and performance-related pay are part of a complex arrangement defining the working relationship between employer and employee, demonstrating not just what the management is trying to achieve but also what the managers believe about the relationship. Incentive schemes frequently represent a working relationship in which manager and worker are far apart, with considerable mutual mistrust and little common interest. The working assumption is that the person doing the work has to be goaded into action.

In contrast performance-related pay arrangements typically embody the view that those who may receive the payments are loyal, keen and hard-working. The possibility of the scheme being manipulated to achieve levels of payment which are not justified is never mentioned, and the working assumption is that the person doing the work is *rewarded*, One approach assumes the worker *will not*; the other assumes that the worker *will*. Incentive schemes are most common among people at the bottom of the organisational hierarchy; performance-related schemes are most common at the top.

In 1988, over a third of male manual employees and over 16 per cent of non-manual males received incentive payments, and the proportion of earnings that were incentives was usually between 15 and 25 per cent. Table 23.1 shows the decline in use of incentive schemes over recent years.

Do incentive schemes work?

The decline in the use of incentive payments suggests that they don't work for the people involved: the slow rate of their decline suggests that they work.

Table 23.1

*Percentage of Workers Receiving Incentive Payments
(DoE, 1984, 1986, 1988)*

	1984 %	1986 %	1988 %
Male manual workers	46.5	42.8	39.0
Male non-manual workers	19.1	16.7	16.3
Female manual workers	35.3	32.3	29.8
Female non-manual workers	13.4	11.4	12.0

we are now able to understand the apparently conflicting prescriptions of people like R. M. Currie who advocated incentive-bonus schemes of various kinds, and Wilfred Brown who recommended that piecework be abandoned. They had each been observing situations in which the particular system they were proposing had been successful, but were not aware that there was something peculiar about those circumstances which contributed to the success of the scheme. (Lupton and Bowey 1975, p. 79)

The first uncertainty is about the *motivational effect*. Do incentives stimulate a higher level of satisfactory output than pay arrangements lacking that feature? There are commonsense reasons to say that they do, as most people welcome extra cash. But earning incentive payments also involves personal costs such as fatigue, the possibility of ill-health and the social opprobrium of your fellow workers, who may begrudge you your success, especially if it is alongside their relative failure. If there is a motivational effect, it will stimulate only the performance of the 'winners', and will demotivate the losers.

An attraction is that incentives assist managers to *control* operations. Individual output has to be measured for incentive payments to be made, and these measurements provide control information for the manager – either to see who is working hard and who is idling, or in order to build up data on how best to distribute tasks among a group of people so that they can all work optimally. This type of information can also demonstrate where there are weaknesses in departmental organisation, and provide some basis for controlling production costs. The history of industrial relations is, however, full of examples of how employees, individually or collectively, set out to beat the system. A control system implies rules, and most of us accept the validity of rules at the same time as we test their flexibility. Especially if the incentive scheme has been devised by management with limited employee involvement in its design, the rules will stimulate a competitive claim for control from employees seeking to optimise their benefits from the scheme rather than the management benefits.

Do incentive payments satisfy the *needs that individual employees bring to their work*? The answer seems to be that they satisfy some, but not the most significant:

> pay can be instrumental for the satisfaction of most needs but it is most likely to be seen as instrumental for satisfying esteem and physiological needs, secondarily to be seen as influential for satisfying autonomy or security needs and least likely for satisfying social or self-actual needs. (Lawler 1971, p. 121)

There are a number of difficulties with incentive schemes, not least of which is that one party to the bargain may be satisfied only at the expense of the other, but more specific problems include the need for *operational efficiency* in a steady state, with materials, orders, equipment and storage space all readily available exactly when they are needed. Furthermore the customer must wait upon the convenience of the production system. These conditions rarely exist: raw materials run out, job cards are not available, tools are faulty or the stores are full. As soon as this sort of thing happens, the incentive-paid worker has an incentive to fiddle the scheme for protection against the operational uncertainties.

The worker will most sedulously resist that *fluctuation in earnings* which is found in all but the most unusual circumstances. Employees will try to stabilise earnings, either by storing output in the good times to prevent the worst effects of the bad or by social control of high-performing individuals to equalise the benefits of the scheme as far as possible. Any one of these tactics reduces the potential management advantages quite considerably, but has relatively little disadvantage to any employee.

Other problems are maintaining *good-quality workmanship* while stimulating speed of operation and ensuring a reasonable *quality of working life* for those doing the work. Incentive schemes work best when work is deskilled: made routine, repetitive and mechanical.

Types of incentive scheme

Most incentive schemes operate through payment by results in one of several ways.

Individual time-saving

It is rare for incentives to be paid per piece produced or task completed, as this provides no security against external influences which depress output. Instead, the incentive is paid for time saved in performing a specified operation. A standard time is derived for a work sequence and the employee receives an additional payment for the time saved in completing a number of such operations. If it is not possible to work, due to shortage of materials or some other reason, the time involved is not included when the sums are done at the end of the day.

Standard times are derived by the twin techniques of method study and work measurement, which are the skills of the work study engineer. By study of the operation, the work study engineer decides what is the most efficient way to carry it out and then times an operator actually doing the job over a period, so as to measure the 'standard time'.

$$\text{Basic standard time} = \frac{\text{observed time} \times \text{observed rating}}{\text{standard rate}}$$

Standard rate (100) is deemed to be the rate at which someone could perform the task with incentive, while normal rate (75) is the rate at which the same person could be expected to perform the same task without incentive. Therefore an observed time of 15 seconds and an observed rating of 70 would produce a basic standard time of 10.5 seconds. It is not regarded as reasonable for someone to maintain basic standard time throughout the day, so a rest allowance of 15 per cent is added. This would produce a standard time, in our example, of 12.07 seconds.

This method can suit a situation where people are employed on

short-cycle manual operations with the volume of output potentially varying between individuals depending on their skill or application.

Group incentives

The same principles can be applied to group rather than individual
output. In many situations it is pointless to operate a scheme
which encourages individuals who are working in harmony to
compete in increasing their individual output. Where jobs are
interdependent, group incentives can be appropriate, although
the pressure on the working relationship may aggravate any interpersonal animosity that exists.

Commission

The payment of commission on sales is a widespread practice that
comes close to performance-related pay in its method. Most of the
drawbacks associated with incentive schemes also apply to commission arrangements, except that they are linked to business won
rather than to output achieved.

Tips

Tipping is generally criticised as being undesirable for those giving
tips, on the grounds that it is an unjustified additional charge for
a service they have paid for already. It is also criticised as being
undesirable for those receiving tips, as it requires them to be
deferential and obsequious. It is also often described as an
employer device to avoid the need to pay realistic wages. This
practice persists only to a limited extent.

Performance-related pay

Incentive schemes are collective and impersonal. The idea of
performance pay is usually to make it individual and personal, so
that some do better than others – or some do worse than others.
Therein lies the problem. If the performance pay arrangement is
to be effective, it must have an apparent impact on individual

performance; but selective individual reward can be divisive and lead to overall ineffectiveness unless everyone perceives the rules to be fair. Overall performance-related pay has its greatest impact when there is scope for expansion of both business and earnings:

> Individualised pay seems tailor-made for a period of competitive expansion . . . By all accounts this has had a considerable initial effect on company performance. But at the same time it produced a tremendous inflationary spiral. The systems introduced have generally been highly geared, with a high pay threshold as a carrot to attract employees and secure acceptance of the new arrangements. Awards for below standard performance have often been higher than the general run of increases in other industries. (IDS 1988, p. 5)

When schemes are individualised, there is raised expectation all round and it is difficult to limit pay rises only to high-performers. If a business is struggling, it cannot afford performance pay, and performance pay is always inflationary.

Twenty years ago, inflation was sometimes attributed to 'consolidation', as the proportion of pay that was basic as opposed to payment by results was progressively increased. Similar issues can arise with performance pay to some senior managers. There have been several instances of company chairmen having a large proportion of their income linked to company performance, and the other directors deciding to reward the chairman with a special payment as compensation for the fact that business results have been disappointing.

Although performance-related pay (PRP) has had a mixed press, it remains an objective in most organisations. The current thinking is in two directions. One is to develop a broader idea of performance *management* rather than solely performance *pay*, and the other is to develop PRP related to teams instead of individuals.

Performance management incorporates performance objectives, training and development plans, and monitoring as well as a pay linkage. A typical sequence is like this.

1 Use job evaluation to establish a pay grade for the job.
2 Devise a development plan for each individual person in the job, including agreed measures and objectives for both training and career development.

3 Evaluate the current performance of the individual, using headings such as:

Business awareness
Teamworking
Decision-making
Cultural commitment
Initiative
Creativity
Safety
Planning

This is done by the use of judgement, either a simple scoring with marks out of ten for each item, or ranking on a scale between outstanding and unacceptable. Sometimes the evaluation is by a single superior, but using a panel – as in job evaluation – is likely to produce less problematic evaluations, as groups will be less prejudiced and more willing to be 'hard markers'.

4 The development plan is then put into operation as a basis for action and development over the next twelve-month period, when the evaluation is repeated.

If this approach is to succeed, it is important to trust it. It must never fall a victim to economies, it must never be fudged, and it must carry the full weight of pay increases. Cost-of-living adjustments of 10% with an extra 1% for PRP will leave performance as an additional criterion. It is only when all pay adjustments are performance-related that performance comes centre stage as the sole criterion for getting more money. That degree of management commitment is rarely found, and it is likely to produce many of the problems in implementation that have been mentioned earlier, but it is only where a management is able and willing to make, and stick with, that single-minded commitment that performance management is likely to work.

Study themes

1 Where manual employees are employed on some form of pay-

ment by results, New Earnings Survey shows that the percentage of average earnings made up by incentive payments is under 20 per cent for men and over 30 per cent for women. How would you explain this difference?

2 The reasons why incentive schemes persist include the following:

- Managements can sometimes avoid a problem by buying a way past it through juggling with the incentive arrangement.
- Manipulating incentive schemes can overcome resistance to change.
- A basic conviction in the minds of many managers that incentive schemes ought to work as they seem basically sensible.

Ask about the incentive scheme where you work, or a scheme of which one of your friends has experience. Which of these three reasons exist? What others are there?

3 Obtain particulars of profit-sharing schemes from the Profit-related Pay Office, Inland Revenue, St Mungo's Road, Cumbernauld, Glasgow G67 1YZ. Would you describe profit-sharing as an incentive or as a pleasant windfall?

4 The American management expert Douglas MacGregor wrote:

> The practical logic of incentives is that people want money, and that they will work harder to get more of it. Incentive plans do not, however, take account of several other well-demonstrated characteristics of behaviour in the organisational setting:
>
> 1 that most people want the approval of their fellow workers and that, if necessary, they will forgo increased pay to obtain this approval;
> 2 that no managerial assurances can persuade workers that incentive rates will remain inviolate regardless of how much they produce;
> 3 that the ingenuity of the average worker is sufficient to outwit any system of controls devised by management.
> (McGregor 1970, p. 71)

Does this apply to performance-related pay?

References

DoE, 1984, 1986, 1988. *New Earnings Surveys 1984, 1986, 1988*. HMSO, London.

Husband, T. M., 1976. *Work Analysis and Pay Structure*. McGraw-Hill, Maidenhead.

IDS, 1977. *Incentive Pay Schemes*. IDS Study 140. Incomes Data Services, London.

IDS, 1985a. *Improving Productivity*. IDS Study 331. Incomes Data Services, London.

IDS, 1985b. *Staff Benefits and Allowances*. IDS Study 332. Incomes Data Services, London.

IDS, 1988. *Performance Pay*, IDS Focus 49. Incomes Data Services, London.

IDS, 1989. *Incentive Bonus Schemes*, IDS Study 443. Incomes Data Services, London.

Lawler, E. E., Jnr., 1971. *Pay and Organizational Effectiveness*. McGraw-Hill, New York.

Lupton, T., and Bowey, A. M., 1975. *Wages and Salaries*, Penguin, Harmondsworth.

McGregor, D., 1970. *The Human Side of Enterprise*. McGraw-Hill, Maidenhead.

Smith, I., 1983. *The Management of Remuneration: Paying for Effectiveness*. Institute of Personnel Management, London.

White, M., 1985. What's New in Pay? *Personnel Management*, February, pp. 20–3.

Whyte, W. F., 1972. Economic incentives and human relations, in Lupton, T., (ed.), 1972. *Payment Systems*, Penguin, Harmondsworth.

Woodley, C., 1990. The cafeteria route to compensation, *Personnel Management*, May, pp. 42–5.

Chapter 24

Benefits and Packages

Employment benefits are clearly separate from incentive and merit pay and from the decisions about the proportion of pay allocated to performance. They are also clearly separate from the legal requirements of employing people. Having said that, however, this still leaves some uncertainty as to what we mean by employment benefits. In this chapter we will therefore identify a range of perspectives on what constitutes employment benefits and the reasons why benefits are used. We will then review a selection of commonly used benefits and explore the newer 'cafeteria' approach to offering benefits packages.

What are employment benefits?

Benefits are any items or services that employers offer to employees although not legally bound to do so. Sometimes these will result from negotiations with unions. Often they will apply across the board at different grade levels in the organisation, or relating to differing levels of service, and are not related to performance. For some benefits, though, there is room for discretion on the part of management.

The most noticeable forms of benefit are those such as company cars and shares, nursery provision, pensions and health insurance. Some of these provisions may incur a contribution from the employee direct to the company, as with most pension schemes and nurseries. Other benefits may incur a tax liability, such as health insurance and company cars.

Other forms of benefit are those which are often seen as part of the contract or employment, such as sick pay, holiday entitlement and flexibility of hours. The degree of generosity of these schemes will be seen as a benefit, or otherwise, by employees.

A further group of benefits are those which ensure that the

employee is not out of pocket due to any obligations or costs incurred as a result of carrying out the organisation's business. In this group would be included subsistence and out-of-pocket expenses, relocation expenses and benefits related to the nature of the business – for example, uniforms required. Again, some of the benefits are hardly a *benefit*, as they represent standard good practice. However, the fact that they are usually of variable value and are grade-linked can turn them into a benefit in reality.

Why use benefits?

Many benefits were traditionally used as a way of giving extra money to employees in a form which was not taxable, and so they were intially seen as a perk for more senior groups of staff. Changes in the tax laws over the past two decades have resulted in these tax advantages being severely limited. There are, however, many other reasons why employers give benefits, and these include using them as follows:

- as a way of encouraging certain types of behaviour – for example, paying for subscriptions to professional associations, paying for part-time further education, paying for dry-cleaning, offering on-site accommodation;
- as a way of encouraging potential employees to join the organisation – for example, relocation expenses, company cars and flexitime;
- as a way of retaining employees and recognising long service – for example, share ownership, pensions, holidays increasing with service and long-service awards;
- as a demonstration of being a caring employer – for example, sick pay, pensions, life insurance and health insurance;
- as a way of recognising status – for example, reimbursement of first-class travel, four- and five-star hotels and executive cars;
- as a way of demonstrating commitment to equal opportunities – for example, nurseries, career-break schemes and flexible hours.

From the employer's point of view, the use of benefits can have tax advantages. For example, employers can claim nursery provision costs against tax, and can claim back VAT on subsistence expenses where this is itemised separately. A useful guide for employers in assessing what VAT they can reclaim is *The VAT Guide* (HMCE 1987). In the case of capital costs, such as company cars, the employer can 'write off' part of the cost of the vehicle, over a four-year period, against profits, thus resulting in a tax saving. The employer can also take advantage of buying items in bulk at a lower price than individual purchasers could obtain.

From the individual's point of view, in spite of contributions he or she may make, or tax penalties, benefits still represent a considerable advantage.

Commonly used benefits

According to Peppercorn and Skoulding (1987), the most commonly used benefit for managers was the company car, offered to almost 70 per cent of their sample survey. This was followed by private health insurance at just under 60 per cent, with share options and non-contributory pensions coming some way behind at just over 30 per cent, as shown in fig. 24.1. The respondents were, however, asked directly only about the use of those benefits contained in the list.

Company cars and mileage allowances

Organisations offer a variety of company car and mileage schemes, but in general they will buy or lease a car in the organisation's name but for the use of the employee. Employees may be offered a range of cars according to their grade, or be given a price ceiling under which they can make their own choice. Depending on the value of the car and the amount of business mileage, a value is attached to this 'benefit in kind' and the employee will pay income tax on this amount. For some employees – for example, sales representatives – a car is an absolute requirement of the job and the high business mileage they cover means that the benefit will have a much smaller tax liability for the employee. For other employees the car may purely be a 'perk' rather than a necessity, in that they are office-based and do little or no business mileage in the year. In these cases the value of the benefit in kind would

Figure 24.1
Commonly used benefits for managers
(from Peppercorn and Skoulding 1987, p. 88)

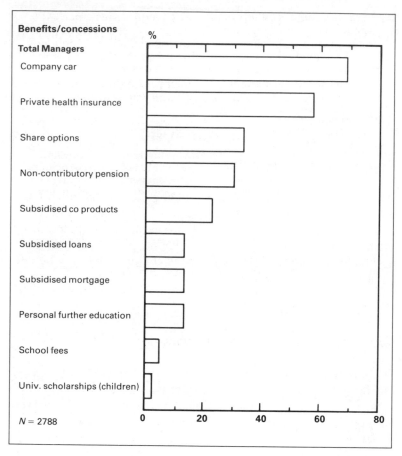

be much higher. Details of the effect that business mileage and cost of car have on the taxable benefit are excellently explained in the Ford Motor Company's yearly publication *The Taxman and the Company Car* (Talkback 1991), and an example of its analyses is shown in fig. 24.2.

Mileage allowances are usually paid according to the cubic capacity of the car. Alternatively, some employers provide free

Figure 24.2

Company car taxation

Taxable benefit is determined by extent of annual business mileage plus the engine capacity or value of car when new as shown in the table below. The taxable benefit for cars over 4 years old is slightly less than the figures in the table.

The amount of tax that company car drivers pay on their taxable benefit depends on their total taxable income. For 1991/2, when this figure exceeds £23,700 then the charge will be at 40%.

TAX YEAR 91/92

	Driving 2,500 or less business miles per annum		Driving between 2,500 and 18,000 business miles per annum		Driving 18,000 or more business miles per annum	
	Car benefit	Private fuel benefit	Car benefit	Private fuel benefit	Car benefit	Private fuel benefit
Original market value less than £19,250: or under 1400cc	£3075	£480	£2050	£480	£1025	£240
Between 1400cc and 2000cc	£3975	£600	£2650	£600	£1325	£300
Over 2000cc	£6375	£900	£4250	£900	£2125	£450
Original market value between £19,251 and £29,000	£8250	£*	£5500	£*	£2750	£*
Original market value more than £29,000	£13 350	£*	£8900	£*	£4450	£*

* Dependent on cubic capacity of car.

(Source: adapted from Ford Motor Company, 1990)

petrol on site. For those employees who do not have a company car and use their own vehicle for business purposes, a much higher rate per mile is paid, to cover depreciation and maintenance costs caused by the higher mileage. As an alternative, some employees are paid a monthly allowance to cover use of their own vehicle, in addition to mileage allowances.

Health insurance

Organisations offering private health insurance will negotiate a group scheme with the insurers to cover all employees to whom they wish to offer this benefit. The taxable benefit which results from this is assessed on what would be the individual subscription rate to the scheme (from around £200 per year), which will be greater when spouse and children are included (up to around £800 per year). Now that health insurance is a taxable benefit, many employers give employees the option of being included rather than automatically doing this.

Pensions and life insurance

These will be covered in detail in chapter 26.

Cheap mortgages and loans

These are most often, but not only, available to employees in the financial services sector. They are normally offered to current employees who have a minimum of, say, three years' service. Loans can vary from small amounts of £100 at a low rate of interest to amounts of over £100 000 at no interest for bridging loans offered to employees who are asked to relocate. These loans are not normally regarded as a taxable benefit, but this would depend on the circumstances.

Nurseries

Nursery places may be provided free to employees, or may be charged for at varying rates. For the employee they would be taxed as a benefit in kind if they were provided free – although this aspect of taxation law may be reviewed in the future. Employers can gain tax relief only on their contribution to the cost of the places. The allocation of nursery places – which are often in limited supply – can become an issue. Some employers use these places to attract women back to work for jobs that cannot otherwise be filled; others have a more egalitarian approach, such as first come first served from current employees.

Relocation expenses

Relocation expenses would normally be paid to any current employee who was required to move area to meet business needs, and also to new employees who were required to move to take up their new post. Expenses paid usually represent reimbursement of such costs as solicitors' bills, estate agents' fees, physical removal costs and necessary travelling before taking up the post. Sometimes allowances are given for fitted items such as carpets and curtains.

Holidays

Holidays are a key benefit, not normally quantified in money terms, and are often taken for granted in the UK as allocations are much more generous than in the United States, say. In the UK, allocations vary from around three to seven weeks, compared with the USA where two to three weeks is common even for senior employees. Employers are increasingly offering some choices between extra pay and extra holidays. So, for example, an extra five days' holiday a year may be taken or the money equivalent. The employee can usually take this in the proportions that he or she wishes – for example, opting for two days' extra holiday and three days' extra money. A different choice can usually be made each year.

Other benefits linked to the nature of the business

Other benefits linked to the nature of the business may include the purchase of company products or services at a discounted rate and the provision of uniforms or other items needed in order to carry out the job. Sometimes on-site accommodation is provided, and this may be taxed as a benefit in kind in some circumstances.

General reimbursement of expenses

This hardly sounds like a benefit, but for some employees it can be seen as such. Employees who stay in hotels to only a small extent on their own account may see a business requirement to run a course in a high-standard hotel as a benefit. Employees who travel second-class on their own account may see first-class travel as a benefit. Principally, though, the level of reimbursement will normally depend on grade, with higher-graded jobs attracting higher levels, in an attempt to provide the employee with no less than is appropriate for an individual of that status. In addition there is the desire, in offering higher-level reimbursement, to minimise the strain and the hassle and to recognise and value the employee's efforts, with the intended result that the work will be conducted in the most effective and efficient manner. Undoubtedly the image of the organisation is also a consideration in this area!

The cafeteria approach to benefit packages

A 'cafeteria' approach to pay and benefits is used to a much greater extent in the USA than in the UK, although there is increasing evidence of, at least, limited systems being offered over here. The most simple form of cafeteria-style pay and benefits is offering the individual a choice between the benefit and its money value. Hilton (1991) quotes the Mortgage Corporation as the only employer in the UK known to have introduced this system over the whole workforce. The West Dorset Mental Health Trust has declared its intention to develop this approach, and it is being considered by Bradford Royal Infirmary. In these approaches, some grades of employee are given the choice between, for example, a pension plan and a money alternative and between additional days' holiday or a money equivalent.

Other types of scheme are more complex and offer the individual a much wider range of choices – for example, Woodley (1990) quotes the example of the Manufacturers National Corporation, based in Detroit. In this case there are a variety of options covering, for example, different types of medical care, dental care and life insurance. More details are given in fig. 24.3. An even more flexible approach is to give the employee a money value or points limit which can be used to purchase the benefits that are of most value to the employee.

Giving individuals a much more significant part in determining the benefits that are available to them enables them to weigh up current needs, long-term security and tax efficiency in making the decisions that suit them best. There is also the advantage that the

Figure 24.3
An example of a cafeteria benefits approach

Manufacturers National Corporation

Manufacturers National Corporation, a bank based in Detroit, has around 6,000 employees, around 5,000 of whom participate in a flexible benefits plan. The main objectives of the plan, introduced in 1983, were long-term cost control, competitive recruitment positioning and a closer fit of benefits to a workforce which is 75 per cent female.

The plan incorporates the following choices:

- Six medical options
- Five dental options
- Ten life insurance options
- Four long-term disability options
- Savings facility for dependant care costs
- Buying or selling 'vacation days'
- Cash alternatives to all of these options.

Kimberley Altenburg, personnel officer, comments that the 'benefit programme has been an effective recruiting tool, especially for middle managers. Our programme is more attractive, especially to women.'

Each individual is allocated annually a 'credit' amount. Each participating employee makes choices at the beginning of each calendar year and can amend those choices only if certain specified events (termed 'family status changes') take place during the year.

When the plan began, choice was restricted so that a number of benefits were compulsory. These restrictions have been removed as the company has felt more comfortable passing full responsibility to employees.

At first the plan was administered by a third party. However, the company had some problems due to lack of control over data and reporting, and it is currently being brought in-house.

New benefits or options have been introduced to increase choice almost every year since implementation. Altenburg says: 'We have somewhat controlled medical costs. More importantly, we have enhanced the perceived value of the benefits package. For example, 50 per cent of eligible employees buy additional vacation days, even at a premium price tag of 120 per cent of a day's price. We are also less conservative now and allow opt-outs from certain coverages to reflect dual-income earners' needs as well as others'.

Implementing and maintaining the plan has not been plain sailing from an administrative and communications point of view, but she says: 'We would never consider returning to a traditional fixed programme. The modern household is simply too diverse today.'

From Woodley (1990) p. 45

message this conveys to them is that the organisation cares about them as an *individual* rather than seeing them as part of a group with identical needs.

Woodley suggests that, in spite of these advantages, cafeteria-style compensation and benefits are not in much evidence yet due to inertia, ignorance, tax complexity, administrative burden and difficulty in communicating the options.

Study themes

1 Read Woodley's article (1990) on cafeteria benefits and write an analysis, to include specific evidence, of the major reasons why full cafeteria pay has not been introduced into your organisation.
2 Design a system to administer cafeteria pay that is as simple as possible for the employee to understand and which minimises the administrative burden.
3 Read Ford's latest guide *The Taxman and the Company Car*. Imagine you were offered a car costing under £19 000 while carrying out your current role. Analyse the advantages and disadvantages for you, together with alternatives you could pursue, and come to a decision about whether you would accept the offer.
4 Interview five members of staff in your organisation. Try to represent five different levels in the organisation. Design a semi-structured questionnaire and use this to uncover:

   (a) what they classify as employment benefits,
   (b) their view of the way these are allocated and the reasons for this,
   (c) the effect that the benefit system has on them.

References

Hilton, P., 1991. Hospital trusts aim for 'cafeteria' pay, *Personnel Plus*, February, p. 1.
HMCE, 1987. *The VAT Guide*, HMSO (for Her Majesty's Customs and Excise), London.

Peppercorn, G., and Skoulding, G., 1987. *Profile of British Industry: the Manager's View*, Ashridge/BIM/Cranfield, Corby.

Talkback, 1990. *Issue no 14*, from Talkback information service, Ford Motor Company, Chelmsford.

Talkback, 1991. *The Taxman and the Company Car*, Ford Motor Company, Chelmsford.

Woodley, C., 1990. The cafeteria route to compensation, *Personnel Management*, May, pp. 42–5.

Chapter 25

Conditions of Employment

Conditions of employment are an intrinsic part of the contract of employment which exists between the employer and employee. In this chapter we shall look at hours of work (including shift working and overtime), holidays, and sickness and maternity pay. Remaining topics will be covered in the following chapters.

Hours of work

Developments in working hours may be traced by examining changes in the length of the working day and week. Historical evidence indicates that from the medieval period onwards the length of the working day has gradually become shorter. This overall reduction has included periods of fluctuation when working hours lengthened or remained stable for long periods.

Trends before the Industrial Revolution are difficult to identify, due to variation in working time between agricultural and manufacturing workers, and between employees and the self-employed (Blyton 1985). Working time in agriculture is traditionally dependent upon the weather, the amount of daylight and cultivation patterns, which are hard to predict. In contrast, working hours in manufacturing conform more closely to predetermined work patterns, and comprise the basis of most studies of working time (see Bienefeld 1972). Such analyses indicate that by the end of the eighteenth century (before the Industrial Revolution) the 10-hour working day was generally accepted as the norm in manufacturing industries in Britain.

The Industrial Revolution itself was characterised by an increase in working hours up to 12 or 13 a day, a deterioration in working conditions and the subsequent rise in the trade union movement. From this point onwards, reductions in working hours have been negotiated through collective-bargaining agreements. By 1875, the

54-hour week (comprised of six 9-hour days, or longer weekdays and a shorter Saturday) was common, and it remained virtually unaltered until the early 1900s.

Changes in working time this century have seen the introduction of the 48, 44, 40, 39 and more recently 38/37 hour week. Factors prompting these reductions in hours have included rises in productivity (influencing reductions in the 1960s); high unemployment (influencing reductions in the 1980s) and, more generally, union pressure and increased use of shift working or overtime. By 1984, the average weekly hours of manual workers were 39.2 (exclusive of overtime). However, these hours were significantly higher than non-manual staff, who averaged 37.1 hours per week. Similar differences were also found between male and female employees, with men working longer weekly hours (DoE 1984). The low inflation levels of the 1980s, together with increases in labour productivity, prompted trade unions to seek a further reduction in working hours to 37 per week. This move was initiated by the engineering unions, and looks likely to spread to other areas of industry.

Shift working

Shift working can be defined as 'a situation in which one worker replaces another on the same job within a 24-hour period' (Ingram and Sloane 1984, p. 168). The reasons for introducing shift working vary from company to company. However, it is likely that the following considerations will be of importance (Palmer and Redmond 1986):

- *Demand requirements*   Consumer needs frequently necessitate round-the-clock coverage – for example, hospitals, delivery and transport services.
- *Capital utilisation*   Many companies rely on intensive use of machinery in order to reduce costs and increase competitiveness.
- *Technical necessity*   For some industries, such as, steelworking, the costs of shutting down and restarting machinery and production are prohibitive.
- *Productivity*   Various levels of productivity are predicted under different shift systems.

Other factors which need to be taken into consideration are the availability and cost of labour, trade union and employee attitudes, legislation, and custom and practice within the industry. These interrelated influences are important cost elements which should be carefully evaluated before the introduction of shift working and its associated premium payments.

Shift work has traditionally been concentrated among manual workers in certain industries, notably mining, steel production, textiles, paper, chemicals and oil-refining. However, recent increases in shift working have been accompanied by a broadening of arrangements to encompass non-manual staff in a variety of occupations, including service and retail.

Examples of shift systems

There are a variety of shift systems in current use in the UK (categorisation from Cook 1954):

- *Alternating day and night shifts*   These involve two groups of staff who spend a period on day hours followed by a period on nights. For example, each employee could spend one month on day hours followed by a fortnight of night work. It is a flexible system, allowing a rotation of shifts.
- *Double day shifts*   These involve two groups of staff, usually working one to two weeks on the morning shift followed by one to two weeks on the afternoon shift. Examples of shift hours are 6.00 a.m. to 2.00 p.m. and 2.00 p.m. to 10.00 p.m.
- *Permanent night shifts*   These are normally a variation of the alternating day and night shifts above, but can be incorporated into double day-shift working.
- *Discontinuous three-shift systems*   These involve three groups of staff working successive weeks (or fortnights) on the morning, afternoon and night shifts. Unlike continuous three-shift systems (discussed below), a break is provided over the weekend.
- *Continuous three-shift systems*   The organisation is covered 168 hours per week. The length of the working week determines the number of crews employed. An average 42-hour week is generally covered by four shift crews. However, recent reductions in the working week to 38/37 hours have led to the intro-

duction of five shift crews. Continuous systems are the most costly, as enhanced payments must be made for weekend working.

- *Evening shifts for part-time employees* Usual hours are 5.00 p.m. to 10.00 p.m. These employees are mainly women who are unable to work normal day hours, due to domestic commitments.

- *Staggered day work* Employees are divided into a number of groups, starting and finishing work at intervals of, for example, 1 hour or ½ hour. This system is often used in seasonal industries.

Despite technical and economic changes, patterns of shift working in the UK have remained fairly stable. However, a review of working patterns was prompted in the early 1980s by a number of factors, including the need to reduce overhead costs, reduction in the working week, improved utilisation of capital assets and economic fluctuations (Atkinson 1982). These led to an evaluation by many companies of shift working schemes, as regards cost-effectiveness and their ability to match working hours to business needs. As a result, some companies introduced five-crew working in continuous shift-work operations, while others have adopted annual or monthly hours arrangements (see chapter 4).

In the future it is likely that successful shift-working schemes will be those which (a) promote flexible working and (b) least disturb conventional work/social/rest patterns. Indeed, proposed European legislation aims to introduce stricter controls on the use of shift and night work. If successful, this would necessitate a major review of current shift patterns, particularly those used in continuous-process industries.

Overtime

> Overtime may be defined as time worked in excess of 'standard' hours, which is generally rewarded either by payment at a premium rate or by subsequent time off in lieu. (Blyton 1985, p. 50)

The amount of overtime worked in the UK varies between industries, companies and employees. In general, those industries with low basic pay rates tend to maintain higher levels of overtime. It also tends to be more widespread among manual as opposed to white-collar workers, men as opposed to women and 'prime age' workers as opposed to their younger or older colleagues. Thus, the typical high-overtime employee is a male manual worker in his thirties or forties.

Despite progressive reductions in basic working hours over the last 40 years, from 44 to 38/37 per week, overtime has continued to increase. Figures show a rise from around 2 hours overtime per week per employee in the late 1940s to an average of 5.4 hours overtime per week in 1985. What are the reasons for this?

Overtime fulfils a number of organisational needs (Smith and Palmer 1981):

- *Extension of total work time* – for example, overtime may be used on a regular basis for cleaning, maintenance, shift working.
- *Flexibility and fluctuations in demand* – overtime allows cyclical changes in demand to be met without recruiting or laying off extra staff.
- *Covering unforseen emergencies* – such as absenteeism, machine breakdown or pressing deadlines.
- *Labour shortages* – problems in recruiting skilled labour may be alleviated through overtime working by existing staff.
- *Employee needs* – for many employees overtime is an important element of the working week, both in terms of time and the opportunity it provides to raise earnings.
- *Cost of employment* – overtime is cheaper than employing extra workers.

Overtime is an expensive labour cost – it is usually paid at premium rates, varying from time-and-a-quarter and time-and-a-half to double, treble and quadruple time. Indeed, a recent study has shown that the majority of organisations wish to reduce the amount of overtime worked (Curson 1986). A variety of methods have been adopted: productivity agreements, flexible hours, additional shift crews, time off in lieu, overtime limitation agreements, use of part-time or temporary workers and subcontractors. While these methods have had a limited effect on the reduction of over-

time working, more fundamental changes are required to remove
it completely. (See chapter 4.)

Holidays

The last few decades have witnessed a significant increase in paid
holiday entitlement for employees. In the mid 1950s, most manual
workers received less than two weeks' paid holiday a year. By the
end of 1983, 95 per cent of manual workers received at least four
weeks' holiday, with 20 per cent enjoying five weeks or more
(DoE, 1984).

However, while the amount of holiday entitlement may have
increased, the degree of flexibility over taking these holidays has
remained limited (Blyton 1985). A number of industries place
restrictions on the period during which holidays may be taken.
For example, many production industries have a 'shutdown'
period in summer and over Christmas. This allows workers discretion over only part of their holiday entitlement. In addition, an
even larger number of companies stipulate that all holidays must
be taken within a 12-month period. This prevents employees from
'carrying over' leave in order to build up longer holidays.

Future developments may well see increased flexibility over
timing of holiday entitlement, such as long-term banking of holidays, and greater provision for unpaid leave.

Sickness benefit

There are two systems of sick pay: State and occupational. While
nearly all employees are eligible for State sick pay, entitlement to
occupational sick pay depends upon working for an employer who
runs a scheme.

State sick pay

State sick pay or Statutory Sick Pay (SSP) was originally intro-
duced under the Social Security and Housing Benefits Act 1982.
Under that scheme, employers took over responsibility from the
State for paying employees sick pay. Important amendments to

the Act came into effect in April 1986 under the Social Security Act 1985.

A summary of the main terms and regulations covering SSP is provided below (for further details see *Croner's Reference Book for Employers* or DSS leaflet N1244, *Statutory Sick Pay – Check Your Rights*).

Periods of incapacity for work (PIW)   A PIW is formed when an employee has been absent from work due to illness or disablement for four consecutive days. It does not matter if these are working days or rest days. No SSP can be paid unless the employee has formed a PIW.

Linked periods   PIWs may be linked to form a single period. PIWs which began/ended on or after April 1986 are linked to form a single PIW, provided they are not separated by more than 56 calendar days.

Qualifying days   SSP is only paid for qualifying days. These should reflect those days on which the employee would normally work. For example, employees working Monday to Friday would have these five days as qualifying days. The arrangements may vary for those employees on shift work.

Waiting days   The first three qualifying days of a PIW are known as waiting days. For linked periods, only the first PIW is subject to this rule. Waiting days do not qualify for SSP.

Entitlement period   An employer's liability to pay SSP ends when:

- the employee is fit to return to work; or
- maximum SSP entitlement of 28 weeks is reached – each PIW starts a new 28-week period of entitlement, provided it is not linked to the previous PIW; or
- the employee's linked PIW reaches three years (even though 28 weeks' SSP may not have been paid); or
- the employment contract is terminated; or
- the employee is taken into legal custody or goes outside the European Community; or
- a pregnant employee enters the 'disqualifying' period – that is,

starts receiving Statutory Maternity Pay, Maternity Allowance, or reaches the sixth week before the expected week of confinement.

Recovery of SSP Provided the correct procedure for payment has been followed, employers may reclaim SSP from the government via National Insurance contributions:

Absence certification The employer must be able to prove to a DSS inspector that all periods of absence have been correctly recorded and evidence of incapacity has been provided. Employers generally require DSS self-certificates (or company self-certification forms) for the first seven days of absence (Form SC1) and doctor's medical certificates thereafter.

Administration When dealing with SSP, employers will need to use the following forms:

- *Leaver's Statement SSP1(L)* This form allows employers to link sickness absence with previous PIWs. This form is issued by employers to leavers if they have been sick in the eight weeks preceding the end of their contract of employment. The form may then be handed over by the employee to a new employer if the individual is sick within eight weeks of starting work. The new employer's liability for SSP is thus reduced.
- *Record Sheet SSP2* Employers are required by law to keep sickness records for three years. Form SSP2 is intended to facilitate the keeping of SSP records. However, some companies have devised their own systems.
- *'Change-over' Form SSP1* Those employees who have reached maximum SSP entitlement or who are excluded from the scheme for some other reason may receive *State Sickness Benefit*. In order to transfer the employee over to the State scheme, the employer should complete 'Change-over' Form SSP1, stating the reasons for exclusion from SSP. This form should then be forwarded by the employee to the DSS. (For further information, see DSS leaflet NI 16, *Sickness Benefit*).

Occupational sick pay

The rules governing occupational schemes vary. Many have particular requirements regarding qualifying periods, length of entitlement, funding and administration (see Torrington and Hall 1987).

The amount of occupational sick pay employees receive usually ranges between State benefit and normal full pay. The most popular schemes provide normal pay for a specified period, usually dependent on an employee's length of service. Some employers pay a flat-rate benefit in addition to payments provided through SSP. Others link payments to the level of an individual's earnings.

The majority of occupational sick schemes are non-contributory and are considered by a growing number of employees to be an important employment benefit.

Maternity benefits

Maternity benefits are covered by the Social Security Act 1986. Two kinds of benefit are available to women under the scheme: Statutory Maternity Pay and Maternity Allowance.

Statutory Maternity Pay (SMP)

This is a weekly payment from the employer to employees who take maternity leave or leave employment because of pregnancy.

Qualification for SMP To qualify for SMP employees must, firstly, satisfy the continuous employment rule. This states that a woman must have been employed by the same employer for at least 26 weeks into the *qualifying week*, which is 15 weeks before the week in which her baby is due (the *expected week of confinement*). A woman not employed during the qualifying week is not entitled to SMP. Secondly, the woman must, on average, earn enough to pay Class-1 National Insurance contributions. This is known as the earnings rule.

Applying for SMP The employer should receive at least 21 days' notice of an employee's intention to stop work to have a baby. The employer will also require medical evidence of the date the baby is due (Maternity Certificate, Form MATB1). This should normally be provided no later than three weeks after the date SMP was due to start.

Payment of SMP   SMP can be paid for a maximum of 18 weeks. This is known as the *maternity pay period* (MPP). SMP is payable from the beginning of the eleventh week before the expected week of confinement, *only* if the employee has stopped work. SMP cannot be paid for any week during which the employee works. A woman may choose to continue working beyond the twelfth week before the expected week of confinement, in which case the MPP will start the week after the week in which the employee last worked. If the employee stops work before the start of the sixth week before the expected week of confinement, payment for the full 18 weeks will be received. However, if the employee works later into her pregnancy, she will lose payment for each week that she works.

There are two rates of SMP:

- *Higher rate*   In order to qualify for the higher rate, a woman must have been employed full-time (at least 16 hours per week) for a continuous period of two years, or part-time (8–16 hours per week) for a continuous period of five years into the qualifying week. The higher rate (90 per cent of average weekly earnings) is payable for the first six weeks of the MPP. The remainder of the MPP is covered by the lower rate.
- *Lower rate*   Employees who do not qualify for the higher rate receive 18 weeks at the lower rate. This is a set rate which is reviewed annually. See DSS NI 196, *Social Security Benefit Rates*, for details.

Maternity Allowance (MA)

This is a weekly benefit paid by the Department of Social Security. Women receive MA only if they are unable to get SMP and have been employed/self-employed and paid sufficient National Insurance contributions. Women who are not entitled to either SMP or MA may be able to claim Sickness Benefit. For further information, see DSS leaflet NI 17A, *A Guide to Maternity Benefits*.

Employment Rights of Pregnant Women

Antenatal care All pregnant employees are entitled to paid time-off to attend antenatal appointments.

Dismissal due to pregnancy Dismissal may be fair in certain circumstances – for example, if pregnancy prevents the employee from carrying out her duties or if continuing work is dangerous or illegal. In such cases the employer should offer an alternative job. If this is not possible, the employee may be fairly dismissed. However, such women may still be entitled to SMP.

Right to return to work Women who have been continuously employed for two years full-time (16 hours per week or more) or five years part-time (8–16 hours per week) by the beginning of the eleventh week before the expected week of confinement have the right to return to work after maternity leave. The woman has the right to return at any time before the end of 29 weeks from the week of confinement, provided she gives her employer 21 days' notice in writing of her intention to return to work. If the original job is not available, a suitable alternative should be offered. Women are not entitled to return part-time if they were previously employed full-time, unless their employer agrees.

Study themes

1 What are the main problems associated with shift working? How can they be overcome?

2 (a) Does your organisation operate an occupational sick pay scheme? Explain how this integrates with SSP. What improvements, if any, would you like to make to your company scheme.

  (b) How are short-term and long-term sickness absence monitored within your organisation? What role does personnel play in relation to the control of sickness absence?

3 For what reasons is overtime used within your organisation? Can you suggest any alternatives?

References

Atkinson, J., 1982. *Shiftworking*, Report no. 45, Institute of Manpower Studies, Falmer.

Bienefeld, M., 1972. *Working Hours in British History: an Economic History*, Weidenfeld and Nicolson, London

Blyton, P., 1985. *Changes in Working Time: an International Review*, Croom Helm, London.

Cook, F., 1954. *Shift Work*, Institute of Personnel Management, London.

Croner's Reference Book For Employers, Croner Publications, Kingston.

Curson, C., (ed.), 1986. *Flexible Patterns of Work*, Institute of Personnel Management, London.

Department of Employment, 1984. *Employment Gazette*, HMSO, London.

Department of Social Security, 1989. *Statutory Sick Pay – Check Your Rights*, Leaflet no. NI 244.

Ingram, A., and Sloane, P., 1984. The growth of shiftwork in the British food, drink and tobacco industries, *Managerial and Decision Economics*, vol. 5, no. 3, pp. 168–76.

Palmer, S., and Redmond, D., 1986. New forms of shiftworking, in Curson (1986).

Smith, M. K., and Palmer, S., 1981. Getting to the bottom of overtime, *Personnel Management*, February, pp. 27–31.

Torrington, D., and Hall, L., 1987. *Personnel Management – a New Approach*, Prentice-Hall, Hemel Hempstead.

Chapter 26

Pensions

Recent years have seen fundamental changes in pension provision. There are a number of reasons for this.

Firstly, the nature of work has changed considerably over the past few decades. Employees no longer expect to spend the majority of their working lives with one employer – there is greater job mobility. In addition, an increased number of women are now entering the labour market. Women often have broken records of service, due to family and domestic commitments. Traditional pension schemes are unable to cater effectively for these new employment patterns (see Torrington and Hall 1987).

Secondly, the government is coming under increasing pressure as regards the funding of State pension schemes. These pension schemes are designed on a 'pay-as-you-go' basis – there is no State pension fund. This means that the money that is paid to today's pensioners comes from the taxes and National Insurance contributions of today's workers. The money that will be paid to today's workers will come from the contributions of the workforce of the future. However, an increasing elderly population and a falling birth rate means that there are fewer workers supporting a growing number of pensioners. This situation is putting the State schemes under tremendous financial strain.

As a result of the above factors, legislation has been introduced

- to allow individuals greater choice and flexibility as regards pension provision,
- to relieve pressure on State schemes by encouraging people to join employer's schemes or to take out personal pensions

This chapter provides a brief description of the various types of pension scheme available, recent changes in legislation and the implications of greater pension choice for employers and employees. For further details, an excellent review of pensions is provided by the Industrial Society (1988). A range of pension leaflets is also published by the DSS. Other useful texts are given in the references.

State basic pension

There are two types of pension available through the State: the basic State flat-rate pension and the State earnings-related pension.

Basic State flat-rate pension

The flat-rate scheme provides a pension which is set by the government on an annual basis. The basic pension is increased in line with price rises, but tends not to rise as rapidly as average earnings.

Entitlement to State benefits, including the basic pension, depends on the number of full *National Insurance contributions* years an individual has accumulated throughout 'working life' – that is, from age 16 to retirement. The State retirement age is currently 60 for women and 65 for men.

From 1975, NI contributions have been collected from employees through the 'Pay-As-You-Earn' (PAYE) system. NI contributions are payable for all earnings falling between the *Lower Earnings Limit* (LEL) and the *Upper Earnings Limit* (UEL). NI contributions are also made by employers for those employees whose earnings are over the LEL.

In order to qualify for *any* State basic pension, an individual must have paid NI contributions for one-quarter of his or her working life. To qualify for *full* State basic pension, full NI contributions must have been paid for roughly nine-tenths of the individual's working life. People earning less than the LEL do not pay NI contributions and will not qualify for basic pension. This includes many part-time workers, the majority of whom are women.

Pension provision for women Women who have paid sufficient NI contributions qualify for State basic pension from age 60. Married women aged 60 or over can get a basic pension based on their husband's NI contributions record if he is receiving a State basic pension. Special provisions are also made for widows and widowers.

The State Earnings Related Pension Scheme (SERPS)

The State Earnings Related Pension Scheme, or SERPS, was introduced in 1978. It is intended to provide employees with an additional State pension related to their earnings. It is paid at State retirement age in addition to the State basic pension.

An individual may be 'contracted-in' or 'contracted-out' of SERPS. All employees with earnings above the LEL who are paying NI contributions are said to be *'contracted-in'* to SERPS and will receive the additional pension on retirement. Alternatively, an employer or employee can choose to be *'contracted-out'* of SERPS, in which case NI contributions are rebated and may be paid into an occupational or personal pension scheme.

As a consequence of the increasing long-term costs of SERPS, the government has introduced legislation (in the Social Security Act 1986) aimed at reducing the benefits derived from SERPS to half their current value by 1998.

Occupational pension schemes

A good occupational pension scheme is an effective way of attracting, retaining and rewarding staff. It may be particularly helpful as regards the retention of senior staff with several years' pensionable service. From April 1988, membership of an occupational pension scheme can no longer be enforced as a condition of employment: employees can choose whether or not to join a scheme.

Most occupational pension schemes provide death benefits and retirement pensions. Some are funded solely by the employer ('non-contributory'), while others require contributions from both employer and employee ('contributory'). There are a number of types of occupational scheme.

Final-earnings schemes

In these schemes, employees receive a guaranteed pension based on their length of service and final earnings on retirement (*defined benefit scheme*). The pension is calculated on the basis of one-sixtieth or one-eightieth of the employee's retirement earnings, multiplied by the number of years' service. Assuming an average working life of 40 years, employees will receive a pension of between half and two-thirds of final earnings. For example, the pension payable on final earnings of £24 000 after 40 years' service for a one-sixtieth scheme would be

$$\frac{£24\,000}{60} \times 40 = £16\,000$$

Final-earnings schemes can participate in SERPS or opt out. Employers operating contracted-out final-salary pension schemes must provide employees with a *Guaranteed Minimum Pension* (GMP) which at least equals the level of benefit that would have been provided by SERPS. NI contributions are lower for employees who are in employers' contracted-out schemes, because the State will not be providing an earnings-related pension for that period of employment. From the 1989/90 tax year onwards, employers have to increase the GMP paid after retirement by 3 per cent a year, or by the Retail Prices Index (RPI), whichever is lower. In addition, under the Social Security Act 1990 the government will require most occupational salary-related pension schemes to increase pensions *above* GMP in line with the rise in the RPI up to a maximum increase of 5 per cent a year.

Money-purchase schemes

In these schemes, members' contributions are invested and on retirement individuals use the accumulated fund, *in respect of their own contributions*, to buy an annuity which will provide a regular income for retirement (*defined-contribution scheme*). The drawback of these schemes is their dependence on stock-market performance - a 'slump' could lead to a devaluation of investments. Some forms of money-purchase schemes guarantee that the capital invested will not decline in value:

- 'with-profits' schemes – profits on investments are averaged over a long period, so the returns are not as volatile;
- 'deposit-based schemes' – interest is built up on capital.

Contracted-out money-purchase schemes (COMPS)   In the past, money-purchase schemes were unable to contract-out of SERPS. However, from 6 April 1988, under provisions introduced by the Social Security Act 1986, employers have been able to run contracted-out money-purchase schemes (COMPS). COMPS are open to those individuals who are not already members of an occupational scheme and to those who are in non-contributory schemes. The minimum amount that may be put into these schemes is the National Insurance contracted-out rebate, which equals the amount by which SERPS contributions are reduced. These minimum payments and their investment return are known as *'protected rights'*. Retirement income based on these protected rights is subject to annual inflationary increases equal to 3 per cent or the rise in the Retail Prices Index, whichever is lower.

Comparison of final-earnings and money-purchase schemes

The advantage to the employer of money-purchase arrangements is that the amount of contributions paid each year is defined and under the employer's control. There is no potential open-ended financial liability as with final-salary schemes.

From the employee's point of view, money-purchase schemes provide no guarantee as to the value of the final pension and no GMP. There is also no protection against stock-market and economic fluctuations. However, members leaving money-purchase schemes early do receive the full value of their contributions. Under final-salary arrangements, employees often lose a large slice of their pension if forced to retire or leave early. The 'portability' of money-purchase schemes is one of their main attractions.

In the future, it is likely that the open-ended commitment and increasing costs associated with defined-benefit pension schemes will spur employers towards defined-contribution or money-purchase schemes (see *FT* 1990).

Average-earnings and revalued-average-earnings pensions

'Average-earnings' pensions are based on the employee's average earnings over the total years of service with an employer.

'Revalued-average-earnings' pensions are based on the actual earnings over the period of service, which are then 'revalued' up to the date of retirement – that is, actual amounts are multiplied by the increase in prices over a certain period in order to maintain their real value in current monetary terms.

Additional Voluntary Contributions

From April 1988, all employers are obliged to provide an Additional Voluntary Contributions (AVCs) scheme for employees in occupational pension schemes. AVCs allow individuals to make extra contributions and to build up their pension.

Under limits imposed by the Inland Revenue, up to 15 per cent of gross earnings can be contributed towards an occupational pension scheme. Thus, if an individual is currently contributing 5 per cent of earnings towards such a scheme, then up to 10 per cent can be put into an AVC scheme. Since tax relief is obtained on these additional contributions, they represent a tax-efficient form of saving.

Types of AVC scheme

- *Added years*   AVCs are used to buy extra years of service in the main scheme
- *Building society plans or deposit administration schemes* Interest is paid on the AVC account, and on retirement the accumulated amount is used to buy an annuity.
- *Unit-linked plans*   AVCs are used to purchase units of stocks and shares. On retirement, the units are cashed in and the money released is used to buy an annuity and/or to provide a lump sum.
- *Insurance company 'with-profits' plans*   These plans provide a termination bonus on retirement, as well as accumulated interest. The total amount is used to purchase an annuity.

From October 1987, employees can choose to contribute to

independent AVC schemes, run by approved financial institutions. These are known as '*Free Standing Additional Voluntary Contributions*' (FSAVCs).

Information on occupational pension schemes

A number of employees' rights were set out in the Social Security Act 1985 with respect to membership of occupational pension schemes. The majority of these measures concerned the provision of additional information.

Under the Act, all new and potential members must be given pension scheme details within 13 weeks of joining the scheme. Details should also be given to recognised trade unions, pensioners, members with deferred pensions, spouses and dependent beneficiaries. All schemes should provide annual reports explaining contributions paid in, benefits paid out and investment performance. In the event of cessation of the scheme, all beneficiaries should be advised.

Despite the increased availability of pension information, the majority of people find pensions difficult to understand. One useful idea, adopted by a number of larger companies, is the production of simplified pension booklets with information presented in a pictorial or 'comic-strip' format (see Hunt 1988). Such publications are more likely to be read and understood by employees than much of the traditional pensions literature. Other methods of communicating pensions information include pension 'surgeries' and newsletters. Some occupational schemes use the annual pension statement as an opportunity to inform members of any improvements or changes to the scheme over the year.

Equalisation of pension rights and pension age

Pension rights   Since the introduction of the Social Security Pensions Act 1975, all occupational pension schemes have had to allow equal access for men and women. However, many of these schemes admit only full-timers. Since 90 per cent of part-timers are female, such schemes indirectly discriminate against women. As many part-time female workers do not qualify for State basic pension either, this creates a bleak situation with regard to retirement provision for women.

Pension age Following a decision by the European Court of Justice in May 1990, occupational pension schemes will have to introduce equal pension ages for men and women. The case involved Douglas Barber, former employee of Guardian Royal Exchange (GRE) who was made redundant at age 52.

> Part of GRE's severance terms on redundancy included an entitlement to immediate retirement pension, provided the individual was at least age 55 in the case of a man, or age 50 in the case of a woman . . . Mr Barber claimed unlawful sexual discrimination. (IRE 1990, p. 3).

The court ruled that occupational pensions constitute pay and that GRE had broken the equal pay rule embodied in Article 119 of the Treaty of Rome. To give women an immediate pension and men of the same age a deferred pension was unfair. The court ruled that the decision would not apply retrospectively.

In the light of this decision, options for pension managers include introducing a standard retirement age of 65 for all employees or bringing the retirement age down to 60. A compromise solution might be a retirement age of 62 or 63. Although the above ruling does not directly affect the State basic pension, there is now pressure on the government to equalise State pension ages.

Future developments may see the introduction of *flexible retirement plans* with an age range of, say, 55 to 65.

Leaving an occupational pension scheme

Employees who leave a pension scheme before reaching the normal retirement age are known as 'early leavers'. Such individuals have a number of statutory rights as regards their pension entitlement:

Pensionable service of less than two years There is no entitlement to a 'preserved' pension (see below); however, from April 1988, employees who leave an occupational pension scheme after less than two years' pensionable service can take a cash refund of contributions. For contracted-out schemes, arrangements can also be made to 'buy back' into SERPS.

Pensionable service of two years or more Employees who leave after two to five years' service will no longer be entitled to a refund. These individuals have a number of choices:

- The employer's pension can be preserved (sometimes referred to as 'frozen' or 'deferred'). This preserved pension will be paid from the date of retirement.
- The value of the accumulated pension can be calculated and a 'transfer value' fixed. This can then be transferred straight into another employer's scheme.
- The 'transfer value' obtained from the employer's pension can be used to start a personal pension.

Early retirement on the grounds of ill health While the majority of occupational pension schemes have special provisions for employees who have to retire early due to ill health, such individuals will not be able to draw State basic pension until age 60 or 65. They may, however, qualify for other State benefits.

Pension funds and trustees

Unlike the pay-as-you-go arrangements for State pension schemes, occupational schemes create pension or 'trust' funds which ensure that pension investments are kept separate from business finances. Thus, if a company goes bankrupt, its independent pension fund cannot be seized to pay debtors. Pension funds consist of (a) contributions from members and employers and (b) income from investments. Benefits are paid from the fund to pensioners and their dependants.

Pension funds are run by trustees, nominated by either employees or employers. The trustees are responsible for

- monitoring the scheme's accounts and investments,
- conveying information to members,
- paying out benefits.

Trustees often rely on pensions experts (consultants, solicitors, actuaries) to advise them with regard to possible investment opportunities and potential risks. The trust assets must be used for the benefit of the members and beneficiaries. Any trustees who fail to act in their members' best interests, or contravene the rules of the trust, may be taken to court and held liable for any losses.

Personal pensions

Personal pensions became available from 1 July 1988. They are intended (a) to give individuals greater flexibility and freedom of choice and (b) to get as many people as possible contracted out of SERPS.

Personal pensions can be taken out with any bank, building society, insurance company or unit trust whose schemes have been approved by the Superannuation Funds Office (SFO) and the Occupational Pensions Board (OPB). These two organisations are responsible for approving applications from financial institutions wishing to offer personal pensions.

The contracted-out version of these new personal pension plans are called *Appropriate Personal Pensions* (APPs). APPs consist of two elements· firstly, the NI contributions made by the employee and employer that would normally have gone towards SERPS and, secondly, the individual's voluntary additional contributions.

On retirement, one-quarter of the total invested fund can be taken as a lump-sum payment. The remainder must be used to buy an annuity which covers a spouse's pension and death benefits. In addition, the annuity must increase annually by 3 per cent or the increase in the Retail Prices Index, whichever is less.

Advantages of personal pensions

1 Personal pensions are fully portable and can be continued when individuals change jobs.
2 As an incentive to join a personal pension plan, APP members who have never been contracted-out, or who have been contracted-out for less than two years, will receive a bonus of 2 per cent of annual earnings from the DSS until April 1993. This will be credited to the member's account at the end of each tax year.
3 There is no limit on pension benefits. Under favourable investment conditions, returns may be high.

Disadvantages of personal pensions

1 The profits accumulated through investment funds are subject to fluctuations in the stock market. There is no guarantee as to the level of retirement benefits.
2 Employees leaving an occupational scheme to take out a personal pension may not be allowed back into the employer's scheme.

   Individuals who leave their employer's scheme, but remain 'contracted-in' to SERPS, can take out 'top-up' personal pensions. However, these schemes are not eligible for the 2 per cent bonus payments from the DSS.
3 While contributions to personal pensions can be lower than those to occupational schemes, the benefits provided by many low-cost personal pension plans are basic, and dependants may not be adequately provided for.
4 Administrative charges and agent's commission may be deducted from pension contributions.

Pension mortgages

A pension mortgage is a loan which enables an individual to purchase or improve a house. It is an 'interest-only' loan where none of the capital is paid off – only interest payments are made on the loan. On an agreed date, a tax-free lump sum, taken as part of the pension on retirement, is used to pay off the outstanding mortgage loan. The remaining pension is used to buy an annuity which provides a regular income throughout retirement.

The advantage of a pension mortgage is that tax-relief is gained both on the mortgage payments and on the tax-free lump sum. The disadvantage is that a repayment date is fixed well in advance of retirement. Unfortunately, it is not possible to take a smaller lump sum and keep the remainder to boost pension payments.

Future problems may arise in connection with the limit on lump sums which can be taken on retirement. This is currently £150 000. With rising house prices, it is unlikely that this amount will be sufficient to pay off mortgages in the future. The Inland Revenue may review this figure, but there is no guarantee that it will be increased in line with rising prices.

Maintenance of pension rights

Under the Social Security Act 1990, a Register was established which enabled members of pension schemes to trace the benefits to which they have become entitled through the course of their working lives. Individuals may request from the Registrar information required to trace their preserved pensions. The Register will cover both occupational and personal pension schemes.

The Act also makes provision for an Ombudsman and Conciliation Service to investigate and assist members with disputes arising from any pension claims. The cost of this service will be covered by a levy imposed on pension schemes.

Study themes

1 Briefly outline the pension provisions your organisation offers its employees.
2 Discuss the advantages and disadvantages of a final-pay occupational scheme compared with a personal pension.
3 Explain the difference between a 'fully approved' and a 'simplified' COMP scheme.
4 What advice with regard to pension arrangements would you give to an individual who is self-employed?

References

Croner's Reference Book for Employers (1991) Croner Publications, Kingston.
Department of Social Security, 1989. *A Guide to Retirement Pensions*, Leaflet no. NP46, April.
FT, 1990. Days numbered for salary-based schemes? *Financial Times*, 10 April.
Hunt, P., 1988. Must pensions always be a turn off? *Personnel Management*, November, pp. 50–2.
Industrial Society, 1988. *The Employer's Handbook to Pensions*, Industrial Society Press, London.
IRE (Industrial Relations Europe), 1990. *Employment Law*, Summer, ECS: The Wyatt Company, S.A.
Torrington, D., and Hall, L., 1987. *Personnel Management: a New Approach*, Prentice-Hall, Hemel Hempstead.
Wilson, J., and Davies, B., 1988. *Your New Pension Choices*, Tolley, Croydon.

Chapter 27

Cost Control

Controlling the cost of payment arrangements is one of the weakest aspects of personnel management, as well as being one of the most important. The most recent examples of this phenomenon have been in the introduction of performance-related pay. The cost of introduction has often been confidently estimated at 2, 3 or 5 per cent, only to turn out at four or five times that amount in practice.

There are various reasons for this. First is the tendency to think that what people are paid is the same as what it costs to employ them – yet even the addition of employer's National Insurance and pension contribution may add 20 or 30 per cent, and every feature of fringe benefits adds more. Secondly, agreement in principle often turns out to be different in practice – and never, ever cheaper! A nice, clean deal between the head-office personnel team and the national officers of the union will be confidently priced at x per cent, but factory personnel officers and production managers will be faced with a series of anomalies and special cases that are most easily dealt with by buying their way past the problem. Thirdly, there is the problem of the accountants, who like to attribute costs in a way that seems to defy the ability of anyone to isolate the true costs of pay. Finally, there is the personnel specialists' distaste for the stark, lifeless business of keeping an eye on the figures.

With the increasing variety of approaches to payment, and the potential of the computer to bring in improved control, this is an area where the personnel specialist can make a major contribution to business effectiveness, ensuring that the positive aspects of human resources management (regarding the people of the business as assets in which to invest) are made possible by elementary good housekeeping.

Elements of pay cost

What are the various features that constitute the cost of employing someone? First are the elements which relate clearly to the individual. Table 27.1 gives illustrations relating to annual amounts for three hypothetical employees: a sales representative, a personal assistant and an electrician. All are typical figures, the National Insurance rates are those that apply from April 1990: 2 per cent on weekly income up to £46 and 9 per cent on earnings above that figure.

Table 27.1
Annual costs (£) for three hypothetical employees

	Sales rep.	Personal assistant	Electrician
Salary	12 000	8 000	10 000
Overtime			1 000
Bonus		250	
Incentive scheme			750
Performance pay	3 000		
Allowances (e.g. London)	1 500	1 500	1 500
Subtotal	16 500	9 750	13 250
National Insurance	1 316	707	1 026
Pension contribution	1 650	975	1 325
Travel, subsistence etc.	5 000	250	250
Total	24 466	11 482	15 851

In addition there is a range of costs that derive from employing people and applying a whole range of options within the pay framework, for example:

- *Payroll administration* involves the running costs of the system that does the weekly or monthly calculation, issue of pay statements, dealing with expenses claims, allowing for changes in National Insurance rates and so forth, as well as the starting and finishing costs of getting someone on and off the payroll.
- *Incentive schemes*, such as that applying to our hypothetical electrician, involve daily administration and calculation as well as the employment of work study and methods officers.
- *Performance-related pay* has considerable administrative costs

attached to it, mainly in managerial time, to establish targets, assess achievement and interview people about their prospective achievements.

- *Share ownership or profit-related pay arrangements* have an associated administrative cost in addition to the proportion of the profits that is diverted to this purpose.
- *Job evaluation* consumes a great deal of time in dealing with individual cases, as well as consultancy fees where these are paid.
- *Fringe benefits* have costs that are not always apparent, especially where they are a feature of the organisation's business, like low-cost mortgages for bank employees. Costs of company cars are much more tangible.

Compa-ratios

One well-used control device is the comparative ratio, or compa-ratio, which is used to check whether salaries in a particular range or grade are too high, too low or about right in relation to objectives. This has had a new lease of life as a control mechanism since the introduction of performance-related pay (PRP), where it is easy to argue that individual pay levels are right but collectively they may be drifting too high. They are also used to check the situation with incremental pay scales.

Let us first consider the PRP example by assuming that there are ten managers on a pay grade which allows a basic salary of £15 000 to £20 000. There is provision for PRP of 0 to 20 per cent, and the targets are an average of £17 500 for basic salary and £19 000 for salary plus PRP. The formula for calculating the compa-ratio is:

$$\text{Compa-ratio} = \frac{\text{average of all salaries in the range}}{\text{target point}} \times 100$$

The actual situation is shown in Table 27.2.

The average salary is £17 700 and the compa-ratio is 97, which is only slightly below the target. The average of salary plus PRP is £20 530 and the compa-ratio is 108, so PRP has gone significantly above target – especially bearing in mind the basic salary compa-ratio.

It may seem strange to calculate a compa-ratio at all, when the

Table 27.2
Hypothetical basic salaries and PRP

Manager	Salary (£)	PRP (£)	Total (£)
Abbott	15 000	2 000	17 000
Blake	16 000	2 000	18 000
Clarke	16 500	2 000	18 500
Davies	17 000	2 800	19 800
Evans	17 000	2 500	19 500
French	18 000	3 000	21 000
Gordon	18 500	3 000	21 500
Hatch	19 000	3 000	22 000
Inch	20 000	4 000	24 000
Jones	20 000	4 000	24 000

cash figures tell the complete story. The reason is that it makes it possible to compare between different grades, where the cash figures will be very different.

Pay comparison

As well as internal comparison, there is a need to make external comparisons too. This is mainly to establish going rates in the labour market, but it is also necessary to check on costs. There are various approaches to pay comparison.

1 Specialist subscription services

There is much data available in general journals and in annual publications concerning specific occupational groups: the subscriptions can be quite expensive. Table 27.3 illustrates sample computer pay rates in several major organisations. It is reproduced from the *Industrial Relations Review and Report Pay and Benefits Bulletin* no. 272 (25 January 1991).

Industrial Relations Review and Report compiled this table using data from the following sources:

- Salaries and staff issues in computing – 1991 report, The National Computing Centre;
- Hay Data Processing Survey – October 1990, Hay-MSL;
- Computer Economics Ltd – November 1990 survey, London,
- *Computer Users Yearbook* – salary survey, London.

Table 27.3
Computer staff pay rates compared

Organisation (sample job)	Minimum £ p.a.	Maximum £ p.a.	Progression	Effective date
British Telecom				
Operator	9 326	11 660	6% p.a.	1-7-90
Programmer	16 353	20 701	Merit	1-1-90
Systems analyst	16 353	20 701	Merit	1-1-90
Civil Service				
Operator	8 822	10 778	3.4% p.a.	1-4-90
Systems analyst	11 398	16 821	2% p.a.	1-4-90
Cooperative Bank				
Operator	7 867	12 284	Merit	1-7-90
Programmer	14 153	21 151	Merit	1-7-90
Systems analyst	17 237	25 797	Merit	1-7-90
Lloyds Bank				
Operator	9 526	14 289	Merit	1-4-90
Programmer	13 068	19 601	Merit	1-4-90
Systems analyst	13 068	19 601	Merit	1-4-90
Sun Life Assurance				
Operator	9 385	13 328	Merit	1-7-90
Programmer	13 787	18 652	Merit	1-7-90
Systems analyst	16 531	22 366	Merit	1-7-90
NWRHA				
Operator	7 440	8 703	4% p.a.	1-4-90
Programmer	10 589	13 619	4% p.a.	1-4-90
Analyst/programmer	13 251	19 800	4% p.a.	1-4-90

2 Salary clubs

Salary clubs are a popular source of local labour-market information. A group of 6–15 employers agree on a method of supplying each other with regular information about pay rates and structures. Composition of the club is important, to ensure that the information obtained is what is needed – either companies competing directly in the particular labour market or similar companies operating in the same product market. Then each employer has to consider carefully where in the pay league it wants to position itself. It is naïve to assume that you must be at the top of the league for all jobs – though you may wish to be at the top for some.

3 Published data – same occupation

Using telephonists as an example, we can see how information can be taken from published data, such as that of Incomes Data Services, in order to establish prevailing rates of pay for members of a working group that can be clearly defined because the skill can be readily transferred between employers. Table 27.4 summarises information published in *Incomes Data Report* during winter 1990/91.

Table 27.4
Published data on pay rates for telephonists, 1990/91

Company/location	Job title	Pay (£ p.a.)
Rhone Poulenc, Dagenham	Receptionist/Telephonist	6945–9401
Ford Dagenham, Bridgend, Halewood etc.	Telephonist	9525–10 365
Clarks Ltd Avon, Devon	Telephonist	6633–8074
Civil Aviation Authority National	Telephonist	8308–9778
Imperial Tobacco Bristol	Telephonist	8578–9545
Debenhams Manchester	Switchboard operator	6 552–6 916

4 Published data – same labour market

There can also be occasions when it is useful to check on comparative pay rates for people doing different jobs but who might just as readily have chosen to work in your organisation – in other words, they are in the same labour market. Nursing auxiliaries can illustrate this method. They are people with no recognised nursing qualifications and who are not in professional training. If we

assume that such employees are predominantly young and relatively unskilled, then we can compare the pay rates for age with
a number of other jobs that this type of person could do. The pay
rates for nursing auxiliaries at 1 April 1990 were

Minimum	1	2	3	4	5	6
£5715	£5940	£6170	£6425	£6680	£6940	£7195

Table 27.5 lists published 1990 pay rates for shop assistants.
This is a very large group, including many 16+ school-leavers,
who constitute the same general labour market from which nursing
auxiliaries might also come.

Table 27.5
Nursing auxiliaries compared with shop assistants

Employment	£ p.a.
Boots the Chemist (age 18+, provincial areas)	5628–7035
BHS (major cities)	5720
Kwik Save (checkout operator)	5772
Debenhams (entry grade, major cities)	6552–6916
NHS nursing Auxilaries	5715–7195

5 Advertisements

For some occupational groups, a means of establishing the going
rate is to sort through advertisements for job vacancies – particularly for professionals, where there may be a journal produced by
the representative body.

Chartered Surveyor Weekly, for example, is the magazine of the
Royal Institution of Chartered Surveyors. A similar publication is
Surveyor. Both carry extensive job advertising, sometimes with
detailed information on salaries and benefits. A systematic comparison of advertisements in these journals could provide a general
indication of pay and conditions prevailing for quantity surveyors.

Analysing job advertisements has strictly limited reliability, as
the sample is only of companies that wish to advertise in a journal,
and who are willing to specify a precise rate of pay. 'Valuable
package with many benefits' is useless to the salary surveyor.

Other problems come from the limited amount of information about the job that can be gleaned from an advertisement, and it is therefore sometimes difficult to match up jobs. Another problem is the fact that the salary is often not quoted for the higher-status jobs. However, when used in conjunction with other types of information, a reasonable picture of the state of the labour market can be built up.

Study themes

1 How much does it cost your employer to employ you?
2 If you wanted to establish a salary club to compare pay and conditions in your locality, which local employers would you approach and why would you select them?
3 Angela Bowey and Tom Lupton (1973) produced a method of pay comparison to be used between organisations. It was not widely adopted at the time. Would it be useful to you now?
4 Using published data, prepare tables showing the current rates of pay in ten organisations, including your own, for the following jobs:

   (a) telephonist,
   (b) HGV driver,
   (c) computer programmer,
   (d) secretary.

   Is your organisation correctly positioned? Are there non-pay factors that justify your rates being higher or lower than initially seems appropriate? What action is needed?
5 In some organisations there has developed the practice of controlling costs by headcount instead of by paybill, the argument being that the actual long-term cost of employing a person is much greater than any simple financial calculation can measure and that the benefits of employing the *right* people greatly outweigh the financial cost. What do you think of that idea?

References

Armstrong, M., and Murlis, H., 1988. *Reward Management*, IPM/Kogan Page, London.

Bowey, A., and Lupton, T., 1973. *Job and Pay Comparisons*, Gower, Aldershot.

E

Health, Safety and Welfare

Chapter 28

The Health and Safety Framework

The ignorance or carelessness of an employer can endanger employees' health by exposing them to hazardous working conditions; the ignorance or carelessness of employees can endanger themselves; and both employers and employees can easily endanger the health and safety of customers, visitors and members of the local community by their ignorance or carelessness. Furthermore, there is always a conflict between the needs of the employer to push for increased output and the needs of the employee to be protected from the hazards of the workplace.

The nature of the problem has changed. A hundred and fifty years ago it was the long hours and heavy physical demands of the factory system. Today the tensions are more varied and more subtle.

Health, safety and welfare

The personnel manager on the one hand is interested in ensuring physical wholeness and benefits and on the other hand is concerned with psychological wholeness. This is partly to protect individuals from hazard, partly an element in the total personnel approach of ensuring commitment and competence. Physical benefits deal mainly with safeguarding health and safety and providing wholesome conditions, such as paid holidays and reduced working hours. Psychological benefits derive from attempts to offer emotional support, such as counselling, information to counter uncertainty or anxiety, and attempts to improve the human relationships centred on the workplace.

Health, safety, welfare and the personnel role

The development of welfare is closely related to the development of personnel management. There was an employee counselling programme running at the Hawthorne plant of the Western Electric Company from 1936 to 1955, and this was found to benefit both the work and the mental health of the employees. As health and safety legislation in the UK has developed, the personnel department has taken on the role of advising managers on the consequences of this, as well as all the other employment law in the same period.

The personnel management view of the welfare issue is uneasy. In many ways it seems to cast the personnel people in the role of social workers who happen to be on the company payroll, rather than people with a strong contribution to make in the main management drive of the business:

> the personnel function seeks to be . . . a full member of the management team, aiming to participate and contribute to the success and survival of the organisation . . . It is the credibility of personnel management in the eyes of other managers that matters, not their credibility in the eyes of the workforce. (Mackay 1986, p. 32)

On the other hand, some imaginative version of the welfare role is central to maintaining the personnel contribution. Some (for example, Kenny 1975) maintain that this is the very essence of personnel management. As the HRM influence increases personnel managers' concern with the management of managers rather than the management of non-managers (Legge 1989), welfare re-emerges in a smart new suit of clothes. Instead of flowers in the canteen and summer weekend trips to the seaside, the talk is of stress counselling, career advice, benefit packaging, health checks and so on. Now we have the idea of cosseting the core employees on whom the future depends, rather than dispensing goodies to the cap-doffing deserving members of the workforce.

This has tended to legitimise welfare once more, with at least some of the benefits being enjoyed by all members of the undertaking, with a change in emphasis from purely physical to both physical and emotional well-being. Welfare is back.

Health and safety has become an area of increasing interest to trade unions. Eva and Oswald (1981) in their book on the trade union approach to health and safety identify a number of health and safety concerns of the unions in the early 1970s:

- Despite health and safety legislation, the number of accidents in the workplace continued to rise.
- New technologies were continually being introduced, creating fresh hazards not covered by existing laws.
- Changing methods caused new diseases to be identified and attributed to working conditions.
- The bulk of the protective legislation, like the Factories Acts, offered example but no protection to the increasing proportion of the working population who were in jobs outside its scope. There were, for example, over 6 million employees in the welfare and State sectors (like schools, hospitals and government services).
- There was growing doubt about the capacity of the factory inspectorate to ensure compliance with legislative requirements.

It is, of course, basic common sense and civilised behaviour for the employer to make effective health and safety provision, whatever the legal obligations – especially as the human and financial costs of error are so great. The tachograph restrictions on the hours that lorry drivers drive are a protection against the fatigue that could lead to fatality. Early stress counselling for members of aircrew could mean the difference between a safe flight and a disastrous accident. But underlying the clear-cut, dramatic incidents that make newspaper headlines are the numbing statistics of the everyday hazards of work. The annual report of the Health and Safety Executive for 1989–90 (1990) included the following:

- the number of deaths down by 10.6 per cent to 623;
- the number of major injuries down by 5.0 per cent to 32 364;
- the number of three-day injuries up by 4.5 per cent to 163 493.

The personnel manager in any large organisation works with a variety of other specialists, including (probably) a safety officer and at least one nurse, and (possibly) a medical officer, a welfare officer and trained counsellors.

Health and safety legislation

The main legislation is contained in the following statutes:

- the Factories Act 1961,
- the Offices Shops and Railway Premises Act 1963,
- the Fire Precautions Act 1971,
- the Health and Safety at Work Act 1974.

The Health and Safety at Work Act (HASWA) is the most pervasive and has updated the other three, and all four are extended and implemented by a range of regulations, which are usually based on European Community directives. The most significant of these is the 1988 Control of Substances Hazardous to Health Regulations, or COSHH.

An associated feature of the legislative scene is the production of codes of practice, though these are not legally enforceable. Section 15 of HASWA explicitly aims gradually to replace the older statutes by new regulations and approved codes of practice.

The Factories Act 1961

Factories Acts have been progressively updated for over 100 years, and they are no longer quite so central to safety provision as they were, but the 1961 Act still governs many conditions in factories 'where two or more persons are employed in manual labour by way of trade or for the purpose of gain' in a range of operations including, for example, building sites, dry docks and film production.

The Act ensures minimum standards of cleanliness, space for people to work in, temperature and ventilation, lighting, conveniences, clothing, accommodation and first-aid facilities. There are further requirements relating to general safety, fire precautions and statutory registers.

The Offices, Shops and Railway Premises Act 1963

The Offices, Shops and Railway Premises Act extends to these premises protection similar to that provided for factories. The general provisions are very similar to those of the Factories Act, dealing with cleanliness, lighting, ventilation and so on.

The Fire Precautions Act 1971

Premises for which a fire certificate is required are listed in the Fire Precautions Act. These include all premises used as places of work. Certificates are issued by the local fire authority, who can stipulate conditions that have to be met before the fire certificate will be issued. These are most often conditions regarding the means of escape from the building, training for employees in what they should do in case of a fire and limits on the number of people to be allowed on the premises at any one time.

The Health and Safety at Work Act 1974

> The objectives of the Act which are very ambitious, include both raising the standards of safety and health for all persons at work, and protection of the public, whose safety and health may be put at risk by the activities of persons at work. Because it is of general application, it brings within statutory protection many classes of persons who were previously unprotected. (Howells and Barrett 1982, p. 1)

HASWA also imposes criminal liability on those who fail to comply with its provisions. It enlarges the authority of some pre-existing bodies and creates others.

The Health and Safety Commission

The Commission has seven to nine members responsible for carrying out the policy of HASWA and providing advice to those with responsibilities imposed upon them by the Act. It issues codes of practice and regulations, as well as having the power to make inquiries and investigations. The main executive body, appointed by the Commission, is the Health and Safety Executive.

The Factory Inspectorate

Factory inspectors were first employed in 1833, but their role was enlarged by the 1974 Act to give them the power to issue improve-

ment and prohibition notices to appropriate employers. They have
the general right to enter employers' premises; carry out investigations; take measurements, photographs and recordings; take
equipment and materials and examine books and documents.
Recently the number of inspectors has increased, from 681 in 1973
to 823 in 1985 and 1239 in 1990.

The Employment Medical Advisory Service

EMAS provides advice to government on industrial medicine and
a team of medical advisers to carry out medical examinations of
employees whose health may have been endangered by their
work.

Enforcement

Enforcement of HASWA and associated provisions is by a varied
and comprehensive range of means that are more extensive than
for previous legislation.

Employer health and safety policy

The Act requires every employer to have a written statement of
policy on health and safety, together with a note of the arrangements for implementation. All employees should be advised of
what the policy is, and it should be kept up to date, because of
the speed with which new and unexpected health hazards develop.

Many employers have inevitably met the letter rather than the
spirit of the law on this matter. Many policies are no more than
ringing phrases; others express a clear intention to safeguard
employee health and safety, but say little about implementation
(Booth 1985). Booth comments that of 121 policy documents
investigated, most expressed a clear commitment to health and
safety, but few contained appropriate details of the necessary
arrangements for implementing the policy. Michael Armstrong
suggests an approach:

> The general policy statement should be a declaration of the
> intention of the employer to safeguard the health and safety

of his employees. It should emphasise four fundamental points: first, that the safety of employees and the public is of paramount importance; second, that safety will take precedence over expediency; third, that every effort will be made to involve all managers, supervisors and employees in the development and implementation of health and safety procedures; and fourth, that health and safety legislation will be complied with in the spirit as well as the letter of the law. (1988, p. 280)

He also provides (ibid. pp. 656–7) a sample of a company policy, which is a useful starting-point, although it is important always to conceive and develop the policy in line with the actual operations of the business, rather than in the abstract.

Managerial responsibility

The management of the organisation carry the prime responsibility for implementing the policy and for operating the plant and equipment in the premises safely – meeting all the Act's requirements whether specified in the policy statement or not.

This is a responsibility imposed on two separate categories of manager:

(a) employer or 'boardroom level manager' duties: these are the duties of officers who act within the 'brain area' of a corporation, formulating corporate strategies and providing the necessary resources for achieving the objectives of the corporation, including its legal liabilities.
(b) manager's duties: the duties of officials employed as line managers who apply the corporate resources and carry out the day to day activities in accordance with policies laid down by the board of the corporation in order to comply with the law. (Howells and Barrett 1982)

Where there is negligence, proceedings can be taken against an individual responsible manager as well as against the employing organisation. The question of liability will depend first on whether or not the employer had explicitly delegated responsibility, whether it was reasonable in the circumstances to delegate the responsibility and whether the person to whom the responsibility had been delegated was negligent.

An appropriate management appointment is of a safety officer, manager or director with specific responsibility for advising 'board-room level managers' on safety policy and who is responsible for the implementation of the policy. This does not necessarily absolve the employer from responsibility, but it can improve safe working.

Employee responsibility

A radical innovation of HASWA was the duty placed on employees while they are at work to take reasonable care for the safety of themselves and others. The employee is, therefore, legally bound to comply with the employer's safety rules and instructions, and a deliberate breach can lead to criminal prosecution.

Employers can also regard misconduct as a fair ground to dismiss employees who refuse to obey safety rules. In *Mortimer* v. *V. L. Churchill* 1979, an employee who refused to wear safety goggles for a particular process was warned of possible dismissal because the safety committee had decreed that goggles or similar protection were necessary. He refused on the grounds that he had done the job previously without the goggles and did not see that they were now necessary. He was dismissed, and the tribunal did not allow his claim of unfair dismissal (see IPM 1986).

Employees also have a duty to cooperate with the employer in safety matters.

Safety representatives

Another novel HASWA device is the power of safety representatives, appointed by the recognised trade union. Safety representatives have a legal duty to consult with employers and are entitled to paid time-off for training to enable them to carry out their functions, which are:

- to investigate potential hazards and dangerous occurrences at the workplace and to examine the causes of accidents at the workplace;
- to investigate complaints by employees on matters of individual health, safety or welfare at work;
- to make representations to the employer on these matters and on general matters affecting the health, safety and welfare of

employees at the workplace;
- to carry out general inspections and inspections following accidents, dangerous occurrence or notifiable disease – including the inspection of documents;
- to represent the employees in workplace consultations with Health and Safety Executive inspectors;
- to receive information from inspectors, and
- to attend meetings of safety committees.

(Condensed from Safety Representatives and Safety Committees Regulations 1977.)

Safety committees

Although the main thrust of the Act to involve the workforce is through the safety representatives, the safety committee is envisaged as the forum through which management and employee involvement is combined to keep under review

> the measures taken to ensure the health and safety at work of . . . employees and such other functions as may be prescribed. (Health and Safety at Work Act 1974, Section 2(7))

The safety representatives have to be consulted about the membership of the committee, and advice on their function and conduct is provided in the guidance notes on safety representatives (Health and Safety Commission 1976).

Research by Leopold and Coyle (1981) showed a great increase in the number of safety committees since the passing of the Act, especially in companies employing fewer than 200 people and in those industries where there was previously a low level of accidents. Despite this development, the level of accidents remains higher in smaller manufacturing establishments than in larger ones. This was confirmed in analysis of the data by the Health and Safety Executive:

> employees in establishments of under 50 people appear to be some 20 per cent more at risk of major injury than those in medium to large establishments (100–1000 people) and some 40 per cent more at risk than those in very large establishments (over 1000 people). Equally those in medium-sized

establishments appear to be around 20 per cent more at risk of major injury than those in very large establishments. (Thomas 1991, p. 21)

Codes of practice

Codes of good practice have been available since well before HASWA, but their use has become much more widespread and it becomes difficult for an employer to find a defence against a charge of negligence if the advice contained in a code has been ignored. They may be issued by the Health and Safety Commission itself, or adopted by it after being prepared by a different body. Codes issued so far relate to:

- time-off for the training of safety representatives,
- the protection of persons against ionising radiation,
- control of substances hazardous to health (various).

Improvement notices and prohibition notices

Inspectors can serve improvement notices on individuals who they regard as being in breach of HASWA or related provisions. An improvement notice specifies the breach and requires its remedy within a stated period. The 'individual' on whom the notice is served is nearly always a member of management, but it could also be an employee who was deliberately disobeying safety instructions.

Alternatively, where there is a risk of serious personal injury, the inspector may issue a prohibition notice, which prohibits an operation or activity being continued until specified remedial action has been taken. There is a right of appeal against both types of notice.

Control of Substances Hazardous to Health Regulations (COSHH) 1988

COSHH comprises 19 regulations and four codes of practice, and represents the most far-reaching health and safety legislation since HASWA. It aims to protect all employees who work with substances hazardous to their health, by placing a requirement on the employer regarding the handling, use and control of such substances. The regulations apply to all workplaces and place a responsibility for good environmental hygiene on both employer and employees. All substances are included, except those having separate regulations, such as asbestos and lead. The regulations have five principal features:

1 *Assessing the risks and identifying what precautions are needed.* This assessment can be a demanding operation. Cherrie and Faulkner (1989) reported that one employer was using 25 000 different substances. Assessors may be employees or external consultants, but employees will need careful training (Mountfield 1989).

2 *Introducing measures to control or prevent the risk* These are likely to involve removing the substance, changing the processes or controlling the substance by, for example, total or partial enclosure of the process or increased ventilation. Such measures should reduce maximum exposure limits (MEL) and meet Occupational exposure standards (OES). For a fuller explanation, see Powley (1989).

3 *Ensuring control measures are used, procedures followed and equipment regularly maintained* Where employees are necessarily exposed to the substance, that exposure should be monitored and recorded.

4 *Carrying out health surveillance* Where a particular substance is known to be dangerous, regular surveillance of the employees involved can identify problems early. Records should be kept and should be accessible to employees.

5 *Employee information and training* Those exposed to risk need to be informed of those risks and trained in appropriate procedures and precautions.

Stress

> Untreated and unresolved crises affect worker productivity and contribute to labour turnover; the annual cost to US business of alcoholism alone is put at $5 billion. The 'hard' costs of ill and unhappy employees (absence, recruitment, and training expenses) are high enough. Still greater are

inefficient and inadequate job performance, discredit to the company and diminished morale engendered among co-workers. The bottom line? Estimated cost for 'emotional problems' in US business and industry is $17 billion a year. (Slaikeu and Frank 1986)

Stress at work was originally discussed only as a problem for executives, partly because of the stereotype of the senior manager working long hours with a high degree of responsibility – to say nothing of business lunches and high living. This remains an aspect of considerable interest (for example, Cooper and Marshall 1980 and Palmer 1989), with the strange corollary that such people feel humiliated if anyone suggests that their job is *not* stressful. Research soon demonstrated that work-related stress is experienced by people in a wide range of occupations, especially in manual work (Cooper and Smith 1985).

Different people react to the same pressures in different ways and to different pressures in different ways, so it is the response of the individual that determines whether he or she displays the symptoms of stress. Stress is not uniform. One person can be stimulated by financial responsibility and anxious in social situations, while another may be stimulated in social situations and find financial responsibility stressful.

Stress is a threat to both physical and psychological well-being, so there is always a potential detriment to the person's working performance as well as to his or her state of mind. Furthermore, stress is something that affects the whole person all the time, no matter what its source. Someone who is experiencing severe stress away from work will be affected at work, and vice versa. Glowinkowski (1985, pp. 1–2) summarises the effects:

> While stress can be short-lived it can represent a continuous burden leading to short term outcomes such as tension, increased heart rate, or even increased drinking or smoking. In the long term, stress is said to cause disorders such as depression, coronary heart disease, diabetes melitus and bronchial asthma . . . Indeed, while stress may be a direct causal factor in heart disease, its effects may be indirect. Stress may increase smoking and cause overeating, which are also high risk factors in coronary artery disease.

Just as most people look forward to the weekend to escape the stresses and strains of working life for a couple of days, we must also bear in mind that those under stress at home may well benefit from the change of pace and problems that work presents. Although we all react differently, there are five main sources of work-related stress:

Workload   There may be too much work, so that a person feels overwhelmed and unable to cope; or there may be too little to do, leading to boredom or the fear of being superfluous. On other occasions the work may be too difficult, or not sufficiently demanding.

Uncertainty   We all like some variety, but may fray at the edges when there is too much. Much of the ever-expanding literature on the management of change is devoted to this apparent problem of overcoming resistance to change, with the resistance being attributed to uncertainty about the implications of the change.

Relationships at work   Few people have sufficient social poise to manage well all their relationships at work, and some will find some aspects very hard to take. Some will dread rows, while others like 'clearing the air'. Some cannot cope with unpopularity or mistrust.

Organisational culture   The experience of working in an organisation invariably limits a person's individual freedom at the same time as extending the range of responsibility. Personal stress is usually reduced by increasing the degree of participation in decisions affecting the job and the place of work.

Balance between work and non-work   There is always a potential conflict of interest between the demands of the job and the demands of home life. This means that there are competing, legitimate demands on time and commitment that can cause considerable stress to the person who seeks to satisfy one set of demands while experiencing guilt or apprehension about failing to satisfy the other set. This usually reaches its peak in middle age, when the career job may be very demanding at the same time as home problems of adolescent children and ageing relatives may also be at their peak.

Employing organisations provide a variety of facilities that may help with stress problems.

Counselling

> Counselling
> - is not thinking or acting for another person, nor is it directing them towards a decision
> - is not repeating cliches about what someone else ought to do
> - is more than simply being sympathetic towards another person's feelings, talking something over or merely the application of techniques
> - does not impose solutions, opinions, values or judgements. It does not minimise, negate or question the worth of what the person wishes to discuss
> - is not about criticising or manipulating the person.
> (Megranahan 1989, p. 3)

There has been resistance to the idea of stress counselling, particularly in traditionally 'macho' areas like manufacturing. To go to a counsellor seemed to be a sign of weakness, but gradually this inhibition is being overcome. The counselling may come from a variety of sources – for example, the 'buddy' or trusted working colleague, the manager or the personnel manager – but it is often more useful to be counselled by someone who is not a part of the job itself, especially if the job is the source of the stress.

Independent counselling could come from the specialists on the payroll who are seen as not being part of the management process, such as the medical officer, occupational health nurse or welfare officer, or from a specialised counsellor. Someone in this type of role would be able just to listen to the problem without judging it, aiming to provide a supportive atmosphere to help a person to find his or her own solution to the problem.

The counsellor should also be well placed to offer advice on practical matters, such as aspects of taxation, social security provision, finance and debt, suggesting other sources of assistance where appropriate. Some of the more specialised problems on which counselling is needed include diet, smoking, alcohol and drug abuse, the control of AIDS and the threat of violence. The medical officer, if there is one, would be well placed to deal with most of these, as well as providing some continuing monitoring of the person's progress.

AIDS is such a frightening epidemic that most managers will no doubt feel that it is best left to social workers and the medical profession. Those with AIDS or carrying the HIV virus probably agree, but there are inescapable issues for managers to consider. Those who travel abroad – espcially men – are often at greater risk of infection than those who stay at home, and the infection risk is highest in certain countries where western visitors are more likely to be travelling on business than as tourists, so there is a need for those travelling on company business to be advised of the risks. More importantly there is the probable experience at work of the AIDS/HIV sufferer. The disease causes such fear that colleagues may refuse to work with the victim or subject him or her to harassment and abuse.

Positive health programmes

Positive health programmes can be used to relieve or prevent stress. The most popular are the various types of dance exercise, like aerobics, which provide excellent exercise to relieve tension and stimulate the circulation. More esoteric are meditation and yoga. Autogenic training is developed through exercises in body awareness and physical relaxation which lead to passive concentration. It is believed that the ability to achieve this breaks through the vicious circle of excessive stress and that, as well as the many mental benefits, there are benefits to the body, including relief of physical symptoms of anxiety and the reduction of cardiovascular risk (Carruthers 1982). Chemo feedback (Positive Health Centre 1985) is an early warning system to pick up signs of unfavourable stress from the completion of a computerised questionnaire together with a blood test. This approach is being offered as a 'stress-audit' on a companywide basis.

Study themes

1 Read Eva and Oswald (1981) and the latest annual report of the Health and Safety Commission. How have health and safety issues changed since the initial analysis by Eva and Oswald?

2 How are the requirements of the Fire Precautions Act 1971 implemented where you work?

3 Devise a health and safety policy for your organisation, including information about:

- specific hazards and how to deal with them,
- management responsibility for safety,
- how the policy is to be implemented.

How does your draft differ from the official policy? How do you explain the differences?

4 Read Powley (1989). What do you understand by MEL and OES?

5 Read Cherrie and Faulkner (1989) and Thomas (1991). How can safety standards in smaller manufacturing companies be improved? Why are they poorer than in larger companies?

6 Read Gill and Martin (1976) and Pirani and Reynolds (1976). What methods are effective in ensuring safe working and what methods are relatively ineffective?

7 Read Booth (1985) and the Royal Society (1983). What do you see as the benefits and drawbacks of risk assessment as an approach to health and safety?

8　　We are buying the skills, energy, industry and commitment of the people who work here. While they are at work we don't feel we've got responsibility to manage their social life, marriages, religious faith or anything else . . .

To what extent do you agree with that opinion expressed by a personnel manager? How do you think employees see the provision of facilities at work to deal with their personal, emotional problems?

9 Is an interest in welfare an advantage or a disadvantage when trying to develop the authority and status of personnel management?

References

Armstrong, M., 1988. *Handbook of Personnel Management Practice*, 3rd edn, Kogan Page, London.

Booth, R , 1985. What's new in health and safety management? *Personnel Management*. April.

Carruthers, M., 1982. Train the mind to calm itself. *General Practitioner*, 16 July.

Cherrie, J., and Faulkner, C., 1989. Will the COSHH regulations improve occupational health? *Safety Practitioner*, February, pp. 6–7.

Cooper, C. L., and Marshall, J., 1980. *White Collar and Professional Stress*. John Wiley, Chichester.

Cooper, C. L., and Smith, M. J., (eds.), 1985. *Job Stress and Blue Collar Work*. John Wiley, Chichester.

Eva, D., and Oswald, R., 1981. *Health and Safety at Work*. Pan Books, London.

Gill, J., and Martin, K., 1976. Safety management – reconciling rules with reality, *Personnel Management*, June, pp. 36–9.

Glowinkowski, S. P., 1985. *Managerial Stress: a Longitudinal Study*. Unpublished PhD thesis, UMIST, Manchester.

Health and Safety Commission, 1976. *Safety Representatives and Safety Committees*. HMSO, London.

Health and Safety Commission, 1978. *Health and Safety in Manufacturing and Service Industries 1976*. HMSO, London.

Health and Safety Executive, 1988. *Introducing COSHH*, HMSO, London.

Health and Safety Executive, 1990. *Annual Report 1989/90*. HMSO, London.

Howells, R., and Barrett, B., 1982. *The Health and Safety at Work Act: a Guide for Managers*. Institute of Personnel Management, London.

IPM, 1986. News and notes: *Mortimer v. V. L. Churchill 1979*. *Personnel Management*, March.

Kenny, T., 1975. Stating the case for welfare. *Personnel Management*, September, pp. 18–21, 35.

Legge, K., 1989. Human resource management: a critical analysis, in Storey, J., (ed.), *New Perspectives on Human Resource Management*, Routledge, London, pp. 19–40.

Leopold, J., and Coyle, R., 1981. A healthy trend in safety committees?, *Personnel Management*, May, pp. 30–32.

Levinson, H., 1964. *Executive Stress*, Harper & Row, New York.

Mackay, L. E., 1986. *The Workforce and the Personnel Function*. Unpublished paper, UMIST, Manchester.

Megranahan, M., 1989. *Counselling*, Institute of Personnel Management, London.

Mountfield, B., 1989. Preparing for COSHH at ICI, *Occupational Health Review*, June/July, pp. 6–7.

Palmer, S., 1989. Occupational stress, *The Safety and Health Practitioner*, August, pp. 16–18.

Pirani, M., and Reynolds, J., 1976. Gearing up for safety, *Personnel Management*, February, pp. 25–9.

Positive Health Centre, 1985. *Chemo Feedback*. Positive Health Centre, London.

Powley, D., 1989. Life under the COSHH, *Manufacturing Engineer*,

September, pp. 24–31.

The Royal Society, 1983. *Risk Assessment: a Study Group Report.* The Royal Society, London.

The Safety Representatives and Safety Committees Regulations, 1977. HMSO, London.

Slaikeu, K., and Frank, C., 1986. Manning the psychological first aid post. *Management Today.* February, pp. 35–6.

Thomas, P., 1991. Safety in smaller manufacturing establishments, *Employment Gazette*, January, pp. 20–4.

Chapter 29

Industrial Safety and Personnel Management

In this chapter we will first consider the incidence and economic/ social costs of industrial accidents and disease. We will then review the changing role of personnel in the development and maintenance of a safe and healthy working environment.

Industrial accidents and disease

Accident statistics

Accident statistics are important indicators of safety standards. Analysis of these figures can provide information about where and why accidents are happening, so that preventative measures in the forms of safety policy and legislation can be accurately directed.

Under the Reporting of Injuries, Diseases and Dangerous Occurrences Regulations 1985 (RIDDOR), employers are required to report to the Health and Safety Executive (HSE) or to local authorities the following:

- fatal accidents – including a death occurring up to a year after the accident;
- major injuries and accidents and certain work-related diseases, as specified by RIDDOR;
- 'over-three-day' injuries – accidents causing more than three consecutive days' incapacity for work;
- dangerous occurrences – incidents which were potentially dangerous.

All accident records must be kept by the employer for a minimum period of three years.

The HSE Annual Reports, which provide the most accurate data regarding accidents to employees at work, give the figures in Table 29.1 for the period 1986–9.

Table 29.1

Accidents to employees at work, 1986–9 (from HSE 1990)

Year	Type of accident		
	Fatal	Major	Over-3-day
1986–7	355	20 246	158 344
1987–8	360	19 609	159 195
1988–9	514*	18 933	155 112

*Includes the 167 fatalities of the Piper Alpha disaster, 6 July 1988.

Without the figures from the Piper Alpha disaster, the fatal injury rate for 1988–9 would have been similar to that for the previous two years, following a declining trend. As far as major and over-three-day injuries are concerned, if we take into account the increase in employment levels over the past two to three years, these figures show an overall reduction in accident incidence rates.

Figure 29.1 (from HSE 1990) shows the 15 industrial areas with the highest fatal and major injury rates. These industries account for 42 per cent of reported fatal and major injuries, while comprising only 14 per cent of total employment figures.

How accurate are these figures? Changes in the reporting arrangements for accidents and industrial diseases may limit the extent to which useful comparisons over time can be made. (The most recent amendments were introduced under RIDDOR, effective 1 April 1986.) Under-reporting is a particular problem in certain industries, such as construction and agriculture, and may lead to difficulties when making comparisons *between* industries. However, this effect is of less importance when making comparisons over time, whether for individual industries or generally.

Causes of accidents

Accidents at work are generally caused by a combination of events. However, analysis of accident statistics has identified a number of contributory factors which can be directly linked to injuries at work (Eva and Oswald 1981):

Figure 29.1

Number of fatal and major injuries per 100,000 employees in the 15 highest-risk industrial sectors (provisional figures 1988/89)

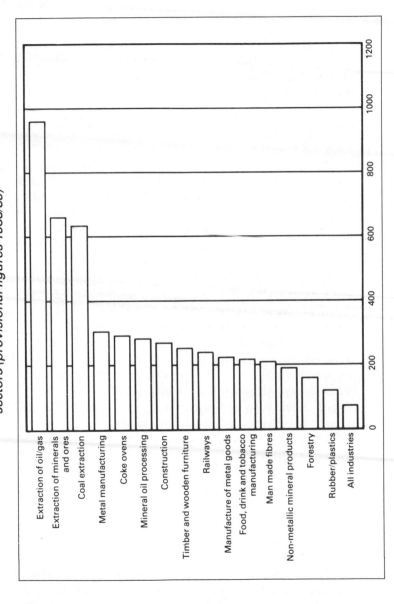

1 Lack of training/supervision and information regarding hazards

Under the Health and Safety at Work Act 1974 (HASWA), employers are obliged to provide employees with adequate information, instruction, training and supervision to ensure safe working practices. Training should be available on a 'refresher' basis in order to keep both workers and supervisors up to date on safety issues.

2 Unsafe design and irregular maintenance of equipment

More attention needs to be paid to the design of machinery. Guards should be fitted to prevent workers from coming into contact with dangerous moving parts. All equipment should be regularly inspected for mechanical faults and for wear and tear.

3 Design of the workplace and work systems

Workplaces should be ergonomically designed to suit the requirements of the workforce, product, process, etc. This should be coupled with safe and effective work systems.

4 Poor working conditions

Environmental hazards at work may include noise, noxious fumes, chemicals, lighting and temperature. Such conditions may contribute to the development of industrial diseases (see below).

5 Inadequate analysis of accident statistics and patterns

See above.

In addition, there is the *human factor* in accident causation. This may include:

- error of judgement or misunderstanding of the instructions given,
- lack of experience or skill,
- deliberate refusal to obey safety rules,

- a basically unsafe attitude to work — as evidenced by those accidents caused through horseplay.

The role of human error in accident causation, with particular respect to management responsibility, is considered in chapter 30.

Occupational diseases

An occupational disease arises out of prolonged exposure to particular working conditions, and normally develops gradually over a period of time. In some cases the link between work and the disease is clear – for example, asbestosis. In other situations, however, occupation may be only one of a number of contributory factors – for example, bronchitis may be caused by working conditions (exposure to dust, extremes of temperature) but it may equally well be due to poor living conditions, smoking etc. Some examples of work-related illnesses are considered below:

Occupational deafness

High noise levels can lead to permanent deafness or to impaired hearing. In addition, noise increases stress, and may cause heart strain, hormone disorders and stomach problems. Occupational deafness is the largest single category of compensated occupational disease. The problem of noise at work can be tackled in a variety of ways: redesign of equipment, sound-proofing, ear-protection, and reduction of exposure time to noise.

Repetitive strain injuries

Repetitive strain injuries (RSI) are a group of musculo-skeletal and tendinous injuries found in the upper limb, shoulder girdle and neck. They are generally caused by making repetitive movements or by having to keep the muscles in a static, tense position for long periods of time. The disease has affected a variety of workers, including assembly-line workers, poultry packers and office staff who use keyboards – for example, typists and computer operators. The introduction of new technology appears to have exacerbated the problem – for example, high-speed keyboards require faster movements and allow for fewer breaks. In addition, such workers are often paid on a bonus basis for meeting particular production targets.

Recent initiatives by the TUC and the Health and Safety Executive to tackle the problem of RSI have come up with the following recommendations (Hill 1989):

- work organisation allowing frequent breaks from the keyboard (at least every hour) and a variety of tasks;
- training for employees regarding the risks of RSI;
- special exercise programmes;
- ergonomic design of tools, workstations and equipment.

Backstrain

It has been estimated that 70 per cent of workers in the UK suffer from backstrain at some point in their lives, leading to a loss of some 15 million working days every year (Eva and Oswald 1981). Most of these injuries are caused by lifting. Remedies include adequate training in lifting and carrying techniques, redesign of work processes to avoid heavy or awkward lifting and, where appropriate, introduction of mechanical lifting and handling equipment.

Passive smoking

Workplace smoking – particularly the effects of 'sidestream' tobacco smoke – has long been a contentious issue. Evidence in the late 1980s from the DHSS-sponsored Independent Committee on Smoking and Health indicated that passive smoking poses a significant health risk to non-smokers. More recently, in August 1990, an asthma sufferer won a ruling against her employer on passive smoking at work. She claimed to have developed acute respiratory problems due to colleagues' smoking. Although the decision was based on special factors, including the claimant's sensitive reaction to cigarette smoke, it is likely that this case will lead to renewed interest in the problem of workplace smoking.

A number of organisations have already introduced smoking policies. A survey of 14 000 office staff found that 14 per cent of companies ban smoking in office areas, and 15 per cent allow smoking only in designated areas (IAM 1987) Employer motives for introducing policies include general concern for improved staff health, reduction of absenteeism through smoke-related illnesses and response to pressure from non-smokers. For further information see *Smoking Policies at Work* (HEA 1987).

Economic and social costs of industrial accidents and disease

It is difficult to place a figure on the financial costs of accidents and industrial diseases, since any estimate would involve a number of factors:

- *Cost to the individual* – physical and psychological effects of accidents or disease, lost earnings;
- *Cost to the employer* – lost production (on average, five days are lost through accidents and disease for every one lost through industrial disputes), hiring and training of replacement labour, repair of machinery, investigation of accidents.
- *Cost to the NHS* – hospitalisation and treatment of serious injuries.

  In addition, there is also the cost of providing victims of accident or disease with *compensation* for their injuries.

Compensation for industrial injuries

There are two main routes that employees may take in order to claim compensation for an industrial injury or disease.

Common law

Employers have an obligation in common law to take reasonable steps to maintain the health and safety of their workers. These should include the provision and maintenance of a safe place of work, a safe system of work, safe machinery and equipment and the employment of competent employees. If an individual is injured in the course of employment, a claim for damages may be brought against the employer through the civil courts. The basis of such claims is generally negligence.

Social security

The State compensation scheme was originally introduced via the National Insurance (Industrial Injuries) Act 1946. This replaced the earlier Workmen's Compensation Acts 1925–1945 under which an employer was liable to pay compensation for death or disablement resulting from employment. The scheme provided comprehensive insurance against (i) personal injury or death by accident arising out of an individual's employment, (ii) prescribed industrial diseases. The State scheme was subsequently changed and consolidated into the Social Security Act 1975. Most recent amendments were introduced via the Social Security Acts 1986 and 1988.

Industrial injuries disablement benefit is payable to individuals injured or disabled as a result of an accident at work. The claim is not affected if the individual continues working or returns to work. The amount of benefit payable is directly related to the degree of disablement suffered by the claimant – for example, total loss of sight or hearing counts as 100 per cent disablement and qualifies for maximum benefit. Benefit is not normally paid for disablement of less than 14 per cent.

Individuals may also qualify for benefit under the industrial injuries scheme is they become disabled by an *industrial disease*. Under the scheme, benefit is payable only to those individuals suffering from a 'prescribed' industrial disease. Diseases are prescribed in connection with a particular occupation or working conditions – for example, mesothelioma must arise from working with asbestos. If there is a long delay between the cause of the disease and its subsequent diagnosis, occupational causation is difficult to prove. It is therefore more than likely that the number of compensation awards grossly understates the true incidence of industrial disease.

The State scheme is additional to the right to sue at common law; however, any benefits payable will be taken into account when assessing damages. (See Selwyn 1982.)

More information on the Industrial Injuries scheme can be found in DSS leaflets N I6, *Industrial Injuries Disablement Benefit*; NI 2, *If You Have an Industrial Disease*; NI 196, *Social Security Benefit Rates*.

Health and safety and the personnel role

Health and safety has not traditionally been at the forefront of the personnel function – issues such as recruitment, industrial relations and management development have tended to push health and safety matters down the personnel manager's list of priorities. However, new regulations on hazardous substances, noise and VDUs, together with impending European legislation, have led to a reappraisal of the importance of health and safety within the personnel context (Falconer 1990). We consider below some of the health and safety issues facing personnel managers, in addition to those mentioned in chapter 28 (Howells and Barrett 1982).

Training

Training of employees is a key requirement of HASWA. Personnel managers need to review all current training programmes and to assess whether any additions or changes should be introduced to cover previously neglected areas:

- *Induction training* All new employees should receive a copy of the company health and safety policy, together with adequate information regarding work systems, safety rules and emergency procedures.
- *On-the-job training* – including the operation of machinery, particular hazards and post-accident procedures. This training should be ongoing and take account of any new equipment or changes in procedure.
- *Requirements of legislation* Employees should be made aware of their statutory requirements under HASWA.
- *Management training* – to enable managers to introduce, maintain and monitor safe systems of work.

Reporting and recording

The personnel manager should ensure the maintenance of all statutory records and complete all reporting required by law – that is, fatal and major accidents, over-three-day injuries and dangerous occurrences.

Relationship with other health and safety specialists

The personnel manager is a key member of the health and safety team. Together with the following professionals, personnel is responsible for advising management on health and safety policy and legislation.

Safety officer

While there is no legal requirement to appoint a safety officer, many large organisations – particularly within the industrial sector – have an officer who is responsible for implementing, operating and monitoring the company's health and safety policy. Trade unions tend to view the safety officer as a member of the management team, or at least as an adviser to management. It is therefore important that safety officers consult with union representatives and employees at all times.

Occupational health services

Many organisations employ medical officers and/or nursing staff to provide a health-care service to employees, to carry out pre-employment screening and to advise on existing or potential hazards. Medically qualified staff can also provide a valuable input to discussions on health and safety, while still being seen by the majority of employees as impartial and detached from management. The relationship between medical officers (and nurses), management, trade unions and employees is a complex one and may occasionally lead to a conflict of interests as regards disclosure of information and medical confidentiality.

Study themes

1 Outline the steps you would take to introduce a smoking policy into your organisation. Useful references: Upton (1988), HEA (1987) and IRS (1987).
2 Read the article by Gill and Martin (1976). Explain the dissonance which occurs between prescribed safety practices and actual working practices. Can you think of any examples within

your own organisation? How can this conflict be resolved?
3 What do you consider to be the main advantages of an occupational health service? Are there any disadvantages?

Check-list

1 Health and Safety at Work

(a) Who is responsible for ensuring that the statutory requirement regarding accident notification is fulfilled?
    Is there an accident log book? If so, where is it kept? When was it last checked?
(b) Are employees aware of the correct procedure for accident reporting? Is this covered during induction?
(c) Does your organisation conduct health and safety inspections? Are new work processes and new machinery checked for potential safety hazards before introduction?
(d) What hazardous operations are carried out within your organisation? Are employees provided with protective equipment? Is it used?

2 Role of health and safety specialists

(a) Who has overall specific responsibility for health and safety within your organisation? Outline the post-holder's main duties.
(b) Do you provide an occupational health service for your employees? If so, are the following covered:

- pre-employment screening?
- health care for company employees?
- advice regarding health and safety hazards?

(c) Explain the relationship which exists between occupational health staff, personnel and line management.
(d) Does your organisation meet the statutory requirements regarding the provision of qualified first-aiders and first-aid equipment?
(e) Who is responsible for keeping medical records? For how

long are these records kept?
(f) Does your organisation have a health and safety policy? Are employees aware of this policy? How often is it reviewed and by whom?
(g) Is health and safety training provided for workers? If so, when? At induction, on-the-job? Is this training ongoing?

References

Eva, D., and Oswald, R., 1981. *Health and Safety at Work*, Pan Books, London.

Falconer, H., 1990. Safe and Sound, *Personnel Today*, October, p. 53.

Gill, J., and Martin, K., 1976. Safety management – reconciling roles with reality, *Personnel Management*, June, pp. 36–9.

HEA, 1987. *Smoking Policies at Work*, Health Education Authority, London.

Hill, C., 1989. Getting to grips with repetitive strain injuries, *Personnel Management*, March, pp. 32–5.

Howells, R., and Barrett, B., 1982. *The Health and Safety at Work Act: A Guide for Managers*, Institute of Personnel Management, London.

HSE, 1990. *Health and Safety Executive Annual Report 1988/89*, HMSO, London.

IAM, 1987. *The 1987 Office Salaries Analysis*, Institute of Administrative Management, Orpington.

IRS 1987. No-smoking policies in the workplace, Health and Safety Information Bulletin 140, pp. 2–6, in *Industrial Relations Review and Report* 397, 4 August 1987, Industrial Relations Services, London.

Selwyn, N., 1982. *Law of Health and Safety at Work*, Butterworth, London.

Upton, R., 1988. Has workplace smoking become a burning issue? *Personnel Management*, January, pp. 44–9.

Chapter 30

Social Problems and Social Responsibility

> In 1969 *Fortune* magazine reported on a survey of the 500 largest business organisations in the United States, examining the question of the social responsibilities of companies. At that time the companies gave, as their top social priorities: supporting education (62%), combating air and water pollution (58%), ensuring equality of pay for minorities (57%), employing the hard-core unemployed (54%). (Jones 1972, p. 22)

Although priorities today may have changed, the majority of organisations accept that, in addition to satisfying the profit and business needs of their shareholders, they also have responsibilities concerning a wide range of other issues. In this chapter we shall examine the social responsibility of organisations with regard to the employment problems of workers with special needs, unsafe working practices, pollution and the environment.

Employees with special needs

The long-term unemployed

Direct government responses to unemployment over the last two decades have included job creation schemes, employment-subsidy schemes, training schemes and youth employment schemes (see Moon and Richardson (1985) for a review).

In 1988 the Conservative government launched the Employment Training scheme (ET) to provide practical and directed training for the long-term unemployed. The practical training involves a work-experience placement within an organisation; the directed training (off-the-job learning) being provided either by a college or by an employer. However, ET has run into some difficulties – many employers do not provide adequate training, and some have simply used trainees as additional unskilled labour. The scheme has also been marked by a high drop-out rate among trainees.

As a result, a number of firms are developing a new approach to training for the long-term unemployed in the form of *customised* training. This involves employers designing courses to meet their own specific requirements. Potential recruits are identified by a community-based organisation which provides additional support both to employers and to trainees. These courses guarantee the trainee an interview after training, and increase possible job opportunities and promotion prospects.

One successful scheme was run jointly by retailers Asda, the Nottingham Task Force and Clarendon College of Further Education. The first two weeks dealt with practical information on job-hunting, job applications and the retail business. The remainder of the course was based in-store under staff supervision. Over 70 long-term unemployed have been recruited to Asda through this scheme (Lowe 1990).

Advantages to employers of such customised training schemes include the opening-up of a new labour source, improved company image in the local community, increased cost-effectiveness and high retention rate amongst trainees. In addition to the long-term unemployed, such courses have also included women returners and members of ethnic minorities. The latest development is a program specially designed for the disabled.

Women returners

Predicted demographic changes and labour shortages suggest that non-traditional sectors of the labour market, such as women with responsibility for children or for elderly or disabled dependants, will be of increasing importance over the next decade.

Women with children   Employers are making increased provision for women to continue working while bringing up a family – for example, career breaks, term-time working and flexible hours (see chapter 4). However, for the majority of women, child-rearing entails a break from working life of five to ten years. What options are open to these women returners?

Some employers have set up training courses in conjunction

with local colleges. Companies sponsor participants for periods of work experience, with the long-term aim of offering permanent recruitment. For example, firms in Northamptonshire have clubbed together to sponsor secretarial training courses at Northampton College (Vize 1990). Many of the women these companies are interested in attracting back to work may already be qualified but are looking for a refresher course to update technical skills and to build up confidence.

Carers Six million people in Britain care for elderly dependants on an unpaid basis. The majority of these carers are middle-aged women. Approximately one-quarter of middle-aged women are carers, compared to 16 per cent of middle-aged men (HMSO 1988). Conservative government policy, as reflected in the White Paper *Caring for people – community care in the next decade and beyond* (November 1989), suggests that the current emphasis on private provision of care will continue. It is thus likely that the above figures will rise.

In order to attract and retain such people as workers, employers will be forced to address the specific problems of 'employee carers'. Worman (1990) describes a range of help programmes open to employers:

- flexible working patterns, including special leave provisions (see chapter 4);
- care support assistance – information regarding care and support services;
- consultation and 'outreach' – discussion with employees and care organisations in the public, private and voluntary sectors, leading to the development of more innovative caring schemes.

Ex-offenders

Ex-offenders are frequently discriminated against by employers (see chapter 19). However, in recent years a number of innovative schemes have been introduced to encourage the recruitment of people with criminal records.

The Apex Trust is a welfare organisation dealing with the rehabilitation of ex-offenders which works closely with employers. The Trust has recently set up a project which offers work placements to prisoners. Training is provided by employers within prisons, together with placements on a day-release basis (Falconer 1990). In addition, Apex is aiming to launch a two-year pilot scheme which will involve the issuing of a new fidelity bond insurance (A fidelity bond is insurance purchased by employers to protect themselves against loss incurred through the dishonest acts of employees). This will be available to employers who recruit ex-offenders but who are not appropriately covered by their current insurance. For further information see *Releasing the Potential: a Guide to Good Practice for the Employment of People with Criminal Records*, (Apex Trust 1990), endorsed by the IPM, TUC and CBI.

AIDS Sufferers

AIDS, or 'Acquired Immune Deficiency Syndrome', can develop in humans following infection by a virus known as HIV. This is transferred either through unprotected sexual intercourse with an infected person or by taking infected blood into one's bloodstream. (Male homosexuals and intravenous drug users are particularly high-risk categories.) The virus causes the body's normal defence system to break down, leaving the individual open to infection. To date no cure has been found, and anyone who develops AIDS will eventually die.

The virus *cannot* be spread by normal everyday work or by social contact with an infected person. Thus, for the majority of workers there is little or no risk of becoming infected. However, there are a few jobs, mainly in health care and public services, which do involve some risk. Workers in such jobs require special training. Failure by an employer to inform staff of the possible risk to themselves and of the necessary precautionary measures is a breach of the Health and Safety at Work Act 1974.

Employers' response to AIDS in the workplace

There is no statutory obligation on the part of employees to disclose their HIV infection or to submit to medical tests for the virus. Although some organisations have screened job applicants for AIDS, this is not an effective way of avoiding the problem: the virus may not show up straightaway, the test is prone to false negatives and positives and there is nothing to prevent an employee from becoming infected after the test.

Employers should not discriminate against employees who are HIV-positive, or against members of high-risk groups such as homosexuals (Munyard 1988). Since in most jobs there is little or no risk of passing the virus on, there is no reason to treat such individuals differently. Employers who avoid recruitment of males on the grounds that a proportion will be high-risk homosexuals and therefore a risk category are likely to fall foul of the Sex Discrimination Act. For example, in 1987 the EOC found that Dan Air had discriminated by refusing to employ male stewards in the belief that they were likely to be homosexual and a possible AIDS risk (Aikin 1988).

Employees may refuse to work with an HIV-infected individual. In such cases the employer should attempt to resolve the case through normal procedures (see *Polkey* v. *A. E. Dayton Ltd* 1987, IRLR 503).

If it is known that an employee is HIV-positive there may be special grounds for moving him or her to alternative duties, but only if that person's health deteriorates or if there is an infection risk to other employees. Generally speaking, an infected employee who is medically fit to work should be allowed to do so. However, if the employee develops one or more of the illnesses associated with AIDS (such as pneumonia or cancer), he or she may be unable to continue working full-time. Such individuals should be treated in the same way as other sick employees – with the same entitlements to sick pay and other ill-health benefits.

Infection with the HIV virus is not grounds for dismissal. Employers need to consider all the circumstances: the individual's ability to continue working satisfactorily; a possible move to different duties; medical advice and whether continuing employment is in the employee's, employer's and public's best interest. If the disease develops and the individual is unable to carry out the job, or the level of absence becomes unacceptable, the contract may be terminated in the usual way, ensuring that a correct procedure is followed.

Employers should ensure that information regarding AIDS and

its transmission is made available to workers, in order to allay fears and to prevent a panic response. A policy of training and communication involving employees, employers and trade unions will be most effective. Some organisations have appointed an AIDS liaison officer to whom employees can turn in confidence. (Several useful publications are available from the Department of Employment and the Health and Safety Executive.)

Accidents and unsafe working practices

A review by the Health and Safety Executive (HSE 1985) of over 1000 fatal accidents found that the majority could have been avoided by the use of reasonable precautions and systems. Management failures, such as unsafe systems of work and inadequate provision of training and supervision, were identified as the causes of 60 per cent of the accidents surveyed.

For example, on 12 December 1988 three commuter trains were involved in a multiple collision at Clapham Junction. As a result, 35 people died and nearly 500 were injured. A subsequent investigation by British Rail identified the cause of the accident as being due to faulty rewiring in a signal box, which had been carried out by a BR technician. However, the chairman of the official inquiry, while placing some of the responsibility for the accident on the technician, felt that BR management were also to blame: the technician in question had not been provided with adequate training or supervision and there was confusion regarding responsibility for checking rewiring work, excessive reliance on overtime and inadequate safety systems (HMSO 1989).

What action can management take?

In a recent article dealing with the question of management accountability for safety, James (1990) highlights two main areas for improvement:

Health and safety monitoring   This should be done on a regular basis and incorporated into the day-to-day management of the organisation. The most popular method used by companies to monitor safety is the collection of accident statistics. However, such information may not always provide an accurate assessment of potential safety hazards. A more effective procedure, recommended by the Health and Safety Executive, is the use of 'safety audit' systems. Audits provide an assessment of how closely workplace behaviour conforms to safety regulations and how effective these operational and managerial procedures are. A number of large employers have recently introduced audits as part of an overall programme to increase management awareness of health and safety issues.

Appraising managers Health and safety should be an integral part of every manager's role and thus form a part of any performance appraisal. This would signal to managers the importance attached to health and safety by the organisation – in effect putting it on an equal footing with commercial and business performance. Such management accountability is necessary if the intentions of a safety policy are to be put into practice.

Environmental issues

In 1990 Shell was fined £1 million for polluting the river Mersey – the highest penalty imposed by a British court for such an offence. The Health and Safety at Work Act 1974 makes special provision for the protection of the public from environmental pollution and hazards created by work organisations. Important issues here include the emission of noxious substances into the atmosphere, radiation levels in and around nuclear installations, and the storage and transport of dangerous substances.

The environment is becoming an increasingly important issue in both politics and commerce. The Environmental Protection Bill recently passed by the House of Commons is likely to increase pressure on the business community to improve its environmental record as regards pollution (air and water), disposal of hazardous waste, nuclear power, energy conservation, etc. Indeed, a report by the Institute of Business Ethics (1990) showed that green issues are beginning to affect many organisations. Over 30 per cent of companies surveyed had introduced an environmental policy.

Benefits to organisations of having a green corporate image include (Crabb 1990):

- improved public and customer relations;
- potential recruits are becoming increasingly aware of environmental issues and are less likely to be attracted to companies with a poor environmental record;
- current staff morale and health may be boosted by 'green' policies – for example, provision of healthy foods in the canteen (McDermid 1989), non-smoking policies and improved office design and layout (Pearce 1987).

The first step for an organisation considering 'going green' is to conduct an environmental audit. This is a comprehensive evaluation of the environmental effects of a company's operations. Examples of the areas that may be covered in an audit are given by Crabb (1990):

- *Atmospheric pollution*   There has been much publicity regarding the harmful effects of CFCs on the ozone layer. IBM (UK) is seeking to reduce the use of CFCs – it no longer purchases polystyrene cups, packaging and aerosols manufactured using CFCs.
- *Waste management*   Efficient disposal of hazardous wastes, including high-temperature incineration, chemical treatment and secure landfill disposal, and recycling of waste such as aluminium, paper and glass. Examples include the use of biodegradable bags by the Body Shop and of bottle banks by J. Tetley brewers.
- *Lead-free petrol*   A growing number of companies are now converting company vehicles to use lead-free petrol and fitting catalytic convertors in order to reduce emissions. By the end of 1991, British Telecom will have converted its entire fleet of 66 000 vehicles to run on unleaded petrol. A few organisations have introduced bicycles for staff use – indeed the London Borough of Sutton is paying the same mileage rates for bicycle use as for cars (Carrington 1990).
- *Energy efficiency*   Savings can be made by encouraging staff to conserve energy – for example, by switching lights off when leaving a room, or by introducing time switches.
- *Purchasing policies*   The use of environmentally friendly products – for example recycled paper, biodegradable plastics and organic food for canteen use.

The environment is certain to remain an important issue. A directive currently under discussion by the European Council member states would require all companies to carry out an environmental audit. In addition, trade unions are becoming involved in green issues, and NALGO, TGWU and TUC are planning courses for union members on the environment.

Conclusion

The time and money invested in social problems and issues can be seen as a direct contribution towards the maintenance of the social fabric on which all businesses depend. Organisations that pioneered advanced policies with regard to race relations, women's rights and health and safety have seen their efforts reinforced through legislation. The radical ideas of today are likely to be the accepted practices of tomorrow.

Study themes

1 As a personnel manager, how would you deal with an employee who is suspected by his co-workers of being HIV-positive? Your answer should include reference to current legislation.
2 Read *Work and the family* (IPM 1990) and *Women and Employment* (DoE/OPCS 1984). What steps do you think employers can take in order to attract to work women with caring or family commitments?
3 Read Webster (1973), Peach and Hargreaves (1976) and Jones (1972). What do you consider to be the important social issues facing organisations today? How have these changed over the last two decades?
4 A recent article regarding European management suggested that:

> Being ethical is becoming big business. If in the past the universal byword for success was profitability, it is now empathy. With more discriminating consumers and more enlightened employees, . . . companies are beginning to realise that they cannot afford to be anything but legal, decent and honest – and must be seen to be so. (*The European*, 11 May 1990)

Evaluate the role of business ethics within the modern organisation. How has this changed in recent years? Useful references include Drummond and Carmichael (1989) and Pocock (1989).

Check-list – social responsibility within organisations

1 Training policies

(a) Consider special training schemes for individuals who have had a break in employment, such as women returners, the unemployed and ex-offenders. What specific problems need to be addressed? How can skills such as communication and confidence-building be incorporated into training?

(b) Does your organisation employ any disabled workers? What problems have you encountered? Devise a policy for the recruitment of disabled employees?

2 Links with the local community

(a) Establish links with local schools and colleges. This could take the form of work-experience placements, schools visits, joint projects, etc.

(b) Does your organisation sponsor local sports teams, charities etc? Evaluate the advantages and disadvantages of corporate sponsorship.

3 Management accountability for health and safety

(a) How are accidents monitored within your company? Is this method accurate – if not, what are the problems? Suggest improvements which could be made to the scheme?

(b) How can health and safety issues be integrated more effectively into the day-to-day responsibilities of line managers? Give examples.

4 Corporate responsibility for the environment

(a) Carry out an environmental audit within your organisation using Crabb's headings (1990).

(b) Is there more your company could do to protect the environment? Draft a proposal for an environmental policy. Evaluate the advantages, disadvantages and costs.

References

AIDS and Employment (1987), Department of Employment and Health and Safety Executive, London.

Aikin, O., 1988. A positive response to AIDS in the workplace, *Personnel Management*, May, pp. 52–5.

Apex Trust 1990. *Releasing the Potential: a Guide to Good Practice for the Employment of People with Criminal Records*, Next Step Training, London.

Carrington, L., 1990. Street cred, *Personnel Today*, October, p. 27.

Crabb, S., 1990. Has industry seen the green light? *Personnel Management*, April, pp. 42–7.

DoE/OPCS *Women and Employment: a Lifetime Perspective*, HMSO, London.

Drummond, J., and Carmichael, S., 1989. *Good Business – a Guide to Corporate Responsibility and Business Ethics*, Hutchinson Business Books, London.

Falconer, H., 1990. Courage of convictions, *Personnel Today*, July, pp. 22–3.

HMSO, 1988. *Informal carers*.

HMSO, 1989. *Investigation into the Clapham Junction railway accident*.

HSE, 1985. *Monitoring Safety*, HSE Occasional Paper 9, HMSO, London.

Institute of Business Ethics, 1990. *Ethics, Environment and the Company*, Institute of Business Ethics, London.

IPM, 1990. *Work and the Family – Care-friendly Employment Practices*, Institute of Personnel Management, London.

James, P., 1990. Holding managers to account on safety, *Personnel Management*, pp. 55–8.

Jones, K., 1972. The company's responsibility in society, *Personnel Management*, October, p. 22.

Lowe, K., 1990. Made to measure but for whom? *Personnel Today*, July, pp. 26–8.

McDermid, K., 1989. Company catering and the 'branwagon', *Personnel Management*, December, pp. 54–9.

Moon, J., and Richardson, J., 1985. *Unemployment in the UK*, Gower, Aldershot.

Munyard, T., 1988. Homophobia at work and how to manage it, *Personnel Management*, June, pp. 46–50.

Peach, L., and Hargreaves, B., 1976. Social responsibility: the investment pays off, *Personnel Management*, June, pp. 20–4.

Pearce, B., 1987. The human factor in office design, *Personnel Management*, October, pp. 56–8.

Pocock, P., 1989. Is business ethics a contradiction in terms? *Personnel Management*, November, pp. 60–3.

Vize, R., 1990. Cooperative society, *Personnel Today*, 29 May–11 June, p. 35.

Webster, B., 1973. The company's role in society, *Personnel Management*, November, pp. 39–43.

Worman, D., 1990. The forgotten carers, *Personnel Management*, January, pp. 45–7.

Index